Taking An ASE Certification Test

This study guide will help prepare you to take and pass the ASE test. It contains descriptions of the types of questions used on the test, the task list from which the test questions are derived, a review of the task list subject information, and a practice test containing ASE style questions.

ABOUT ASE

The National Institute for Automotive Service Excellence (ASE) is a non-profit organization founded in 1972 for the purpose of improving the quality of automotive service and repair through the voluntary testing and certification of automotive technicians. Currently, there are over 400,000 professional technicians certified by ASE in over 40 different specialist areas.

ASE certification recognizes your knowledge and experience, and since it is voluntary, taking and passing an ASE certification test also demonstrates to employers and customers your commitment to your profession. It can mean better compensation and increased employment opportunities as well.

ASE not only certifies technician competency, it also promotes the benefits of technician certification to the motoring public. Repair shops that employ at least one ASE technician can display the ASE sign. Establishments where 75 percent of technicians are certified, with at least one technician

certified in each area of service offered by the business, are eligible for the ASE Blue Seal of Excellence program. ASE encourages consumers to patronize these shops through media campaigns and car care clinics.

To become ASE certified, you must pass at least one ASE exam and have at least two years of related work experience. Technicians that pass specified tests in a series earn Master Technician status. Your certification is valid for five years, after which time you must retest to retain certification, demonstrating that you have kept up with the changing technology in the field.

THE ASE TEST

An ASE test consists of forty to eighty multiple-choice questions. Test questions are written by a panel of technical experts from vehicle, parts and equipment manufacturers, as well as working technicians and technical education instructors. All questions have been pre-tested and quality checked on a national sample of technicians. The questions are de-

© Advanstar Communications Inc. 2014.3

Customer Service 1-800-240-1968
FAX 218-740-6437
E-mail PassTheASE@advanstar.com
URL: www.PassTheASE.com
**A9 - LIGHT VEHICLE
DIESEL ENGINES**

rived from information presented in the task list, which details the knowledge that a technician must have to pass an ASE test and be recognized as competent in that category. The task list is periodically updated by ASE in response to changes in vehicle technology and repair techniques.

There are five types of questions on an ASE test:
- **Direct, or Completion**
- **MOST Likely**
- **Technician A and Technician B**
- **EXCEPT**
- **LEAST Likely**

Direct, or Completion

This type of question is the kind that is most familiar to anyone who has taken a multiple-choice test: you must answer a direct question or complete a statement with the correct answer. There are four choices given as potential answers, but only one is correct. Sometimes the correct answer to one of these questions is clear, however in other cases more than one answer may seem to be correct. In that case, read the question carefully and choose the answer that is most correct. Here is an example of this type of test question:

A compression test shows that one cylinder is too low. A leakage test on that cylinder shows that there is excessive leakage. During the test, air could be heard coming from the

tailpipe. Which of the following could be the cause?
A. broken piston rings
B. bad head gasket
C. bad exhaust gasket
D. an exhaust valve not seating

There is only one correct answer to this question, answer D. If an exhaust valve is not seated, air will leak from the combustion chamber by way of the valve out to the tailpipe and make an audible sound. Answer C is wrong because an exhaust gasket has nothing to do with combustion chamber sealing. Answers A and B are wrong because broken rings or a bad head gasket would have air leaking through the oil filler or coolant system.

MOST Likely

This type of question is similar to a direct question but it can be more challenging because all or some of the answers may be nearly correct. However, only one answer is the most correct. For example:

When a cylinder head with an overhead camshaft is discovered to be warped, which of the following is the most correct repair option?
A. replace the head
B. check for cracks, straighten the head, surface the head
C. surface the head, then straighten it
D. straighten the head, surface the head, check for cracks

The most correct answer is B. It makes no sense to perform repairs on a cylinder head that might not be usable. The head should first be checked for warpage and cracks. Therefore, answer B is more correct than answer D. The head could certainly be replaced, but the cost factor may be prohibitive and availability may be limited, so answer B is more correct than answer A. If the top of the head is warped enough to interfere with cam bore alignment and/or restrict free movement of the camshaft, the head must be straightened before it is resurfaced, so answer C is wrong.

Technician A and Technician B

These questions are the kind most commonly associated with the ASE test. With these questions you are asked to choose which technician statement is correct, or whether they both are correct or incorrect. This type of question can be difficult because very often you may find one technician's statement to be clearly correct or incorrect while the other may not be so obvious. Do you choose one technician or both? The key to answering these questions is to carefully examine each technician's statement independently and judge it on its own merit. Here is an example of this type of question:

A vehicle equipped with rack-and-pinion steering is having the front end inspected. Technician A says that the inner tie rod ends should be inspected while in their normal running position. Technician B says that if movement is felt between the tie rod stud and the socket while the tire is moved in and out, the inner tie rod should be replaced. Who is correct?
A. Technician A
B. Technician B
C. Both A and B
D. Neither A or B

The correct answer is C; both technicians' statements are correct. Technician B is clearly correct because any play felt between the tie-rod stud and the socket while the tire is moved in and out indicates that the assembly is worn and requires replacement. However, Technician A is also correct because inner tie-rods should be inspected while in their normal running position, to prevent binding that may occur when the suspension is allowed to hang free.

EXCEPT

This kind of question is sometimes called a negative question because you are asked to give the incorrect answer. All of the possible answers given are correct EXCEPT one. In effect, the correct answer to the question is the one that is wrong. The word EXCEPT is always capitalized in these questions. For example:
All of the following are true of torsion bars **EXCEPT**:
A. They can be mounted longitudinally or transversely.
B. They serve the same function as coil springs.
C. They are interchangeable from side-to-side
D. They can be used to adjust vehicle ride height.

The correct answer is C. Torsion bars are not normally interchangeable from side-to-side. This is because the direction of the twisting or torsion is not the same on the left and right sides. All of the other answers contain true statements regarding torsion bars.

LEAST Likely

This type of question is similar to EXCEPT in that once again you are asked to give the answer that is wrong. For example:

Blue-gray smoke comes from the exhaust of a vehicle during deceleration. Of the following, which cause is **LEAST** likely?
A. worn valve guides
B. broken valve seals
C. worn piston rings
D. clogged oil return passages

The correct answer is C. Worn piston rings will usually make an engine smoke worse under acceleration. All of the other causes can allow oil to be drawn through the valve guides under the high intake vacuum that occurs during deceleration.

PREPARING FOR THE ASE TEST

Begin preparing for the test by reading the task list. The task list describes the actual work performed by a technician in a particular specialty area. Each question on an ASE test is derived from a task or set of tasks in the list. Familiarizing yourself with the task list will help you to concentrate on the areas where you need to study.

The text section of this study guide contains information pertaining to each of the tasks in the task list. Reviewing this information will prepare you to take the practice test.

Take the practice test and compare your answers with the correct answer explanations. If you get an answer wrong and don't understand why, go back and read the information pertaining to that question in the text.

After reviewing the tasks and the subject information and taking the practice test, you should be prepared to take the ASE test or be aware of areas where further study is needed. When studying with this study guide or any other source of information, use the following guidelines to make sure the time spent is as productive as possible:

- Concentrate on the subject areas where you are weakest.
- Arrange your schedule to allow specific times for studying.
- Study in an area where you will not be distracted.
- Don't try to study after a full meal or when you are tired.
- Don't wait until the last minute and try to 'cram' for the test.

REGISTERING FOR ASE COMPUTER-BASED TESTING

Registration for the ASE CBT tests can be done online in myASE or over the phone. While not mandatory, it is recommended that you establish a myASE account on the ASE website (www.ase.com). This can be a big help in managing the ASE certification process, as your test scores and certification expiry dates are all listed there.

Test times are available during two-month windows with a one-month break in between. This means that there is a total of eight months over the period of the calendar year that ASE testing is available.

Testing can be scheduled during the daytime, night, and weekends for maximum flexibility. Also, results are available immediately after test completion. Printed certificates are mailed at the end of the two-month test window. If you fail a test, you will not be allowed to register for the same test until the next two-month test window.

TAKING THE ASE TEST – COMPUTER-BASED TESTING (CBT)

On test day, bring some form of photo identification with you and be sure to arrive at the test center 30 minutes early to give sufficient time to check in. Once you have checked in, the test supervisor will issue you some scratch paper and pencils, as well as a composite vehicle test booklet if you are taking advanced tests. You will then be seated at a computer station and given a short online tutorial on how to complete the ASE CBT tests. You may skip the tutorial if you are already familiar with the CBT process.

The test question format is similar to those found in written ASE tests. Regular certification tests have a time limit of 1 to 2 hours, depending on the test. Recertification tests are 30 to 45 minutes, and the L1 and L2 advanced level tests are capped at 2 hours. The time remaining for your test is displayed on the top left of the test window. You are given a warning when you have 5 minutes left to complete the test.

Read through each question carefully. If you don't know the answer to a question and need to think about it, click on the "Flag" button and move on to the next question. You may also go back to previous questions by pressing the "Previous Question" button. Don't spend too much time on any one question. After you have worked through to the end of the test, check your remaining time and go back and answer the questions you flagged. Very often, information found in questions later in the test can help answer some of the ones with which you had difficulty.

Some questions may have more content than what can fit on one screen. If this is the case, there will be a "More" button displayed where the "Next Question" button would ordinarily appear. A scrolling bar will also appear, showing what part of the question you are currently viewing. Once you have viewed all of the related content for the question, the "Next Question" button will reappear.

You can change answers on any of the questions before submitting the test for scoring. At the end of the examination, you will be shown a table with all of the question numbers. This table will show which questions are answered, which are unanswered, and which have been flagged for review. You will be given the option to review all the questions, review the flagged questions, or review the unanswered questions from this page. This table can be reviewed at any time during the exam by clicking the "Review" button.

If you are running out of time and still have unanswered test questions, guess the answers if necessary to make sure every question is answered. Do not leave any answers blank. It is to your advantage to answer every question, because your test score is based on the number of correct answers. A guessed answer could be correct, but a blank answer can never be.

Once you are satisfied that all of the questions are complete and ready for scoring, click the "Submit for Scoring" button. If you are scheduled for more than one test, the next test will begin immediately. If you are done with testing, you will be asked to complete a short survey regarding the CBT test experience. As you are leaving the test center, your supervisor will give you a copy of your test results. Your scores will also be available on myASE within two business days.

To learn exactly where and when the ASE Certification Tests are available in your area, as well as the costs involved in becoming ASE certified, please contact ASE directly for registration information.

The National Institute for Automotive Service Excellence
101 Blue Seal Drive, S.E. Suite 101
Leesburg, VA 20175
1-800-390-6789
http://www.ase.com

Table of Contents
A9 - Light Vehicle Diesel Engines

The Building Blocks of Our Success

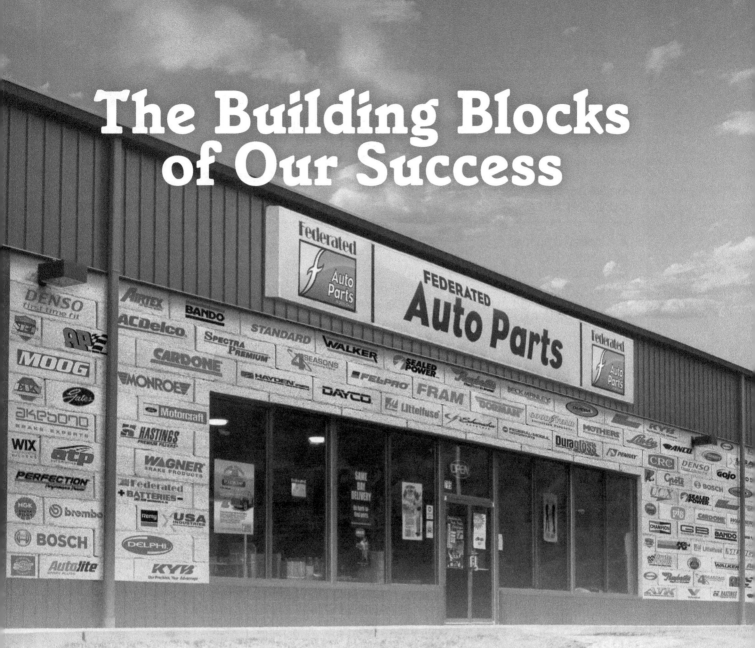

At Federated Auto Parts, you know you will always get great service and support from the most knowledgeable people in the business. You also know that you will get the best brand name, premium quality auto parts available. Parts that you can trust will help you get the job done right.

Light Vehicle Diesel Engines

TEST SPECIFICATIONS
FOR LIGHT VEHICLE DIESEL ENGINES
(TEST A9)

CONTENT AREA	NUMBER OF QUESTIONS IN ASE TEST	PERCENTAGE OF COVERAGE IN ASE TEST
A. General Diagnosis	9	18%
B. Cylinder Head And Valvetrain Diagnosis And Repair	5	10%
C. Engine Block Diagnosis And Repair	5	10%
D. Lubrication And Cooling Systems Diagnosis And Repair	6	12%
E. Air Induction And Exhaust Systems Diagnosis And Repair	12	24%
F. Fuel System Diagnosis And Repair	13	26%
Total	**50**	**100%**

The test could contain additional questions that are included for statistical research purposes only. Your answers to these questions will not affect your test score, but since you do not know which ones they are, you should answer all questions in the test. The 5-year Recertification Test will cover the same content areas as those listed above. However, the number of questions in each content area of the Recertification Test will be reduced by about one-half.

The following pages list the tasks covered in each content area. These task descriptions offer detailed information to technicians preparing for the test, and to persons who may be instructing Light Vehicle Diesel Engine technicians. The task list may also serve as a guideline for questions writers, reviewers and test assemblers.

It should be noted that the number of questions in each content area may not equal the number of tasks listed. Some of the tasks are complex and broad in scope, and may be covered by several questions. Other tasks are simple and narrow in scope; one question may cover several tasks. The main purpose for listing the tasks is to describe accurately what is done on the job, not to make each task correspond to a particular test question.

LIGHT VEHICLE DIESEL ENGINES TEST
TASK LIST

A. GENERAL DIAGNOSIS
(9 questions)

Task 1 - Verify the complaint and road/dyno test vehicle: review driver/ customer concerns and vehicle service history (if available); determine further diagnosis.

Task 2 - Record vehicle identification number (VIN). Identify engine model, calibration and serial numbers to research applicable vehicle and service information, service precautions and technical service bulletins; determine needed actions.

Task 3 - Perform scan tool check and visual inspection for physical damage and missing, modified or tampered components; determine needed repairs.

Task 4 - Check and record electronic diagnostic codes, freeze frame and/or operational data;

monitor scan tool data; determine further diagnosis.

Task 5 - Clear diagnostic trouble codes (DTCs) and verify repair.

Task 6 - Inspect engine assembly and components for fuel, oil, coolant, exhaust or other leaks; determine needed repairs.

Task 7 - Inspect engine compartment wiring harness, connectors, seals and locks; check for proper routing and condition; determine needed repairs.

Task 8 - Listen for and isolate engine noises; determine needed repairs.

Task 9 - Isolate and diagnose engine related vibration problems; determine needed actions.

Task 10 - Check engine exhaust for odor and smoke color; determine further diagnosis.

Task 11 - Check fuel for contamination, quantity and consumption;

determine needed actions.

Task 12 - Perform crankcase pressure test; determine further diagnosis.

Task 13 - Diagnose surging, rough operation, misfiring, low power, slow deceleration, slow acceleration and shutdown problems; determine needed actions.

Task 14 - Check cooling system for freeze point, level, contamination, temperature, pressure, circulation and fan operation; determine needed repairs.

Task 15 - Check lubrication system for contamination, oil level, temperature, pressure, filtration and oil consumption; determine needed repairs.

Task 16 - Diagnose no cranking, cranks but fails to start, hard starting and starts but does not continue to run problems; determine needed actions.

Task 17 - Diagnoses engine problems caused by battery condition, connections or excessive key-off battery drain; determine needed repairs.

Task 18 - Diagnose engine problems resulting from an undercharge, overcharge or a no-charge condition; determine needed action.

B. CYLINDER HEAD AND VALVETRAIN DIAGNOSIS AND REPAIR
(5 questions)

Task 1 - Remove, inspect, disassemble and clean cylinder head assembly(s).

Task 2 - Inspect threaded holes, studs and bolts for serviceability; service/replace as needed.

Task 3 - Measure cylinder head thickness and check mating surfaces for warpage and surface finish; inspect for cracks/damage; check condition of passages; inspect core and gallery plugs; determine serviceability and needed repairs.

Task 4 - Inspect valves, guides, seats, springs, retainers, rotators, locks and seals; determine serviceability and needed repairs.

Task 5 - Inspect and/or replace injector sleeves, glow plug sleeves and seals; pressure test to verify repair (if applicable); measure injector tip, nozzle or prechamber protrusion where specified by manufacturer.

Task 6 - Inspect and/or replace valve bridges (crossheads) and guides; adjust bridges (crossheads) if applicable.

Task 7 - Reassemble, check and determine required cylinder head gasket thickness; install cylinder head assembly and gasket as specified by manufacturer.

Task 8 - Inspect pushrods, rocker arms, rocker arm shafts, electronic wiring harness and brackets; repair/ replace as needed.

Task 9 - Inspect, install and adjust cam followers and retainers; adjust valve clearance.

Task 10 - Inspect, measure and replace/reinstall overhead camshaft and bearings; measure and adjust end-play.

Task 11 - Inspect and time drive gear train components (includes gear, chain and belt systems).

C. ENGINE BLOCK DIAGNOSIS AND REPAIR
(5 questions)

Task 1 - Remove, inspect, service and install pans, covers, ventilation systems, gaskets, seals and wear rings.

Task 2 - Disassemble, clean and inspect engine block for cracks; check mating surfaces and related components for damage or warpage and surface finish; check deck height; check condition of passages, core and gallery plugs; inspect threaded holes, studs, dowel pins and bolts for serviceability; service/replace as needed.

Task 3 - Inspect and measure cylinder walls for wear and damage; determine needed service.

Task 4 - Inspect in-block camshaft bearings for wear and damage; replace as needed.

Task 5 - Inspect, measure and replace/reinstall in-block camshaft; measure/and correct end-play; inspect, replace/reinstall and adjust camshaft followers (if applicable).

Task 6 - Clean and inspect crankshaft and journals for surface cracks and damage; check condition of oil passages; check passage plugs; measure journal diameters; check mounting surfaces; determine needed service.

Task 7 - Determine the proper select-fit components such as pistons, connecting rod and main bearings.

Task 8 - Inspect and replace main bearings; check cap fit and bearing clearances; check and correct crankshaft end-play.

Task 9 - Inspect and time the drive gear train components (includes gear, chain and belt systems).

Task 10 - Inspect, measure or replace pistons, pins and retainers.

Task 11 - Measure piston-to-cylinder wall clearance.

Task 12 - Identify piston, connecting rod bearing and main bearing wear patterns that indicate connecting rod and crankshaft alignment or bearing bore problems; check bearing bore and bushing condition; determine needed repairs.

Task 13 - Check ring-to-groove fit and end gaps; install rings on pistons. Assemble pistons and con-

necting rods and install in block; check piston height/protrusion (if applicable); replace rod bearings and check clearances; check condition, position and clearance of piston cooling jets (nozzles).

Task 14 - Inspect crankshaft vibration damper.

Task 15 - Inspect flywheel/flexplate and/or dual-mass flywheel (including ring gear) and mounting surfaces for cracks, wear and run-out; determine needed repairs.

D. LUBRICATION AND COOLING SYSTEMS DIAGNOSIS AND REPAIR
(6 questions)

Task 1 - Verify engine oil pressure and check operation of pressure sensor/switch and pressure gauge; verify engine oil temperature and check operation of temperature sensor.

Task 2 - Inspect, measure, repair/ replace oil pump, housing, drives, pipes and screens; check drive gear clearance.

Task 3 - Inspect, repair/replace oil pressure regulator valve(s) and bypass valve(s).

Task 4 - Inspect, clean, test, reinstall/ replace oil cooler, bypass valve, lines and hoses.

Task 5 - Inspect turbocharger lubrication and cooling systems; repair/replace as needed.

Task 6 - Change engine oil and filters; add proper type, viscosity and rating of oil.

Task 7 - Inspect and reinstall/ replace pulleys, tensioners and drive belts; adjust drive belts and check alignment.

Task 8 - Verify coolant temperature and check operation of temperature and level sensors/ switch, and temperature gauge.

Task 9 - Inspect and replace thermostat(s), bypasses, housing(s) and seals.

Task 10 - Flush and refill cooling system; add proper coolant type; bleed air from system.

Task 11 - Inspect and replace water pump, housing, hoses and idler pulley or drive gear.

Task 12 - Inspect radiator, pressure cap and tank(s); pressure test cooling system and radiator cap; determine needed repairs.

Task 13 - Inspect, repair/replace fan, fan hub, clutch, controls and shroud.

E. AIR INDUCTION AND EXHAUST SYSTEMS DIAGNOSIS AND REPAIR
(11 questions)

Task 1 - Inspect and service/replace air induction piping, air cleaner, and element; determine needed actions.

Task 2 - Perform intake manifold pressure tests; inspect, test, clean, and/or replace charge air cooler and piping system; determine needed actions.

Task 3 - Inspect, test, and replace turbocharger(s) (including variable ratio/geometry, VGT), pneumatic, hydraulic, vacuum, and electronic controls and actuators; inspect, test, and replace wastegate and wastegate controls.

Task 4 - Inspect, test, and replace intake manifold(s), variable intake manifold(s), gasket(s), actuators, temperature and pressure sensors, and connections.

Task 5 - Perform exhaust back-pressure and temperature tests; determine needed actions.

Task 6 - Inspect and repair/replace exhaust manifold(s), gaskets, piping, mufflers, and mounting hardware.

Task 7 - Inspect, test, and repair/replace preheater/inlet air heater and/or glow plug system and controls.

Task 8 - Inspect, test, and replace exhaust aftertreatment system components and controls, including diesel oxidation catalyst (DOC), selective catalyst reduction (SCR), diesel exhaust fluid (DEF), diesel particulate filter (DPF); check regeneration system operation.

Task 9 - Inspect, test, service, and replace EGR system components including EGR valve(s),EGR cooler by-pass valve(s), EGR cooler(s), piping, electronic sensors, actuators, controls, and wiring.

Task 10 - Inspect, test, and replace airflow control (throttle) valve(s) and controls.

Task 11 - Inspect, test, and replace crankcase ventilation system components, including sensors, filters, valves, and piping.

F. FUEL SYSTEM DIAGNOSIS AND REPAIR
(13 questions)

Task 1 - Inspect, clean, test and repair/replace fuel system tanks, vents, caps, mounts, valves, single/dual supply and return lines and fittings.

Task 2 - Inspect, clean, test, repair/ replace fuel transfer and/or supply pump, strainers, fuel/water separators/indicators, filters, heaters, coolers, ECM cooling plates (if applicable) and mounting hardware.

Task 3 - Check fuel system for air; determine needed repairs; prime and bleed fuel system; check, repair/ replace primer pump.

Task 4 - Inspect, test, repair/ replace low pressure regulator supply and return systems.

Task 5 - Inspect, reinstall/ replace high-pressure injection lines, fittings, seals and mounting hardware.

Task 6 - Inspect, adjust, repair/ replace electronic throttle and PTO control devices, circuits and sensors.

Task 7 - Perform on-engine inspections, tests and replace high-pressure common rail fuel system components and electronic controls.

Task 8 - Perform on-engine inspections, tests and replace hydraulic electronic unit injectors (HEUI) components and electronic controls (rail pressure control).

Task 9 - Perform on-engine inspections, tests and replace pump-line-nozzle fuel system (PLN-E) components and electronic controls.

Task 10 - Perform on-engine inspections, tests and replace electronic unit injectors (EUI) components and electronic controls.

Task 11 - Inspect and replace electrical connector terminals, pins, harnesses, seals and locks.

Task 12 - Connect diagnostic tool to vehicle/engine; access, verify and update software calibration settings; perform ECM relearn procedures as needed.

Task 13 - Use a diagnostic tool (hand-held or PC based) to inspect and test electronic engine control system, sensors, actuators, elec-tronic control modules (ECMs/PCMs) and circuits, determine further diagnosis.

Task 14 - Measure and interpret voltage, voltage drop, amperage and resistance readings using a digital multimeter (DMM) or appropriate test equipment.

Task 15 - Diagnose engine problems resulting from failures of inter-related systems (for example: cruise control, security alarms/theft deterrent, transmission controls, electronic stability control, non-OEM installed accessories.

We employ technicians certified by the National Institute for

AUTOMOTIVE SERVICE EXCELLENCE

Let us show you their credentials

The preceding Task List Data details all of the relevant subject matter you are expected to know in order to sit for this ASE Certification Test. Your own years of experience as a professional technician in the automotive service industry should provide you with additional background.

Finally, a conscientious review of the self-study material provided in this Training for ASE Certification unit will help you to be adequately prepared to take this test.

General Diagnosis

A gasoline engine requires the right air/fuel mixture and a well-timed spark to obtain good performance and low emissions, while a diesel engine needs the proper volume of air and a timely injection of high-pressure fuel to achieve the same. And just as gasoline engines today use electronic controls instead of carburetors and breaker points to attain these goals, so too are modern diesels electronically rather than mechanically controlled.

All modern computerized engine control systems have self-diagnostic capabilities. Gasoline engine vehicles were the first to have this feature, but now modern diesel engine vehicles share this technology. OBD II (On Board Diagnostics generation two) was required by CARB (California Air Resources Board) and EPA (U.S. Environmental Protection Agency) on light-duty (less than 8,500 lb. GVWR) diesel vehicles beginning in 1997. As of 2007, all 8,500-14,000 lb. GVWR diesel vehicles must also be OBD II compliant.

On-board diagnostics are a tremendous aid to the technician when diagnosing a performance problem, but it is important to remember that very often there is a mechanical defect that is the root cause. A DTC (Diagnostic Trouble Code) could ultimately be caused by a worn camshaft lobe or burnt valve.

DIAGNOSTIC PROCEDURE

Any diagnostic process should include the following elements:
1. Identifying the problem
2. Verifying the problem
3. Determining the cause
4. Making the repair
5. Testing the repair.

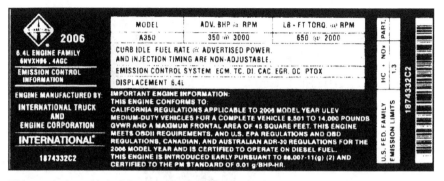

This underhood label from a Ford pickup includes a list of major emission system components. *(Courtesy: Ford Motor Co.)*

Begin by interviewing the customer. Have them describe the symptoms in as much detail as possible. When do they occur, and how long have they been occurring? What does the customer have to do to experience the problem? Is there a temperature, running time, time spent without running, speed, or road condition prerequisite?

If possible, road test the vehicle to verify the complaint. In some cases, a driveability complaint may turn out to be nothing more than a customer's unrealistic expectation of their vehicle's performance capabilities (particularly if they have never owned a diesel engine vehicle before). A road test will allow you to evaluate the reliability of the complaint, and then determine the appropriate course of action.

Check the vehicle's service history to look for similar complaints in the past. Has the vehicle been well maintained and if not, could the lack of maintenance be a contributing factor to the customer's complaint?

Record the vehicle's VIN (Vehicle Identification Number) and identify the engine and any other relevant serial numbers. Use this information to search for TSBs (Technical Service Bulletins) that may reveal updated repair information regarding the symptoms or system in question. Doing research at this point could save valuable time that would otherwise be needlessly spent trying to achieve a diagnosis. Check for recalls and service campaigns, which may indicate that the problem is in fact a defect that the vehicle manufacturer will correct. Some investigation here could save your customer from unnecessarily paying for a repair.

Checking TSBs is particularly important these days since so many driveability problems are now resolved by reprogramming the PCM (Powertrain Control Module) or ECM (Engine Control Module). Connect a scan tool to the DLC (Diagnostic Link Connector) to check the current calibration identification. If a TSB indicates an updated calibration is required, the PCM/ECM must be reprogrammed.

Perform a visual inspection under the hood to check for obvious problems. Check the accessory drive belt(s) for looseness, cracks, glazing or fraying. A loose alternator belt

The VIN (Vehicle Identification Number) is stamped on a metal tab attached to the instrument panel in a place where it is visible through the windshield from outside the vehicle. The illustration shows a typical location for an engine serial number. These numbers will be necessary when searching for applicable TSBs (Technical Service Bulletins). *(Courtesy: Ford Motor Co.)*

could be the cause of a charging system problem. Check the battery cables and all electrical wires and connections for damage and secure connections. Quite often a problem in a computerized engine control system circuit is not caused by a component but rather by broken or abraded wires or by loose or corroded connector pins.

Scan Tool Diagnosis

As indicated above, all currently manufactured light- and medium-duty diesel engine vehicles must be OBD II compliant. OBD II became necessary to ease vehicle serviceability, because the systems that were monitored and even the number of pins and location of the DLC varied from manufacturer to manufacturer on earlier on-board diagnostic systems.

With OBD II, all components and systems that affect a vehicle's emissions output are monitored. All emissions-related failures have common DTCs and definitions. A universal 16-pin DLC, with dedicated pin assignments, must be located under the dash on the driver's side of the vehicle and be easily accessible. And it must be possible for a generic scan tool to connect to the DLC, retrieve OBD II DTCs and clear them from the computer's memory.

The PCM/ECM on OBD II vehicles performs continuous tests on emissions-related systems and components. These tests are known as 'monitors'. Some monitors run all the time and are called 'continuous' monitors. Others are run once per drive cycle and are referred to as 'non-continuous' monitors.

A drive cycle consists of a set of conditions necessary to run the monitor to completion. This usually involves operating the vehicle under specific operating conditions. Always refer to the vehicle shop manual, as each monitor has a specific 'enable criteria' — the conditions that must be met for a monitor to

be completed — and the criteria varies among models and manufacturers.

There are three kinds of tests that can be performed during a monitor. The first is where the PCM/ECM tests a component's electrical circuit for opens and shorts to power or ground. The second involves comparing data between sensors to see if the information is rational and makes sense. In the last type of test, the PCM/ECM checks the function of output devices, either passively or actively. Passive testing is waiting for an actuator to receive a command from the PCM/ECM during normal operation and then checking sensory data that would indicate proper operation. Active testing is where the computer takes control of the actuator for testing purposes only.

If the monitor results indicate a failure, a fault will be recorded in the PCM/ECM's memory. For some faults, the PCM/ECM will set a DTC and turn on the MIL (Malfunction Indicator Light) or CHECK ENGINE light. However, for most DTCs the PCM/ECM must see the same fault occur during two 'trips'. A trip is a completed drive cycle. After the first trip, the fault is recorded as 'pending'. Once the PCM/ECM sees the same fault the next time the monitor runs, the PCM will turn on the MIL. If the same fault is not seen during the next monitor, the pending code will be cleared.

If the MIL is turned on because of a particular DTC, and the monitor responsible for that DTC runs three times in a row without seeing the failure, the PCM/ECM will then turn off the MIL. However, the DTC will remain in the PCM/ECM's memory until a certain number of warm-up cycles occur.

Diesel engines use a number of monitors that are similar to those used on gasoline engines, and there

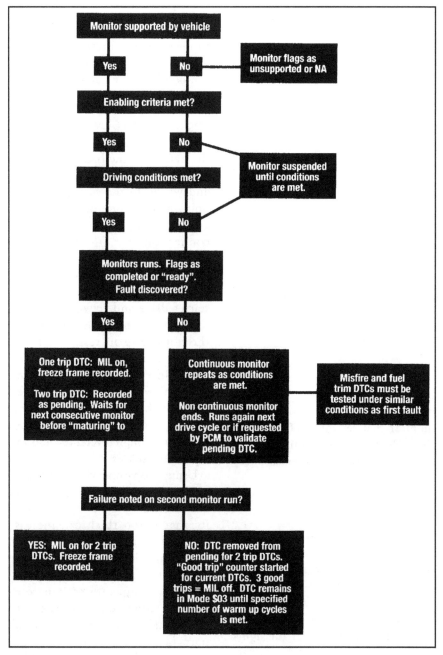

OBD II monitor flowchart.

has a major impact on emissions, a monitor is used to check its operation.

To retrieve any stored and/or pending DTCs and check monitor status, connect the scan tool to the DLC. If a code has turned on the MIL and it is related to a continuous monitor, check and record the freeze frame information. This will give you an idea of the operating conditions that were present when the fault occurred.

OBD II trouble codes consist of one alpha character followed by four digits. The alpha character indicates the area of the vehicle where the failure occurred. This includes (B) Body, (C) Chassis, (P) Powertrain, and (U) Network. The first digit of the DTC denotes the origin of the code. Codes authored by the Society of Automotive Engineers (SAE) are identified by a zero (0). These codes are known as generic DTCs since they are the same for every vehicle. Manufacturer specific codes are indicated by the number one (1). These DTCs are part of the manufacturer's enhanced diagnostic software, and vary between brands. The second digit in the DTC identifies the system experiencing the problem, while the last two digits correspond to a specific code definition.

When checking monitor status, 'complete' or 'ready' indicates monitors that have run successfully. 'NA' or 'not available' indicates monitors that are not used on this particular vehicle. Monitors shown as 'not ready' or 'incomplete' means that either the drive cycle criteria have not been met and the monitor isn't finished or a related monitor has recorded a fault.

Just because a monitor has not completed does not mean that it cannot be useful in achieving a diagnosis. Examine the vehicle service information to see how the system operates. Look for information on

are also components usually associated with gasoline engines that are used to perform monitoring functions on diesel engines. For instance, the MAF (Mass Air Flow) sensor is used with diesel engines to monitor the EGR (Exhaust Gas Recirculation) system. The MAF sensor measures the airflow into the engine while the EGR valve is closed, then an associated drop in airflow is expected to occur as the EGR valve opens.

As would be expected, diesel engines also have unique monitors not used on their gasoline engine counterparts, such as the EGR cooler monitor. The EGR system plays a major role in controlling NOx (Nitrogen Oxide) emissions on a diesel engine. Very high rates of EGR flow are required, so it is necessary to cool the EGR gases to achieve the desired affect. Since the EGR cooler

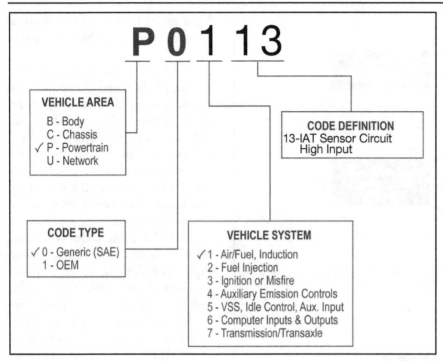

P 0 1 1 3

VEHICLE AREA
B - Body
C - Chassis
✓ P - Powertrain
U - Network

CODE DEFINITION
13-IAT Sensor Circuit
High Input

CODE TYPE
✓ 0 - Generic (SAE)
1 - OEM

VEHICLE SYSTEM
✓ 1 - Air/Fuel, Induction
2 - Fuel Injection
3 - Ignition or Misfire
4 - Auxiliary Emission Controls
5 - VSS, Idle Control, Aux. Input
6 - Computer Inputs & Outputs
7 - Transmission/Transaxle

OBD II trouble code description.

conditions that are necessary for a monitor to complete. Here you may find that a fault derived from one monitor is keeping others from completing. Also look for what various incomplete monitors have in common.

The scan tool should also be used to check data from the PIDs (Parameter Identifications) to see if sensor and actuator values are within their intended range. In theory, out-of-range sensor and/or actuator values should always be accompanied by a DTC. However, this is not always the case. This is why it's important to compare actual scan data readings to the desired values listed in the service manual. Although scan data is a valuable source of diagnostic information, never replace suspect components based on this information alone. This is especially true when diagnosing no-code complaints. Always confirm the accuracy of the scan readings by performing additional tests using the appropriate equipment.

Once repairs are completed, use the scan tool to clear codes and reset all monitors. Operate the vehicle

in a manner necessary to satisfy the drive cycle requirements for the monitor that set the DTC in question. Recheck the monitor status and check for pending codes to see if the fault returned.

Symptom Diagnosis

Engine Will Not Crank

If nothing happens when the key is turned to the Start position, turn the headlights on and turn the key to Start again. If the headlights do not dim, check for an open circuit in the starting system. If the lights go dim, test the battery. If the battery tests OK, check the condition of the cables and wiring to the starter and solenoid, making sure all connections are clean and tight.

If the wiring connections are OK, next check the starter solenoid function. If the solenoid tests OK, perform the starter current draw test. Make sure that the starter is mounted securely and that the starter drive and flywheel/flexplate ring gear are not binding. Perform the voltage drop test. If current draw is excessive and voltage drop

is within specification, the starter is defective or there is a mechanical problem that is preventing the engine from turning over. If the engine can be rotated by hand through several revolutions, replace the starter.

Engine Cranks Slowly

If the engine cranks slowly, test the battery. If the battery tests OK, check the condition of the cables and wiring to the starter and solenoid, making sure all connections are clean and tight. If the wiring connections are OK, perform the starter current draw test.

Make sure that the starter is mounted securely and that the starter drive and flywheel/flexplate ring gear are not binding. Perform the voltage drop test. If current draw is excessive and voltage drop is within specification, the starter is defective or there is a mechanical problem that is causing the engine to bind. If the engine can be rotated by hand through several revolutions, replace the starter.

Using the wrong viscosity engine oil in extremely cold weather can also cause slow cranking. A viscosity that is too thick can increase drag on the reciprocating assembly, and along with the reduced battery output that naturally occurs during very cold temperatures, can combine to reduce cranking speed to the point where the engine won't start. Changing to a lighter weight oil may be all that's necessary to improve cold cranking, however always refer to the manufacturer's specifications for the recommended oil.

Engine Cranks Normally But Will Not Start

A no-start condition on a vehicle that cranks properly could be caused by a sensor or actuator failure in the electronic engine control system, contaminated fuel, low or no fuel pressure, glow plug failure, an air inlet and/or exhaust restriction, loss of compression or low oil pressure on HEUI (Hydraulic Electronic Unit Injector) fuel systems.

Use a scan tool to check for DTCs. For example, on certain engines no CMP (Camshaft Position) sensor signal while cranking will cause a no-start and should set a code.

Make sure there is fuel in the tank and check its condition. Just like lubricating oil, diesel fuel thickens as the temperature drops. Diesel fuel has 'cloud' and 'pour' points at which the fuel begins to gell and restrict fuel flow. Using the proper grade of fuel for the temperatures encountered will prevent this, and some vehicles may be equipped with fuel heaters. Water can also contaminate the fuel, usually from condensation that forms during cold weather. The water can then freeze in the filter and/or fuel/water separator and cause a blockage.

If there is fuel of sufficient quantity and quality, check the pressure in the low-pressure and high-pressure fuel circuits and compare with specifications. If fuel pressure is low, check for restrictions in the pump, lines and filters. Also check for air in the fuel.

Most diesel engines use glow plugs to aid cold starting. Check for voltage to each glow plug with the ignition key on. If there is no voltage, check the glow plug control module connections and wiring. Individual glow plugs can be checked by measuring their resistance and comparing with specifications.

Check the air inlet system for a dirty air filter, collapsed intake hose or other restriction. Some diesel engines are equipped with air restriction indicators, or filter minders, located on the air cleaner housing. A manometer can also be used to measure intake restriction. Check the exhaust system for collapsed, crushed or kinked pipes, and clogging from excessive carbon buildup. If the source of a suspected restric-tion is not obvious, a manometer can be used to check for restriction.

Check engine compression using a suitable compression tester and compare measurements with specifications. If compression is within minimum parameters, it should not prevent the engine from starting. However, if measurements between cylinders vary more than 20%, it will cause the engine to run rough.

On engines, with HEUI systems, there is a minimum injector oil pressure specification below which the injectors will not be enabled. Check the oil pressure while cranking the engine and compare with specifications.

Engine Starts But Will Not Stay Running

An engine that starts but will not continue to run may have an intermittent electronic engine control system failure, air in the fuel, a restricted fuel return line or clogged fuel filter, or an air inlet restriction.

Use a scan tool to check for current and pending DTCs. Since intermittent problems are often caused by damaged wiring and connectors, tapping and wiggling wiring harnesses and connectors can also get problems to reoccur and reset codes.

Check the fuel system for air leaks between the supply and injection pumps. If air is suspected to be in the fuel system, there are usually bleeders located on the filter and injection pump for purging. Crank the engine to build pressure and, working from the tank forward, loosen the bleeder screws until only fuel flows from the opening. Then, tighten the bleeder screws.

A clogged fuel filter can be determined by connecting a fuel pressure gauge in-line on either side of the filter and then comparing the input-side and output-side readings with specifications. If the pressure drop across the filter is not within specifications, the filter must be replaced.

This same procedure can be used to detect restrictions elsewhere in the system.

Engine Misfires

An electronic engine control system failure, air in the fuel, an air inlet or exhaust system restriction, a clogged fuel filter, defective injector or low compression could cause a misfire.

Use a scan tool to check for current and pending DTCs.

An infrared thermometer can be used to help determine a bad cylinder, since the exhaust runner for a non-contributing cylinder should be much cooler than the others during the first few minutes of engine operation.

The injection to each cylinder can also be disabled. Methods vary for disabling the injectors according to fuel system type. A scan tool can be used to disable electronic injectors. A failed injector will have little or no affect on engine performance or rpm.

Engine Lacks Power

Failure to develop normal power could be caused by a failure in the electronic engine control system, contaminated fuel or low fuel pressure, injection and/or injection timing malfunctions, an air inlet and/or exhaust system restriction, low compression or insufficient turbo boost.

Use a scan tool to check for current and pending DTCs.

Check fuel quality and check for restrictions and air in the fuel system. Check the injection pump output pressure.

On older, mechanical systems the injection pump timing is set by aligning marks on the pump and gear housing. On electronically controlled systems, the PCM/ECM controls injection timing based on inputs from the CMP and/or CKP (Crankshaft Position) sensors and injection control pressure sensors. In theory, a malfunction in the system should set a DTC, but this may not be the case. If a problem is suspected, study the vehicle service information to determine the control system strategy and perform tests as necessary.

One or two cylinders with low compression will cause misfire and rough running. If there is uniform low compression on all cylinders, this could be a sign of worn rings on an extremely high-mileage or abused (run without enough oil) engine or it could also be an indication of valve timing that is out of specification.

Insufficient turbo boost could be caused by a clogged air filter or other air intake restriction, air leaks downstream from the compressor, damage to the compressor from dirt or lubrication failure, or wastegate malfunction. On many modern diesels, the wastegate is controlled by the PCM/ECM based on input from pressure, temperature and engine speed sensors.

Engine Smokes

A properly operating diesel at normal operating temperature should have a clear exhaust stream. Any coloration to the exhaust stream would be indicative of an engine problem.

Black smoke is an indication of a rich running engine. The technician may also experience eye discomfort when working on the vehicle if this condition exists. Rich conditions are more common than lean conditions, and may be caused by defects such as leaking injectors, clogged air cleaners or collapsed air intake hoses.

Blue smoke exists when the engine is getting oil in the combustion process. Oil burning can be the result of valve guide wear, turbocharger seal failure or worn piston rings. If the source of oil burning is traced to piston rings, it can lead the technician to the root cause of a performance defect, since worn piston rings can also affect compression and compression is the source of ignition on a diesel engine.

White smoke is an indication of a lean condition. Defects such as low fuel pressure or a crimped fuel line can cause this. Bad glow plugs or a faulty glow plug control module can also cause white smoke on engine startup.

The technician should also make sure to distinguish between white smoke and steam, which would indicate that water is entering the combustion process. This would usually lead to a cooling system problem.

ENGINE NOISE

The typical diesel engine emits a characteristic 'clatter', particularly when warming up. This is caused by the sudden ignition of diesel fuel in the combustion process. Gear-driven injection pumps and valvetrains as well as increased piston-to-wall clearance (compared with gasoline engines) can also contribute noise. Always use fuel with the required cetane rating to help minimize combustion noise. Since diesel engine noises can be disguised by the engine's normal operating sound, it is important to know the difference between a proper functioning diesel engine and one that exhibits problem sounds.

Generally, noises are caused by too much clearance between parts or loss of oil pressure. The following common engine noises can be caused by any of these parts:

Crankshaft Noises
- Main bearings
- Connecting rod bearings
- Pistons
- Wrist pin
- Crankshaft end-play.

Valvetrain Noises
- Bearing noise
- Rocker arms, shaft, ball and seat
- Pushrods

- Tappets and camshaft
- Timing gears and chain.

Other Noises
- Loose or broken brackets
- Oil pump failure.

In order to successfully diagnose noises, you must pay close attention to the frequency at which the noise occurs and how the frequency changes as you vary engine load and engine rpm. Also note how factors such as temperature and oil pressure affect the noise. A stethoscope can be used to find the location of a noise.

Bearing Noises

Main bearing noise is caused by too much bearing clearance due to worn bearings or crankshaft journals or a lack of lubrication. It is usually indicated by a dull or deep-sounding metallic knocking. When you increase rpm or engine load, the knocking usually increases in frequency. The noise is usually most obvious right after the engine starts up, when the engine is under a heavy load, or during acceleration. Along with the knocking sound, the engine may also exhibit low oil pressure.

Connecting rod noise, which is also caused by excessive bearing clearance or lack of lubrication, is much less intense than main bearing noise. This noise usually sounds like a light metallic rapping that is most noticeable when the engine is running under a light load at relatively slow speeds. This knock becomes louder and occurs more frequently when the speed of the engine is increased. When you eliminate the injection to the cylinder with a rod knock, the sound diminishes.

Crankshaft End-Play Noise

Crankshaft end-play noise occurs when there is excessive clearance between the crankshaft thrust bearing and the machined faces of the crankshaft thrust journal, allowing the crankshaft to move back and forth.

When crankshaft end-play is excessive, the engine may make a deep knocking sound that is usually most obvious at idle but diminishes when a load is placed on the crankshaft, such as when the clutch is disengaged on a manual transmission vehicle.

Where space allows, you can verify excessive crankshaft end-play by fitting a dial indicator to the tip of the crankshaft. Using a prybar, carefully pry the crankshaft back and forth and note the reading on the dial indicator. Compare the reading with specifications.

Piston Noise

Excessive piston-to-wall clearance can cause piston slap. This is caused by side-to-side movement of the piston within the cylinder bore, and sounds like a dull or muffled metallic rattle at idle or during light engine loads.

Very faint piston slap may disappear after the engine warms up and the piston expands. In this case, the piston-to-wall clearance usually isn't severe enough to worry about. However, piston slap that continues after the engine warms up should be corrected. Note that unlike a connecting rod bearing noise, piston slap does not quiet down and may in fact grow louder when you eliminate fuel injection to that cylinder.

A knocking noise can be caused by excessive carbon buildup in the combustion chamber where the piston contacts the carbon at TDC (Top Dead Center).

Piston Pin Noise

When piston-to-piston pin clearance is excessive, the pin makes a light but sharp metallic rapping at idle. The sound may be more obvious during low-speed driving. Eliminating fuel injection to a cylinder with a loose piston pin will change the frequency and possibly the in-

tensity of the rapping noise.

Valvetrain Noise

Valvetrain noise can be caused by excessive valve clearance in adjustable valvetrains, worn components like rocker arms, shafts, lifters and camshaft, or lack of lubrication. It is usually indicated by a light ticking noise at idle that occurs at a frequency slower than engine rpm. This is because the valvetrain operates at half the crankshaft speed.

Hydraulic Lifters

A noisy hydraulic lifter usually makes a consistent ticking sound. Try sliding a feeler gauge between the valve stem and the rocker arm. If this eliminates the ticking, it confirms that there is excessive clearance in the valvetrain.

With the engine running, you can also press down on the pushrod end of each rocker arm with a piece of wood or a hammer handle. If this stops or reduces the ticking, you have pinpointed the faulty lifter. Always check valve adjustment and inspect valvetrain parts for wear or damage. Worn valvetrain parts can mimic the noise of bad hydraulic lifters.

Other Noises

A high pitched squealing noise when the engine is accelerated indicates a loose or glazed drive belt.

A thumping noise at the back of the engine that is most noticeable when the vehicle is in Park or Neutral can be caused by loose torque converter bolts or a loose or cracked flexplate.

ENGINE VIBRATION

A misfire in one or more cylinders can cause vibration, but so can parts that turn with the engine and components that come in contact with other parts.

Check the crankshaft vibration damper and pulleys for damage and, if equipped, check the flexplate for missing balance weights. Make sure

that rotating accessories and their brackets are attached securely.

Check for loose turbocharger mounts and turbocharger damage. Bearing failure could cause the rotating assembly to contact the housing and cause an imbalance.

Check the exhaust pipes and other components connected to the drivetrain and make sure they are not misrouted and contacting the frame or suspension.

CYLINDER COMPRESSION, LEAKAGE AND PRESSURE TESTS

Perform the compression test with the engine at the temperature recommended by the manufacturer. Some specifications are for a cold engine while others are for an engine at normal operating temperature. Remove all of the glow plugs or injectors, depending on how the compression gauge will be attached, and disable the fuel system. Be sure the battery is strong enough to maintain the same cranking speed throughout the test. Use a battery charger if the battery is questionable.

Connect the compression gauge to the cylinder being tested, crank the engine through five or six com-

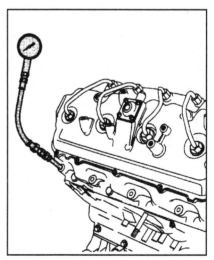

Checking compression with the gauge connected to a glow plug hole. (Courtesy: GM Corp.)

pression strokes and note how the gauge responds. A healthy cylinder usually builds most of its pressure on the first compression stroke and continues building to a good compression reading. Service manuals usually list compression pressure specifications as well as allowable deviations from them. In general, if measurements between cylinders vary more than 20%, it will cause the engine to run rough.

When compression is low in two adjacent cylinders, the head gasket may be blown or the block cracked between those two cylinders. Low compression on all cylinders could be a sign of worn rings on an extremely high-mileage or abused (run without enough oil) engine. It could also be an indication of valve timing that is out of specification.

To determine where compression is leaking, perform a cylinder leakage test. Bring the piston in the weak cylinder up to TDC on the compression stroke and pump compressed air into the cylinder. Where the air leaks out shows you the location of the compression leak.

Air that causes bubbles in the radiator coolant indicates a cracked head, cracked block and/ or a blown head gasket. Air coming from the glow plug or injector hole in an adjacent cylinder means a blown head gasket. Air that is blowing out of the intake system confirms that an intake valve is leaking, while air that comes out of the tailpipe means that an exhaust valve is leaking. Air coming from the dipstick tube or oil fill indicates leaking rings and/or worn pistons.

A crankcase pressure test can also be used to determine the condition of the cylinder bore, rings and pistons. Follow the manufacturer's instructions for its use, but in general the PCV system must be sealed and the tester attached to the oil fill tube. Compare the pressure reading with the manufacturer's specifications.

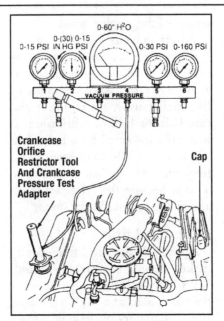

Measuring crankcase pressure. *(Courtesy: Ford Motor Co.)*

ENGINE LEAKS

Fuel Leaks

Since the fuel system is under pressure when the engine is running, the source of a fuel leak is usually not difficult to find. Fuel can leak from damaged lines or O-rings or from loose fittings. Inspect fuel lines for cracks, corrosion and damage from abrasion. Make sure all fittings are properly installed and tightened. Components like pumps, filters and filter/water separators can also be the source of a fuel leak.

If you suspect a leak because air keeps getting into the system but are unable to find it, disconnect the fuel line from the tank and pressurize the system with low-pressure air (no more than 15 psi). Then apply soapy water to line connections, filter canisters, fuel/water separators and all other potential leak sources. Repair leaks as necessary and bleed the system.

Oil Leaks

Oil leaks are most often caused by hardened or worn out seals and gaskets, or leaking oil pressure sending units. However, engine oil leaks can also be caused by something

technicians often overlook — excessive crank-case pressure, which can be caused by worn rings or excessive cylinder wall clearances or a restricted crankcase breather tube. These problems allow an unusual amount of combustion blowby gases to enter the crankcase, where the gases can push oil past seals and gaskets that are in good condition.

To find the source of an oil leak, bring the engine to normal operating temperature and then park the vehicle over a large piece of paper or old sheet. Wait several minutes, and then check for dripping fluids.

Of course, engine oil may not be the only fluid leaking from the vehicle, so you'll need to become familiar with the color, feel and smell of different fluids. Engine oil will be brown, dark brown or black and feel slippery. Automatic transmission fluid will be red or dark brown and smell differently than engine oil. Antifreeze can be green, orange or rust colored and, while slippery, will have a different feel than engine oil. Power steering fluid can be red or clear and will feel like transmission fluid. A clear or dark brown fluid that is significantly less slippery than engine oil is probably brake fluid or hydraulic clutch fluid.

Check for leaks at sealing surface areas, fittings and sending units. If the source of the leak cannot be found, thoroughly clean the engine and surrounding components and apply powder to the suspected leak area. Operate the vehicle for several miles at normal operating temperature and again check for leaks, which will be indicated by discolorations in the powder.

For hard to find oil leaks, add a fluorescent dye to the engine oil that is visible with a black light. Run the engine for a while and then pass the light around the engine. The dye should pinpoint the source of the leak.

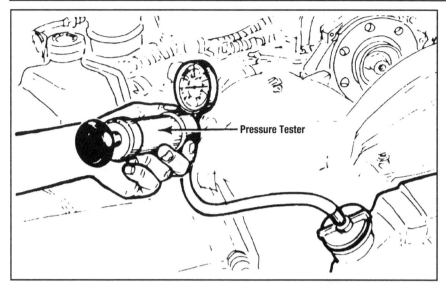

Pressure testing the cooling system. Watch the gauge needle for an indication of a cooling system leak.

Coolant Leaks

Visually inspect for coolant leaks at the radiator and heater hoses, water pump, radiator, intake manifold, sensor fittings, water control valves and heater core. Attach a suitable pressure tester to the coolant filler neck and apply pressure equal to the pressure rating marked on the radiator cap (make sure the cap is the correct one for the vehicle!). The pressure should remain at that level if there are no leaks in the cooling system. If the pressure drops, check for leaks in the same areas.

External coolant leaks are relatively easy to find. But, what if you pressurize the cooling system with a cooling system pressure tester, the pressure drops, and no coolant appears outside the engine? This indicates that the coolant leak is inside the engine and is most likely caused by a defective intake manifold or timing cover gasket, blown head gasket, cracked cylinder head or cracked block. Inspect the engine oil for signs of coolant; if it is thick and milky, that's a dead giveaway.

Symptoms will vary depending upon the severity of an internal coolant leak. When coolant leaks into a cylinder, it may create white exhaust smoke. It may also cause misfiring, especially when the engine is cold.

If coolant is leaking into a cylinder, combustion gases will also be able to escape into the cooling system. When combustion gas escapes into the cooling system, it can cause big air bubbles to appear in the radiator coolant when the engine is running. It can also pressurize the coolant recovery reservoir.

One common internal coolant leak detection procedure uses a chemical that is sensitive to combustion gas. With the engine running, place a vial of the chemical over the radiator neck and draw vapors from the top of the radiator into the vial. If the chemical changes color, you know that combustion gases are leaking into the cooling system.

Sometimes when you disable cylinders, the bubbles appearing in the radiator will diminish when you eliminate the cylinder that has the coolant leak. Disabling the leaking cylinder may also reveal little or no rpm drop compared to the other cylinders.

If the radiator is cool enough to do so, remove the radiator cap. Then perform a leakdown test on the suspected cylinder. If pumping air into that cylinder produces bubbles in the radiator coolant, you know that the leak is in that cylinder. If you also find that air escapes from an adjacent cylinder, you know that the head gasket has blown out between those two cylinders and has caused both a compression leak and a coolant leak.

DIESEL FUEL

There are different grades and ratings for diesel fuel. Number 2 grade is the standard fuel and is used during the summer months. All diesel fuels have what are called 'cloud' and 'pour' points. The cloud point refers to the temperature at which the fuel begins to thicken and 'cloud'. The pour point is the temperature at which the fuel will no longer flow. Number 1 grade fuel, which has a lower pour point, or a mixture of grade's 1 and 2, is used in the colder, winter months to aid starting.

Cetane is the ignition value of diesel fuel, somewhat like octane for gasoline. Most number 2 grade diesel fuel available for highway vehicles has a cetane rating of 40-55. Most electronically controlled diesels require fuel with a cetane rating of at least 45. Fuels with higher cetane ratings improve cold starting and reduce white smoke.

As of this writing, Ultra Low Sulfur Diesel (ULSD) fuel is being phased in at service stations across the United States, and will be the only fuel available for highway use after December 1, 2010. Diesel engine vehicles manufactured after 2007 are designed to operate with ULSD fuel. Using fuel with lower sulfur content will substantially reduce particulate emissions (soot) in diesel engine exhaust.

Diesel fuel is susceptible to contamination from water and microorganisms. Water usually comes from condensation that forms during cold weather. The water can then freeze in the filter and/or fuel/water separator and cause a blockage. Certain microbes can actually live in a diesel fuel system and feed on diesel fuel. These microbes can form colonies that can grow rapidly during warm weather, eventually clogging fuel lines, filters, injection pumps and injectors.

Place a fuel sample taken from a point before the filter/water separator into a clean glass container and allow it to settle for a few minutes. Fuel that is cloudy is an indication of water contamination, while microbes will appear as jelly-like particles floating on the surface. If there is contamination, the fuel tank should be drained and the system cleaned and treated with a biocide to kill the microbes.

LUBRICATING SYSTEM

On any engine it is important to use the proper weight and grade of engine oil, maintain the oil level and change it according to schedule, but it is particularly so on modern electronically controlled diesel engines.

Using the wrong weight oil in the colder, winter months may cause hard or no starting. A multi-viscosity oil that is fine during warmer weather may become too thick when the temperature drops, increasing drag on the reciprocating assembly. Cranking speed may be reduced to the point where it is too slow to start the engine. Always refer to the manufacturer's service information to make sure that when the oil is changed, the proper oil is used for anticipated temperatures.

Beginning in 2007, all new diesel engines were required to use API (American Petroleum Institute) service category CJ-4 lubricating oil. This new grade became necessary to protect emissions equipment like EGR systems and DPFs (Diesel Particulate Filters) installed on newer electronically controlled diesel engines. CJ-4 oil has maximum limits for phosphorus, sulfur and sulfated ash content. These limits will help maintain the life of the emissions control equipment, to help ensure the vehicle will remain emissions regulations compliant. According to API, CJ-4 exceeds the performance criteria of earlier grades and may be used in older vehicles. However, always consult the vehicle manufacturer for recommendations.

Maintaining the proper oil level and changing the oil according to the manufacturer's maintenance schedule is especially important on engines with HEUI systems. The fuel injectors on these engines are actuated by high-pressure crankcase oil.

When checking the engine oil level, examine the oil on the dipstick. If the oil smells like diesel fuel, it could be from faulty injector seals. Just because the oil is dark doesn't mean that there is a problem, as oil will quickly darken during normal engine use. However, if the oil appears milky, there is probably coolant in the oil, which could be caused by a blown head gasket, cracked block or defective oil cooler. Of course, the only way to be absolutely sure regarding the oil's integrity is to send a sample to a lab for analysis.

The oil pressure can be checked by installing a suitable mechanical gauge in place of the oil pressure sending unit. Refer to the manufacturer's specifications for pressure and for the temperature and rpm at which pressure should be measured. Oil temperature can be checked by inserting the gauge's temperature probe into the dipstick tube.

Oil Consumption

The three common causes of excessive oil consumption are oil leaks, valve guide/valve seal problems, and piston ring problems.

When an engine is using oil, inspect it visually for serious oil leaks first. Check the crankcase ventilation system as a matter of routine. If you don't, the oil leaks may reappear in spite of the new seals and gaskets you install.

A careful road test can be a critical diagnostic step in determining the cause of the oil burning. Note when the oil smoke is most intense. Typically, bad piston rings/cylinder wear will make the engine smoke at all speeds. When a vehicle suffers from worn valve guides and/or bad valve stem seals, you'll see exhaust smoke during acceleration after the engine has been idling and immediately after engine startup.

Before you blame either the valve guides or the valve seals for an oil consumption problem, verify that all of the oil return holes are clean. If oil cannot drain freely back into the crankcase, it can accumulate in the head and travel down the valve guides into the combustion chambers, increasing oil consumption and causing exhaust smoke. Valve stem seals are designed to keep normal amounts of lubricating oil from entering the combustion chamber, but seldom work well when submerged in oil.

COOLING SYSTEM

Begin cooling system inspection by checking the coolant appearance, level and freeze protection. The coolant should appear clean and translucent; a cloudy or muddy appearance is evidence of contamination. Check the coolant level in the expansion or overflow tank. The coolant should be at the level indicated for the temperature of the coolant.

Check coolant concentration using a hydrometer. A hydrometer uses a calibrated float to measure the specific gravity of a liquid. The specific gravity of coolant changes according to the antifreeze concentration; the specific gravity increases as the concentration of the antifreeze increases.

It is best to obtain a coolant sample directly from the radiator, as the overflow tank may have recently been topped off with water or pure antifreeze. Always use caution when removing the radiator cap from a pressurized system; only remove the cap when the system is cold. Draw the coolant into the hydrometer and read the specific gravity on the float. The protection level should be at least –34ºF (–37ºC), which represents a 50/50 mixture of antifreeze and water.

Visually inspect the cooling system for problems. Check for signs of coolant leaks at all hose connections, core plugs (freeze plugs), head gasket(s), thermostat housing, water pump and radiator. Inspect all hoses for cracks, ballooning or brittleness and replace if necessary. If the hoses feel soft or mushy when they are squeezed, replace them.

Check the radiator for restrictions in the air passages through the core. Clean the fins of debris, bugs or leaves that may have been drawn in while driving. Sometimes, debris may collect between the radiator and condenser. Make sure all fins are intact, and not bent so as to misdirect air flow. Distorted fins can be straightened using a suitable tool, however, be careful when straightening because the fins are very delicate.

Inspect the radiator for damage and any signs of leakage from the core tubes, radiator tanks and hose collars. Look inside the radiator for large amounts of mineral deposits at the ends of the core tubes, as mineral buildup can cause an internal restriction. If blockage inside the radiator is suspected, an infrared surface thermometer can be used to scan the surface of the radiator when the engine is hot and idling. The radiator should be warmest near the inlet and gradually cool toward the outlet. If there are areas that are considerably cooler than the inlet, then there may be restrictions at those areas.

Check the radiator cap rating to make sure it is the right one for the vehicle. Check the cap's relief valve

spring action, and inspect the seal for brittleness. Check the filler neck on the radiator or surge tank mating surface.

Check the water pump drive belt for wear, glazing and belt tension. A slipping belt will not turn the pump impeller at the proper speed to circulate coolant. If the engine is equipped with a mechanical fan, a slipping belt will cause the fan to turn too slowly, not draw enough air through the radiator, and possibly cause the engine to overheat. Replace or adjust the belt as necessary.

Check for a coolant leak from the vent hole at the bottom of the water pump shaft housing. Check the water pump bearings by grasping the fan or pulley and attempt to move the impeller shaft back and forth. If there is any movement, the water pump bearings are defective. Remove the drive belt and turn the pulley by hand. The pulley should turn smoothly. If there is noise and/or binding, the bearings are defective. Replace the pump if it leaks or the bearings are defective.

Inspect the fan for missing, cracked or bent blades. If equipped with a fan clutch, check the back of the clutch for an oily film, which would indicate that fluid is leaking and replacement is necessary. Turn the fan and clutch assembly by hand; there should be some viscous drag, but it should turn smoothly during a full rotation. Replace the fan clutch if it does not turn smoothly or if it does not turn at all. It should also be replaced if there is no viscous drag when hot or cold.

If the fan is electric, make sure it runs when the engine warms up and also when the A/C is switched on. Make sure the fan shroud is in place and not broken.

Start the engine and listen for unusual noises. A hammering sound may indicate a restriction in the water jacket or air in the system. Squealing noises indicate a bad

belt or water pump bearing damage. Gurgling from the radiator may point to air in the system.

The engine's operating temperature can be verified by installing a mechanical gauge or by using an infrared surface thermometer.

BATTERY

Preliminary Inspection

WARNING: The sulfuric acid in battery electrolyte an cause serious injury if it contacts the eyes or skin. To prevent injury, always wear skin and eye protection when servicing the battery. Batteries give off hydrogen gas, which is highly explosive. Never smoke or allow flames near a battery.

Visually inspect the battery, looking for damage to the battery case and damage or corrosion on the battery terminals and cables. If the battery case is damaged and there is any evidence of leakage, the battery must be replaced. Check the battery's date of manufacture. Just because the battery is near the end of its service life does not mean that it will necessarily test bad, however the age of the battery must be considered when deciding whether replacement is necessary.

Corrosion on the battery case, and battery tray and hold-down, can be cleaned with a solution of baking soda and water. Make sure the battery tray is in good condition and the battery is mounted securely, without over-tightening the battery hold-down.

If the battery terminals and cables are corroded, remove the cables, negative cable first, and clean the terminals and cables with a battery brush. Before disconnecting the battery cables, keep in mind that computers, programmable radios, and other solid-state memory units may have their memories erased by disconnecting the battery. In addition, the engine and transmission on some vehicles may perform erratically when first started and must undergo a relearning process, once the battery is reconnected. To prevent this, a 12-volt power supply from a dry cell battery can be connected to the cigarette lighter or power point connector to maintain voltage in the system while the battery is disconnected.

Inspect the entire length of the battery cables for heavy corrosion, frayed wires and damaged insulation, and replace as necessary. Secure the cables to the battery terminals after cleaning, and apply a coating of petroleum jelly to the terminals to minimize further corrosion.

If the battery has removable vent caps, check the electrolyte condition and level in each battery cell. Look for cloudy or muddy discoloration of the fluid. Discolored fluid is a sign of recent deep cycle discharge action. Add distilled water to the proper level, if necessary. In general, the electrolyte should be 1/4 - 1/2-in. (6.35 - 12.70mm) above the plates.

Battery Ratings

Batteries are classified according to physical size, Cold Cranking Amps (CCA) and Reserve Capacity (RC). Cold Cranking Amps are the number of amps a fully charged battery can deliver for 30 seconds at 0°F, while maintaining a voltage of 7.2 volts. Reserve Capacity is the number of minutes the battery can deliver 25 amps at 80°F while maintaining a voltage of 10.5 volts.

Battery State-of-Charge

A hydrometer can be used to check the specific gravity of the battery's electrolyte if the vent caps are removable. The glass tube of the hydrometer is scale-calibrated to read specific gravity in a range of about 1.100 to 1.300.

The floats in the hydrometer are calibrated with 80°F (27°C) being the exact reference point. For each 10°F variation above or below the 80°F (27°C) mark, 0.004 specific gravity points are added (for temperatures above 80°F) or subtracted (for temperatures below 80°F).

A battery with a specific gravity reading of 1.260 (usually stated as twelve-sixty) is generally regarded as fully charged, while a battery with a reading of 1.070 (ten-seventy) is generally regarded as fully discharged. It follows that 1.120 is one-quarter charged; 1.170 is half-charged; and 1.215 is three-quarters charged. A maximum of 0.050 (50 points) difference between cells is all that is allowed. Any difference greater than this calls for further testing of the battery, and the battery may have to be removed from service.

When checking specific gravity, hold the hydrometer in a vertical position and insert the draw tube into the battery. Draw just enough electrolyte into the tube to permit the float to move freely without touching the top, bottom, or sides. Note that there are times when electrolyte readings are inaccurate. One is just after adding water to the battery. After adding water, it is recommended to wait at least one day, or until the vehicle has been operated for a while to check specific gravity. Another time is during or just after charging. After charging, it is recommended to wait at least 15 minutes prior to checking specific gravity. Still another time is just after the battery has been subjected to a high rate of discharge, such as after prolonged cranking.

The electrolyte cannot be checked on sealed maintenance-free batteries. However, some of these batteries have a built-in hydrometer. Although the readings can vary according to manufacturer, usually a good battery is indicated by a green or light-colored dot in the center.

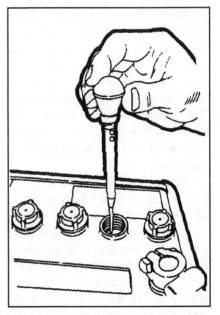

Checking electrolyte specific gravity with a hydrometer.

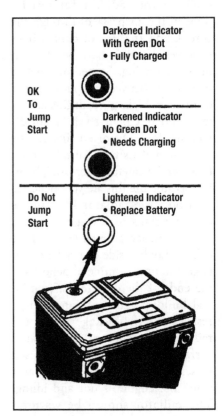

Charge indicator on a sealed maintenance-free battery.

If the indicator is dark, the battery may be jumped or recharged. If the indicator is clear or light yellow, the fluid level is below the level of the hydrometer; the battery should not be charged and should be replaced. Always refer to the label on the battery or the battery manufacturer's instructions to interpret battery condition using the built-in hydrometer. Also, be aware that the built-in hydrometer indicates the condition of only one cell.

At 70°F (21°C) and with all accessories turned off, a healthy fully charged battery should produce 12.6 volts when measured with a voltmeter at the battery terminals. Check the open circuit voltage of the battery to determine if it must be charged before further testing. Remove the surface charge from the battery by turning on the high beams for 10 seconds, then wait a few seconds before checking the battery voltage. Make sure all accessories are off, then measure the voltage at the battery terminals with a voltmeter. If the voltage is less than 12.4 volts, the battery must be charged before proceeding with further testing.

Battery Capacity Testing

Of the many ways to rate the condition of a battery, perhaps the most revealing is to measure its ability to hold up under a high-rate discharge test. This will tell not only if the battery will do the job which it is expected to do, but also if other conditions are within general allowable tolerances.

Connect the battery load tester to the battery terminals. Turn the load control knob to draw current equal to three times the ampere-hour (amp/hr) rating or one-half the CCA (Cold Cranking Amps) rating. The battery rating is usually given on the battery case, case top or label, and some labels will indicate the load that should be placed on the battery. Maintain the load for 15 seconds, then check the voltage reading. On a good battery, the voltage should be 9.6 volts or higher, however the voltage may be slightly lower if the ambient temperature is less than 70°F (21°C).

If a battery fails a load test, but was deemed OK for testing when the state-of-charge was checked, connect a voltmeter and battery charger to the battery and charge the battery for three minutes with the charger set at 40 amps. If after three minutes the voltage reading is greater than 15.5 volts, replace the battery.

Key Off Battery Drain

Excessive circuit drain when the vehicle is not running can lead to battery depletion, even if the battery is in good condition and the charging system is in proper working order.

The main reason for a very slight draw on the battery is the fact that major computerized systems in the vehicle need voltage at all times in order to function properly. Components such as computer memories and stored diagnostic data must be kept whether the vehicle is running or not. The digital clock and other such items also draw a very small current while the vehicle is off. This is not a problem for today's vehicles as long as the drain is not excessive.

Sometimes, it's hard to tell whether there is a key off battery drain because the drain won't be enough to completely discharge the battery while the vehicle is off. The only way this type of drain manifests itself is by excessive battery water usage and the fact that the battery doesn't last as long as it should with a known good charging and starting system. Always use the manufacturer's suggested key off drain specifications when trying to determine the proper amount of current that computer systems and accessories should draw when the vehicle's engine is not running.

Using a 12-volt test light in series with a battery cable is not the most accurate way to check for key off battery drain. The most effective way of checking this condition is to use an ammeter in series with

the negative battery cable and the negative battery post. This enables full battery voltage to the vehicle during the measurement. Another method that can be used is to measure voltage drop across a 1-ohm resistor connected in series between the negative battery cable and the negative battery post, using a DMM (Digital Multimeter).

NOTE: Make sure the ignition switch is in the OFF position at all times during testing. In addition, all courtesy and accessory lights must be off.

If an excessive drain is displayed, remove the fuses from the fuse block one at a time. When the specific fuse powering the circuit with the drain is removed, the high voltage reading will stabilize to a normal reading.

Using a wiring diagram, note the specific circuits that run to the particular fuse that was pulled. Reinstall the fuse and allow the DMM to read the excessive draw. Now, disconnect each circuit to further isolate the current draw. When the draw returns to normal, you've found the circuit that's causing the problem.

If the drain is not found using this procedure, use a wiring diagram and locate all circuits connected to the battery that use a fusible link. Disconnect the circuits, one at a time, to isolate the circuit with the excessive draw. A fusible link is a fused wire that protects a particular circuit from high currents, and may be either in a harness, or mounted separately, and performs the same function as the fuse in a fuse block.

STARTING SYSTEM

Starter Current Draw Test

Perform a starter current-draw test with a high-amperage-rated ammeter designed for this purpose. Allow the engine to warm up to normal

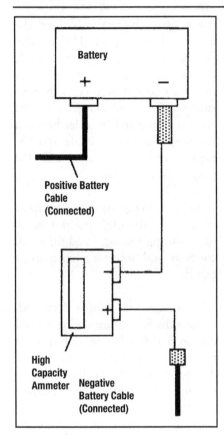

Battery electrical drain check.
(Courtesy: GM Corp.)

operating temperature, then disable the fuel system. Connect the ammeter's inductive pickup to the negative battery cable or connect the ammeter in series with the negative battery cable. Also, connect a voltmeter across the battery terminals.

With the test connections made and all electrical loads off, crank the engine over with the starter. Starter current draw when cranking the engine over should be around 150 amps for a 4-cylinder engine, 200 amps for a 6-cylinder and 250 amps for a V8, however, some permanent magnet type and gear reduction starters can draw more. Always refer to the specifications in the vehicle service manual. Battery voltage should remain above 9.6V, and the engine should spin rapidly.

Higher than normal current-draw readings may be caused by a short circuit in the starter motor or mechanical problems causing binding in the engine. Amperage that is too low may be caused by starter circuit resistance.

Voltage Drop Test

Connect the voltmeter black lead to the battery cable connection at the starter. Make sure the test point is positioned after the starter relay. Now, disable the fuel system and crank the starter motor. As you crank the engine, touch the red lead of the voltmeter to the positive post of the battery. Quickly switch the voltage scale knob of the voltmeter to progressively lower scales until a reading can be seen. Be sure to remove the red voltmeter lead from the battery post before you release the starter engagement, or you could damage the meter.

If the voltage drop exceeds 0.5V for the entire starter circuit, repeat the test, moving the black lead toward the battery one connection at a time. When you get past the bad one, the voltage drop reading will sharply decline. Once the high resistance connection is identified, clean the connection or replace the part causing the problem. Refer to the proper service manual for the manufacturer's maximum acceptable voltage drop specifications.

Starter Ground And Connection

To check the starter ground circuit, first place the black lead of the voltmeter on the negative battery post. Now, using the same technique you used on the supply voltage circuit, crank the starter and place the red lead on the starter housing. Read the voltage drop. If you find a high resistance at the starter mounting, the presence of engine-to-starter shims, or an engine-to-battery ground cable that produces more than the voltage drop recommended by the manufac-

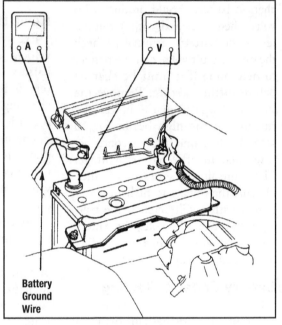

Performing a starter current draw test.
(Courtesy: Honda Motor Co.)

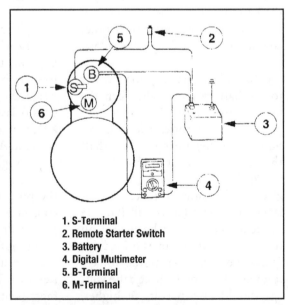

1. S-Terminal
2. Remote Starter Switch
3. Battery
4. Digital Multimeter
5. B-Terminal
6. M-Terminal

Performing a starter voltage drop test.
(Courtesy: Ford Motor Co.)

turer, check carefully for a poor connection or even corrosion.

Locate the problem by moving the red lead closer to the battery post in steps. Repeat the voltage test each time. Don't forget to remove the red lead before you stop cranking the engine!

Now check the control circuit. Locate the starter relay or solenoid and place the black voltmeter lead on the relay control voltage terminal. Crank the engine over and place the red lead to the positive battery terminal to check the voltage drop. This checks the circuit through the ignition switch, neutral safety switch and wiring harness.

Remember to check the relay ground. Quite often, relays are mounted on non-metallic inner fender panels and require a good ground to the metal car body.

Starter Relay

Some starting systems use a relay between the ignition switch and starter solenoid. When the ignition key is turned to start, current flows to the relay, closing the relay contacts. When the relay contacts close, current from the battery flows to the starter solenoid.

To test the relay, measure the voltage at the relay switch terminal and starter terminal and compare to specifications. If the voltage is less than specified at the switch terminal, there is a problem in the control circuit upstream of the relay. If the voltage is as specified at the switch terminal but not at the starter terminal, the relay should be replaced.

The starter relay can be mounted in the engine compartment on the firewall or inner fender, or plug into an underhood fuse and relay box. To replace the former type, disconnect the negative battery cable and mark and remove the wires from the relay. Loosen the fasteners and remove the relay from its mounting. Before installing a replacement relay, check all cables and connections for corrosion

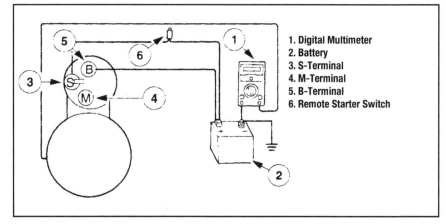

Testing the starter ground circuit. *(Courtesy: Ford Motor Co.)*

1. Digital Multimeter
2. Battery
3. S-Terminal
4. M-Terminal
5. B-Terminal
6. Remote Starter Switch

and proper routing. Clean and make repairs as necessary. To install the relay, reverse the removal procedure.

Starter Solenoid

A starter solenoid is an electromagnetic switch. It may be remotely mounted away from the starter, on the firewall or inner fender, or it may be mounted on the starter motor. Remote mounted solenoids open or close the battery-to-starter circuit. Starter mounted solenoids do this as well, but also push the starter drive gear into mesh with the flywheel/flexplate ring gear.

When voltage is provided to a starter mounted solenoid from the ignition switch or starter relay, the starter solenoid is energized, creating a magnetic field in the solenoid coil and drawing in an iron plunger core into the coil. A lever connected to the starter drive engages the drive gear with the flywheel/flexplate ring gear. When the iron plunger core is all the way into the coil, its contact disc closes the circuit between the battery and the starter motor terminals. Current flows to the motor and the drive gear turns the flywheel/flexplate.

As current flows to the motor, the solenoid pull-in coil is bypassed and the hold-in coil keeps the drive gear engaged with the flywheel/flexplate. The gear remains engaged until the ignition switch is released from the start position.

The starter solenoid can be tested in the same manner as the starter relay. The solenoid can also be tested using a jumper wire between the battery and solenoid 'S' terminals. If the engine cranks, there is a problem in the starter control circuit. If the solenoid makes a clicking sound, it is operating properly and the problem may be with the starter. If no sound is heard, the solenoid is defective and should be replaced.

To replace a remote solenoid, disconnect the negative battery cable and mark and remove the wires from the solenoid. Loosen the fasteners and remove the solenoid from its mounting. Before installing a replacement solenoid, check all cables and connections for corrosion and proper routing. Clean and make repairs as necessary. To install the solenoid, reverse the removal procedure.

To replace a starter-mounted solenoid, disconnect the negative battery cable, then mark and remove the wires from the solenoid. If necessary, remove the starter from the vehicle. Remove the mounting bolts for the solenoid. You may have to rotate the solenoid to remove it from the starter, as some solenoids have a tab that fits in the starter housing. In addition, the plunger spring puts a slight tension on the solenoid.

When installing the solenoid, make sure the spring is in place between the plunger and the solenoid body. Hold the solenoid and compress the spring. If necessary, locate the tab and rotate the solenoid into position. Install the solenoid mounting bolts. If removed, install the starter motor. Reconnect the starter wires and the negative battery cable and check for proper operation.

Neutral Start Switch

The neutral start switch prevents vehicles with automatic transmissions from starting in gear positions other than Neutral or Park. The switch can be located on the steering column, shift lever or transmission.

To check the switch, apply the brakes and move the gearshift lever through each position while holding the ignition key in the Start position. If the starter operates in gear positions other than Neutral or Park, the switch may only need adjustment.

To adjust the switch, place the transmission in Park and loosen the switch mounting screws. Turn the ignition key to the start position and move the switch until the starter operates. Hold the switch in that position, release the ignition key and tighten the switch mounting screws. Check switch operation.

To electrically test the switch, touch a 12-volt test light to the switch output wire while moving the gearshift lever through each position. The test light should be on only when the gearshift is in Neutral or Park. If the light works otherwise, check the device that actuates the switch. If that is OK, replace the switch.

Clutch Switch

The start/clutch interlock switch is a safety device that prevents the engine from starting with the transmission in gear. It prevents the starter from operating unless the clutch pedal is depressed.

The switch is open when the clutch pedal is in the released posi-

tion, interrupting current flow in the starter circuit. When the clutch pedal is depressed, the switch closes, allowing current flow in the circuit. If the starter engages with the clutch pedal released or if it does not engage with the pedal depressed, first check the switch adjustment. Refer to the service manual for specifications.

If adjustment is correct, check for voltage to the input side of the switch. If voltage is present at the input side, there should be no voltage at the output side of the switch when it is in the open position (pedal released), but there should be voltage at the output side when the switch is closed (pedal depressed). Replace the switch if it does not perform as specified.

CHARGING SYSTEM

A charging system can malfunction in several ways: there can be no charging, low charging or overcharging conditions. A no-charging or low charging condition can be caused by a broken or slipping alternator drive belt, defective voltage regulator, defective diodes or stator windings, an open alternator field circuit, excessive resistance or an open in the wiring between the alternator and battery, and sulfated battery plates.

Overcharging can be caused by a defective voltage regulator, a shorted field wire and a battery that is internally shorted.

A system that is not charging or undercharging is usually indicated by a discharged battery that does not have enough power to operate the starter or causes the starter to crank slowly, dim headlights, a dash warning light that illuminates or flickers or an ammeter that indicates low charging. Overcharging is indicated by short light bulb life and a battery that continually needs water.

Undercharging can cause the battery plates to sulfate and can cause a high water content in the electro-

lyte, allowing the battery to freeze in cold weather. Overcharging can cause severe corrosion and warpage to the battery positive plates, excessive heat in the battery that can also damage plates, and electrolyte depletion, which can also cause premature deterioration of the active material in the battery plates.

Voltage is regulated by varying the amount of field current flowing through the rotor. More field current results in higher voltage. Input voltage to the alternator, the sensing voltage, is used to regulate output voltage. If sensing voltage is below the regulator setting, the field current is increased to raise the charging voltage output. Sensing voltage that is higher results in less field current and reduced voltage output.

Historically, voltage regulation was controlled by a voltage regulator, but on most newer vehicles, regulator function is part of the PCM/ECM. Voltage regulators on older vehicles were electromechanical and external to the alternator. Electromechanical regulators were replaced by electronic regulators, which can be mounted externally or inside the alternator. If an internal regulator malfunctions, the entire alternator unit is usually replaced.

Preliminary Inspection

Perform a visual inspection to check for obvious problems. Check the alternator drive belt for evidence of cracking, fraying, glazing or other damage and replace as necessary.

If the belt is adjustable, belt tension can be checked using the deflection method or by using a belt tension gauge. Locate a point midway between the pulleys on the longest accessible belt span. If using the deflection method, push on the belt with your finger using moderate pressure and measure the belt deflection. If you are using a belt tension gauge, position the gauge and measure the amount of force necessary to deflect the belt. Compare your reading with specification.

Belt tension should also be checked on vehicles with automatic belt tensioners to make sure the tensioner is functioning properly. Some automatic tensioners are equipped with belt length indicator and minimum and maximum acceptable marks, the theory being that if the correct length belt is installed on the engine and the mark is within range, belt tension is correct.

To adjust V-belt tension, loosen the adjuster pulley, or alternator pivot and adjuster bolts, then use a suitable prybar to move the pulley or alternator until the belt tension is correct. Tighten all fasteners and recheck belt tension. Make sure the alternator is mounted securely in its mounting brackets.

Inspect and test the battery according to the procedures outlined previously in this study guide. Check the condition of the battery cables and system wiring, making sure all connections are clean and tight.

General Testing

Use an inductive probe to check the alternator output at the alternator output wire while the charging system analyzer places a calibrated load on the charging system. If no analyzer is available, place the voltmeter on the proper scale for battery voltage and connect the red lead to the positive cable. Connect the black lead to the negative cable.

Start the engine. The base voltage reading should increase by approximately 2 volts if the charging system is working properly, but be sure to consult the appropriate service specification.

Now, place a load on the alternator by turning on the headlights, or substitute a carbon pile load connected across the battery terminals.

Increase the engine speed to about 2000-2500 rpm. The voltage should now read between 13.8V and 14.5V. Switch your meter to the AC scale and be certain that your AC ripple current is not excessive, indicating a failed rectifier diode(s). Use available specifications for the vehicle you are testing.

Isolation Testing

If the amp reading is low, testing must be performed to isolate the problem. Alternator output is controlled by the strength of the field current. By replacing the regulator with manual control of the field, diagnosis of the alternator and regulator circuits can be accomplished.

How you substitute and full-field voltage-check the alternator depends on the type of field circuits in the unit. If the alternator is an A-type, the field is grounded AFTER the field (externally grounded). Key on, engine off, you will have a voltage indication on both of the field terminals. If it's a B-unit, the field is controlled BEFORE the field, (internally grounded) by controlling current on the positive side, while the ground on the other side of the field is constant. Check a service manual to determine the exact type of alternator installed in the vehicle on which you are working.

To test an externally-grounded unit (After), make sure all lights and accessories are off. Set the engine rpm to 1500-2000 rpm. Now ground the field according to the manufacturer's recommended procedure. Full amperage output should be indicated if the alternator is in good condition and being driven properly. Listen for noises while the alternator is under full load.

Test an internally-grounded unit (Before) by supplying full-field voltage to the field terminal of the alternator. Use a full fielding device or a jumper wire to send battery voltage to the field winding for a moment, and watch for a rise in system voltage.

If the alternator produces rated amperage, the regulator circuit is out of adjustment or defective. Perform voltage and continuity checks at the regulator harness plug. Make sure the regulator has an adequate voltage supply from the vehicle harness and that the wires connecting the regulator and the alternator are in good condition.

Charging Circuit Voltage Drop

Excessive resistance in the voltage and/or ground sides of the charging circuit can cause a low charging rate due to the difference between alternator output and electrical system voltage requirements. Charging system voltage drop is usually caused by a defective, incorrect or corroded cable from the alternator to the battery, or a poor ground connection on the negative side of the circuit.

To check for high resistance in the voltage side of the system, connect the voltmeter negative lead to the positive battery cable end. Next, connect the positive lead to the opposing cable end at the alternator. Read the voltage drop and compare with the manufacturer's specifications. Normally, the voltage drop should not exceed 0.2 volts.

To check for high resistance in the ground side of the system, connect the voltmeter negative lead to the negative battery cable end. Next, connect the positive lead to the alternator grounding point (usually the alternator bracket). Read the voltage drop and compare with the manufacturer's specifications. Normally, the voltage drop should not exceed 0.1 volt.

Notes

Cylinder Head And Valvetrain Diagnosis And Repair

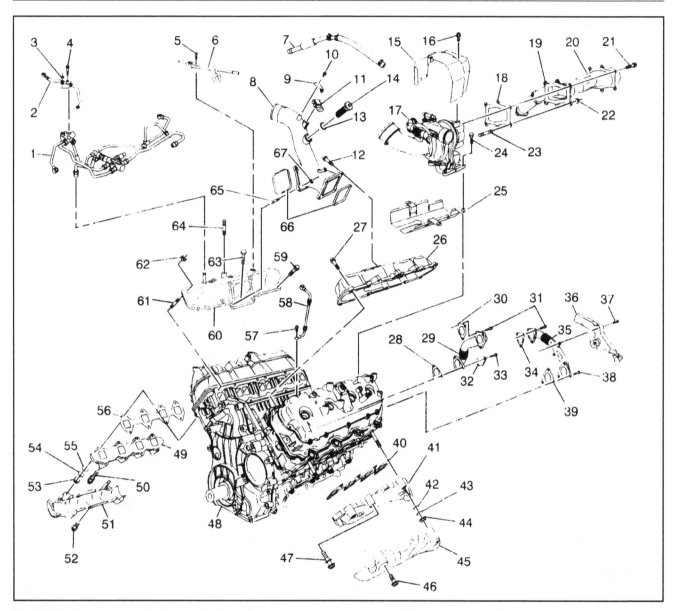

Typical V8 diesel engine intake and exhaust components. *(Courtesy: GM Corp.)*

CYLINDER HEAD REMOVAL

Always wait until the engine has cooled before removing the cylinder head(s). Disconnect the negative battery cable and label and disconnect the necessary electrical connectors. Drain the cooling system.

Disconnect the necessary intake hoses/ducts and exhaust pipes from the turbocharger, if equipped. After removal, cover the turbocharger openings to prevent the entrance of dirt and foreign objects. Disconnect the oil and coolant lines to the turbocharger and remove the turbocharger from the vehicle.

Disconnect and remove the necessary fuel lines, junction blocks, rails, etc, and remove the intake manifold. Remove the exhaust manifold.

Label and disconnect the electrical connectors for the fuel injectors and glow plugs. Remove any hoses, brackets or other components mounted on the valve covers. Remove the valve covers and any acces-

LEGEND FOR PREVIOUS ILLUSTRATION

1. Fuel Pipes Assembly
2. Fuel Inlet Distribution Block
3. Fuel Inlet Distribution Block Nut
4. Fuel Inlet Distribution Block Bolt
5. Fuel Pipe Bolt
6. Fuel Pipe
7. Pcv Hose
8. Intake Manifold Tube
9. Turbocharger Boost Sensor Bracket
10. Turbocharger Boost Sensor Bolt
11. Turbocharger Boost Sensor
12. Intake Manifold Tube Bolt
13. Intake Heater Gasket
14. Intake Heater
15. Turbocharger Heat Shield (Upper)
16. Turbocharger Heat Shield Bolt
17. Turbocharger
18. Exhaust Outlet Adapter Gasket
19. Exhaust Outlet Adapter
20. Heat Shield
21. Heat Shield Bolt
22. Exhaust Outlet Adapter Nut
23. Exhaust Outlet Adapter Stud
24. Turbocharger Bolt
25. Turbocharger Heat Shield (Lower)
26. Intake Manifold
27. Intake Manifold Bolt
28. Exhaust Pipe Gasket
29. Exhaust Pipe
30. Exhaust Pipe Gasket
31. Exhaust Pipe Bolt
32. Exhaust Outlet Bracket
33. Exhaust Pipe Bolt
34. Exhaust Pipe Gasket
35. Exhaust Pipe
36. Heat Shield
37. Heat Shield Bolt
38. Exhaust Pipe Bolt
39. Exhaust Pipe Gasket
40. Exhaust Manifold Gasket
41. Exhaust Manifold
42. Exhaust Manifold Washer
43. Exhaust Manifold Beveled Washer
44. Exhaust Manifold Nut
45. Heat Shield
46. Heat Shield Bolt
47. Exhaust Manifold Bolt
48. Engine Assembly
49. Exhaust Manifold
50. Exhaust Manifold Bolt
51. Heat Shield
52. Heat Shield Bolt
53. Exhaust Manifold Nut
54. Exhaust Manifold Beveled Washer
55. Exhaust Manifold Washer
56. Exhaust Manifold Gasket
57. Turbo Oil Supply Line Eye Bolt
58. Turbo Oil Supply Line
59. Intake Manifold Bolt
60. Intake Manifold
61. Intake Manifold Stud
62. Intake Manifold Nut
63. Intake Manifold Bolt
64. Intake Manifold Stud
65. Intake Manifold Tube Stud
66. Intake Manifold Tube Gasket
67. Intake Manifold Tube Nut

sories and brackets that are mounted on the cylinder head(s).

On OHC (Overhead Camshaft) engines, remove the timing belt or timing chain sprocket(s) from the camshaft(s). Use wire or another suitable device to keep the belt or chain attached and positioned on the sprocket(s), to aid reassembly. If the timing belt is to be completely removed from the engine, mark the direction of belt rotation for assembly reference.

On OHV (Overhead Valve) engines, loosen or remove the rocker arms or remove the rocker arm shafts. Remove the pushrods. Re-

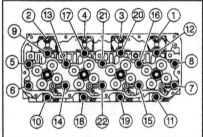

Many components like cylinder heads and manifolds have a manufacturer-specified mounting bolt removal sequence. The sequence shown is the reverse order of the cylinder head bolt torque sequence, but always refer to the manufacturer's service information, as the reverse of the tightening sequence may not always be the case. *(Courtesy: GM Corp.)*

move the fuel injectors.

Loosen and remove the cylinder head bolts. Remove the bolts in the sequence specified by the manufacturer; if one is not given then remove them in the reverse order of the torque sequence. If the cylinder head will not break loose from the engine block, first make sure all head bolts have been removed, then use a prybar inserted into a port to work the head loose.

Inspect the condition of all fasteners and components during the cylinder head removal process. Keep all parts in order so they can be reinstalled in their proper locations. Look for worn and broken parts, and damaged threads. Note the location of threads that must be repaired.

Examine the gaskets and mating surfaces of the intake and exhaust manifolds. Look for cracks, warpage and evidence of leaks and poor sealing. Carefully inspect the head gasket and look for signs of leakage.

DISASSEMBLY

Before you take anything apart, carefully inspect the head for obvious damage such as a broken casting, cracks, stripped threads, broken studs, etc. and for missing components. Serious damage like a crack or broken casting may make the head unsuitable for reconditioning. Also look for any markings indicat-

ing the head has been milled or fitted with a cam with oversized journals.

First remove all components necessary to gain access to the valve components as well as components that are not integral to the cylinder head. Identify the locations of all parts, prior to removal, for assembly reference. Photographs, drawings, tags, etc. are methods that can be used for reference.

Remove all housings, covers, sensors, timing and oil pump drive components. These parts cannot be left on the cylinder head as they could be damaged during the reconditioning process. Inspect all parts for wear and damage as they are removed.

Remove all fittings, core plugs, relief valves, restrictors and oil gallery plugs. Core plugs, also known as freeze plugs, are usually exposed

A slide hammer can be used to remove core plugs from the cylinder head. *(Courtesy: Ford Motor Co.)*

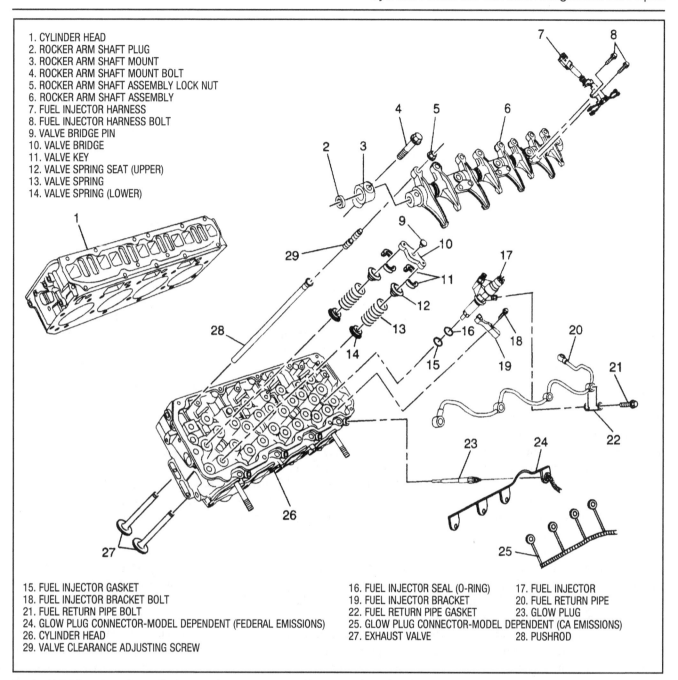

1. CYLINDER HEAD
2. ROCKER ARM SHAFT PLUG
3. ROCKER ARM SHAFT MOUNT
4. ROCKER ARM SHAFT MOUNT BOLT
5. ROCKER ARM SHAFT ASSEMBLY LOCK NUT
6. ROCKER ARM SHAFT ASSEMBLY
7. FUEL INJECTOR HARNESS
8. FUEL INJECTOR HARNESS BOLT
9. VALVE BRIDGE PIN
10. VALVE BRIDGE
11. VALVE KEY
12. VALVE SPRING SEAT (UPPER)
13. VALVE SPRING
14. VALVE SPRING (LOWER)

15. FUEL INJECTOR GASKET	16. FUEL INJECTOR SEAL (O-RING)	17. FUEL INJECTOR
18. FUEL INJECTOR BRACKET BOLT	19. FUEL INJECTOR BRACKET	20. FUEL RETURN PIPE
21. FUEL RETURN PIPE BOLT	22. FUEL RETURN PIPE GASKET	23. GLOW PLUG
24. GLOW PLUG CONNECTOR-MODEL DEPENDENT (FEDERAL EMISSIONS)	25. GLOW PLUG CONNECTOR-MODEL DEPENDENT (CA EMISSIONS)	
26. CYLINDER HEAD	27. EXHAUST VALVE	28. PUSHROD
29. VALVE CLEARANCE ADJUSTING SCREW		

Typical V8 diesel engine cylinder head components. *(Courtesy: GM Corp.)*

to coolant and can corrode from the inside. A core plug may look fine on the outside but in reality be paper thin from corrosion, so to be safe all core plugs should be replaced. Relief valves, oil gallery restrictors and gallery plugs must be removed to allow thorough cleaning of the oil galleries. If any gallery plugs are left in place, dirt and sludge could remain in the head and the wet sludge could also attract abrasives from the

cleaning process. The combination of dirt and abrasives can be carried throughout the engine by the oil when the engine is restarted, with disastrous consequences. Stubborn oil gallery plugs can be heated with a torch and quenched with paraffin wax or in extreme cases, drilled and the remainder removed with a screw extractor.

Any studs should be removed on an as-required basis. If the studs in-

terfere with or could be easily damaged during the reconditioning process, then they should be removed. However, some studs may be difficult to remove without breaking them and attempts to remove them may cause more problems than leaving them in place would.

As you disassemble the valvetrain components, line up the parts to keep them in order. This is especially important on OHC engine

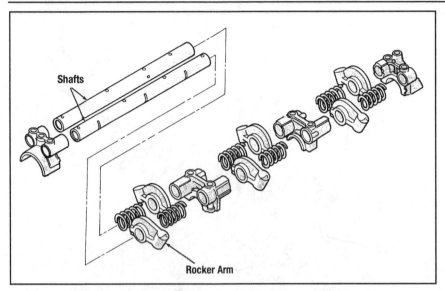

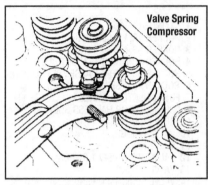

Compressing the valve spring with a valve spring compressor.

Valvetrain components develop wear patterns, so all parts should be kept in order as they are removed. Inspect all components as they are removed for signs of obvious wear and damage. Even if wear to these parts is found to be within specification, they should still be reassembled in their original order. *(Courtesy: Chrysler LLC)*

parts that contact the camshaft. These parts include rocker arms and bucket-type valve adjusting shims, which wear mate to the cam lobes during engine operation. Keeping the parts in order can also help you spot problems. For example, a rounded or mushroomed valve stem tip can also result in a badly worn valve guide or a damaged rocker arm. A bad hydraulic lifter could be the cause.

On OHC cylinder heads, the camshaft can be mounted in a removable carrier or it may slide into the camshaft bearings from the front or rear of the cylinder head, but in most cases the camshaft is retained by removable bearing caps. Before removing the camshaft from the cylinder head, make sure the camshaft bearing caps are marked for correct installation direction and position. Gradually and evenly loosen the camshaft bearing cap bolts to gradually remove the pressure on the camshaft exerted by the valve springs. Follow the bolt loosening sequence if one is specified by the manufacturer. Failure to properly loosen and remove the camshaft bearing cap

bolts can result in camshaft or cylinder head casting breakage. Examine the bearing caps as they are removed for wear and damage. On most engines, the camshaft will ride directly on the cylinder head and bearing caps, however some engines have replaceable insert cam bearings. These must be removed prior to cleaning operations.

Using an appropriate valve spring compressor, compress the valve springs and remove the keepers with needlenose pliers or a magnet. Release the compressor and remove the valve spring, retainer and oil seal from each valve stem.

Before removing the valves, measure the valve stem installed height if the valve stem installed height specification is not available. This dimension will be used for later reference during assembly. Height is measured with the valve closed. It is the distance from the spring seat to the tip of the valve stem. Also measure and record the valve protrusion or recession in relation to the head gasket mating surface of the head.

When a valve will not slide out

but sticks in the guide, do not drive it out. A mushroomed valve stem will ruin the inside of the guide if it is pounded out. To remove a mushroomed valve without damaging the guide, hold the valve shut and file the edge of the stem tip until the valve can slide easily through the guide.

Sometimes an injector sleeve will pull out of the cylinder head when removing an injector. In this case examine the seating surface of the fuel injector sleeve and the fuel injector sleeve bore in the head for debris or damage. If the injector sleeve bore is damaged, the cylinder head may need to be replaced.

CLEANING

The method of cleaning selected should remove all grease, carbon and dirt from the head and valve components without damaging the metal. It will also vary according to the available equipment and the degree of grime. The head may only require gasket scraping, carbon removal with a scraper or wire wheel, followed by solvent cleaning. Chemical or thermal cleaning is less labor intensive but requires special equipment.

If an aluminum head is to be chemically cleaned in a hot tank, cold tank, or jet spray washer, the chemical must be aluminum safe. Caustic soda dissolves aluminum.

Thermal cleaning in an oven will bake off the grease and oil in a head leaving behind a dry powdery ash residue. This residue is removed by washing, airless shot blasting, or glass beading. With aluminum heads, baking temperatures should generally be reduced from the usual 650-750°F (344-399°C) down to 400-450°F (205-232°C). Higher temperatures can cause valve seats to fall out.

Components like injector and glow plug sleeves, as well as pre-combustion chambers, may require removal for certain cleaning techniques. Always refer to the manufacturer's recommendations.

When cleaning heads with an airless shot blaster or glass beads, all of the blast material must be removed from the head cavities after cleaning. Glass or steel cleaning media can cause severe engine damage. A tumbler is commonly used for this purpose. Steel shot is too abrasive to use on soft aluminum heads. An alternative is to use aluminum shot. It's softer and is less apt to cause damage if a particle finds its way into the engine. Glass beading can be used on aluminum to remove carbon and hard, dry deposits. Crushed walnut shells and plastic media are other alternative soft cleaning materials.

Note: Glass beads are especially prone to sticking to wet surfaces inside oil galleries. This method should not be used on an aluminum head that is not completely dry.

Parts like valves, valve springs and retainers can be cleaned by hand with parts cleaning solvent or in a media tumbler. If valves are cleaned in a media tumbler, then the stems must be protected to keep them from being nicked and becoming rough.

INSPECTION

Crack Inspection

After the head has been thoroughly cleaned, inspect it for cracks. Cracks are generally caused by thermal stress, but sometimes result from casting imperfections. The most common places where cracks form are between the valve seats, in the exhaust ports, near the valve guides, and under the spring seats. When cracks extend into the cooling jacket, they often leak coolant into the combustion chamber. Due to the breakdown in lubrication, ring, cylinder, and bearing damage usually results. Cracks that are not leaking coolant are still considered a potential problem because cracks tend to grow. They may begin to leak eventually.

Crack inspection can be done in several ways: using fluorescent dyes, magnetic crack detection equipment, pressure testing or vacuum testing. Magnetic crack detection can only be done on ferrous (iron and steel) parts. Dye penetrants can be used on aluminum castings since they are not magnetic. Pressure testing and vacuum testing can be used to check for cracks and porosity in iron and aluminum heads.

Magnetic particle detection is a fast and easy way to find hairline cracks in cast iron heads. The magnetic field created by the tester attracts iron powder applied to the head. A secondary magnetic field is created at the location of a crack. Additional powder accumulates around this field, outlining the crack. This technique will not reveal a crack that is parallel to the magnetic field. A second magnetic check is made by turning the tester 90 degrees. This can catch any cracks that might have been missed on the first try. It is difficult to find internal cracks in water jackets and ports with this technique.

Dye penetrant is a method of crack detection that can be used on aluminum. Dye is sprayed on the surface and allowed to dry. Then the excess is wiped from the surface. A developer is sprayed on to make the cracks visible. A black light can be used with some dyes for greater visibility.

Pressure testing is another crack detection method that is good at revealing hard-to-see internal leaks. After plugging all the external openings of the water jacket, the head is lightly pressurized (usually less than 30 psi) with air. A soapy water solution is sprayed on the head to check for leaks. Bubbles highlight leaks.

Pressure testing can also be used to see if injector and/or glow plug sleeves are leaking. If a sleeve is leaking and replacement is required special tools may be necessary. After removal, examine the seating surface of the fuel injector sleeve and the fuel injector sleeve bore in the head for debris or damage. If the injector sleeve bore is damaged, the cylinder head may need to be replaced. After installation, pressure test the head again to ensure the new sleeve is sealing.

Vacuum testing is a quick way to determine if a head is cracked or porous. The cylinder head is placed combustion chamber side down on a foam pad lightly coated with oil, to seal the coolant passages. Smaller foam pads on metal backing plates are then used to seal off the remaining coolant passages. One of the pads is attached to a hose that is connected to a vacuum pump. When all pads are in place, the cylinder head is then held down against the main pad and the vac-

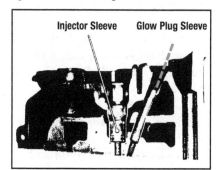

Cross section of a cylinder head showing the fuel injector and glow plug sleeves. These sleeves seal coolant from the injector and glow plug and transfer heat from the injector to the coolant. *(Courtesy: Ford Motor Co.)*

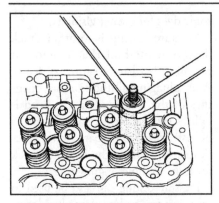

Using a special tool to remove an injector sleeve from a cylinder head. *(Courtesy: GM Corp.)*

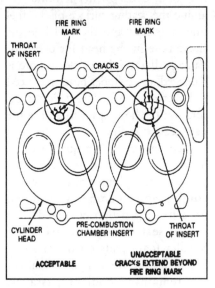

An example of acceptable and unacceptable cracks in precombustion chambers. *(Courtesy: Ford Motor Co.)*

uum pump is started. If a steady vacuum can be maintained for a certain period of time, then the head is not cracked or porous. If the head will not hold vacuum, then it can be pressure tested to find the source of the leak.

When a crack is found in a head, a decision must be made before proceeding further. If there are extensive cracks that would be difficult or impossible to repair, the head must be replaced with a new or used casting. If a crack appears to be repairable, the head can be salvaged using one of several repair techniques: epoxy or heat setting caulk, pinning, lock stitching or welding.

Some cracks in precombustion chambers are acceptable. Refer to the manufacturer's service information to see what level of cracks are acceptable.

Warpage Inspection

Clean any remaining dirt and gasket material that may be left over from the cleaning process from all of the cylinder head gasket mating surfaces. Inspect the gasket mating surfaces for scratches, gouges and other damage that could prevent a gasket from sealing. Minor imperfections can be removed by resurfacing, but severe damage may require that the head be replaced.

Check the head surface for flatness with a straightedge and feeler gauge. Always refer to the factory specifications for flatness since some engines are not as tolerant of distortion as others are. If distortion exceeds the factory limits, the head will have to be resurfaced. Some diesel engine manufacturers do not recommend resurfacing; if warpage exceeds specification the head must be replaced.

Aluminum heads are much more vulnerable to warping than cast iron because aluminum has a much higher coefficient of expansion. When mated to a cast iron block, an aluminum head tends to expand in the middle as it gets hot. Under normal conditions, the clamping force of the head bolts keeps the metal from moving excessively. But if the head overheats, it usually bows up in the middle, resulting in permanent warpage and/or cracking. Severely warped aluminum heads should be straightened before they are resurfaced.

On OHC heads, warpage affects the concentricity of the cam bores. If the warpage is severe enough, it can result in rapid bore wear, loss of oil pressure and possible binding or cam breakage. OHC cam bore alignment can be checked easily before disassembly by turning the cam to see that it rotates freely.

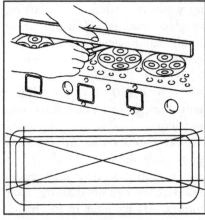

To check cylinder head warpage, place a straightedge across the head gasket surface. This should be done in diagonal directions and on each side of the combustion chambers, checking for gaps at several points along the head. *(Courtesy: GM Corp.)*

If the cam does not rotate freely, check the cam bores for wear and check the camshaft runout at the center journal. If the cam bores are OK, runout is within specification, and the camshaft does not turn easily, the head can be straightened. Straightening should be done before resurfacing or cam align boring the head. This minimizes the amount of metal to be removed. Align boring may be needed after straightening or welding to restore the cam bores.

Heads can be resurfaced by grinding, milling, or belt sanding to eliminate warpage and restore a proper surface finish. Proper surface finish is critical for head gasket sealing. The surface finish must be correct for the type of gasket that will be used, particularly with multi-layer steel gaskets, or the gasket will not seal properly. Refer to the gasket manufacturer's specifications for surface finish requirements.

The surface finish can be checked after milling or grinding using a profilometer or comparator gauge. A profilometer has a stylus that sweeps across the surface to be measured. The vertical movement of the stylus is recorded and used to calculate a roughness measurement. A comparator gauge is a metal card with sample patches of various surface textures to visually compare with the head surface.

The amount of material that can be removed from a head surface is limited. Too much resurfacing can increase compression excessively, create valve-to-piston interference problems, or change the valve timing on OHC engines. Many diesel engine manufacturers specify a minimum head thickness. The head is measured from the cylinder head gasket mating surface to a particular point on top of the casting. Different thickness head gaskets are usually available, but these are usually meant to compensate for piston protrusion above the cylinder block deck.

Resurfacing a direct injection diesel cylinder head will affect the distance that the injector tip extends into the combustion chamber. The injector tip location must be measured and compared with specifications for injector tip protrusion/ recession. Follow the manufacturers instructions for restoring the injector tip location. This usually involves replacing the injector sleeves.

On some engines equipped with them, the precombustion chambers can remain in place when the head is resurfaced. However, on others the manufacturer may recommend they be removed and machined separately. Precombustion chambers are threaded or pressed into the head.

Some diesel cylinder heads have fire ring grooves machined in the head, which align with fire rings used with the head gasket. Resurfacing the cylinder head will reduce the depth of these grooves. The grooves must then be machined to restore the depth to specification. Refer to the manufacturer's specifications for fire ring groove depth.

Milling the heads may change the alignment between the heads and intake manifold on V6 and V8 engines.

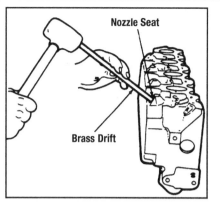

Removing a pressed-in precombustion chamber with a hammer and brass drift. *(Courtesy: Ford Motor Co.)*

Excessive metal removal would require proportional amounts of metal to be machined off the manifold if the ports in the heads and manifold are to match up.

On pushrod engines, another change brought on by resurfacing head(s) is a decrease in the distance between the lifters and rocker arms. Excessive resurfacing can upset the valvetrain geometry, causing the rocker arm to contact the valve stem tip improperly, resulting in excessive valve and guide wear. On non-adjustable valvetrain engines, excessive resurfacing can cause the location of the hydraulic lifter plungers to be too low within the lifter bodies. Shorter than stock pushrods can be used to compensate for resurfacing and restore proper valvetrain geometry.

Valves

The valves should be carefully inspected and cleaned. Hard carbon deposits can be removed from the valve head with a wire buffing wheel or glass bead blaster. Do not glass bead the valve stems.

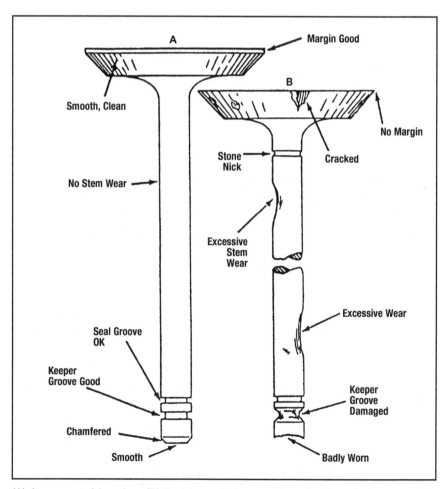

(A) An acceptable valve. (B) Problems that prevent a valve from being reused.

The following are conditions which would require a valve to be replaced: cupped heads, evidence of necking (stretching and narrowing of the stem neck just above the head), pitting, burning, cracks, worn keeper grooves, too narrow a margin on the valve head, or a worn or bent stem.

Stem diameter should be measured with a micrometer and compared to specifications. Measure the valve in a worn area and compare that to an unworn area of the stem below the keeper groove. Some valve stems are ground with about 0.001-in. (0.025mm) taper. Stems on these valves are smaller at the combustion chamber end. Carefully check the keeper grooves for wear, too.

Most exhaust valves are made of a higher quality stainless steel. Always replace stainless steel exhaust valves with ones of at least the same or better steel. Check a valve to see if it is magnetic. Stainless is non-magnetic. Some exhaust valves are spin welded of two pieces (head and stem are different). Check the stem and valve head with a magnet. The valve head of a premium valve will be non-magnetic. The valve stems of these valves are sometimes magnetic. Some valves also have a spin welded hardened stem tip. Intake valves are occasionally of a stainless grade, too.

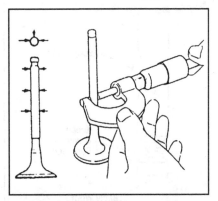

Checking valve stem wear with a micrometer.

Valve Guides

Every head will show a certain amount of valve guide wear. Severe wear can indicate inadequate lubrication, problems with valve geometry, and/or wrong valve stem-to-guide clearance (too much or too little).

Inadequate lubrication can result from oil starvation in the upper valvetrain, from low oil pressure or an obstructed oil passage. Inadequate guide lubrication can also be caused by using the wrong type of valve seal or using a positive seal in combination with an original equipment O-ring seal. Insufficient lubrication results in stem scuffing, rapid stem and guide wear, and valve sticking. Ultimately, the valve will fail due to poor seating and the resultant overheating.

Valve geometry problems include incorrect installed valve height, out-of-square springs, and misaligned rocker arms (which push the valve sideways every time it opens). The resulting uneven guide wear leaves an egg-shaped hole. This leads to increased stem-to-guide clearance, poor valve seating, and premature valve failure.

A certain amount of clearance between the guide and valve stem is necessary so that oil can lubricate the stem and guide, and to allow for thermal expansion of the valve stem. Exhaust valves require more clearance than intake valves because they operate at higher temperatures and expand more. But the stem-to-guide clearance must also be tight enough to control oil consumption and to prevent exhaust gases from going up the stem and damaging the valve seal and spring. Varnish and carbon deposits can also build up on stems when there is excessive clearance. This can cause valve sticking.

Too little clearance can lead to scuffing, rapid stem and guide wear, and sticking (which prevents the valve from seating fully). A sticking valve can run hot, causing the valve to burn. The lower end of the guide is often relieved (made larger) for a distance of about 3/8-in. (9.525mm) during guide machining to prevent valve sticking.

Too much clearance can create oil control problems. Oil drawn into the engine past worn guides can cause the engine to smoke, and contribute to a rapid buildup of carbon deposits on the backs of the intake valves and in the combustion chamber.

Inadequate valve cooling is another problem that can result from excessive valve stem-to-guide clearance. A valve loses much of its heat through the stem. If the stem fits poorly in the guide, heat transfer will be reduced and the valve will run hot. This can contribute to valve burning, especially with exhaust valves (which don't have the benefit of intake cooling from fresh air and fuel).

Different engines have different valve stem-to-guide clearance requirements. Always refer to the factory recommendations. Exhaust guides usually require more clearance than the intakes because the valves expand more due to the hot exhaust gases. Heads with sodium-filled exhaust valves usually require extra clearance to handle the additional heat conducted up through the valve stems.

The type of guide also influences the amount of clearance needed. Bronze guides are said to be able to handle about half the clearance specified for cast iron guides or integral guides, with less tendency to seize. A knurled guide, one with oil retention grooves, or a bronze threaded liner, provides better lubrication than a smooth guide. Consequently, clearances for these types of guides can be kept closer to the low side of the listed tolerance. As extra assurance against valve sticking, do not go tighter than the specified minimum valve stem-to-guide clearance.

The design of the engine's valve guide seal is also a factor to consider when determining clear-

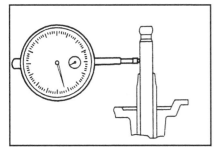

Checking valve guide wear with a dial indicator. *(Courtesy: GM Corp.)*

ances. Compared to deflector O-ring or umbrella type valve seals, positive valve seals reduce the amount of oil that reaches the valve stem. A guide with a deflector/O-ring valve seal may need somewhat tighter clearances than one with a positive valve seal to control oil consumption.

Guide clearance can be checked after cleaning the valve stem and guide with solvent and a brush to remove all gum and varnish. Insert the valve into its guide and hold it at its normal opening height. Rock it from side to side (in the same direction that the rocker arm would push on it) while checking play with a dial indicator. The amount of actual clearance is one half of the TIR (Total Indicator Reading).

When valve stem-to-guide clearance exceeds the specified limits, measure the valve stem with a micrometer to see if it is worn exces-sively. The I.D. (Inside Diameter) of the guide can be measured with a split-ball gauge and micrometer, a go/no-go gauge, or a special valve guide dial indicator. A guide will typically show the most wear at the ends and the least wear in the middle. This is called bellmouth wear.

Valve Springs

Thoroughly clean and visually inspect the valve springs. Do not reuse a valve spring that has shiny ends or is shiny between the coils. These are indications of a weak spring. Also do not reuse a spring that is rusted, nicked, or has deep scratches. Such flaws focus stress and can cause the spring to break.

Check the valve springs for ten-

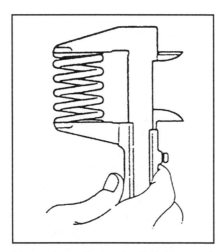

Measuring valve spring height.

sion, squareness and height. Start by checking the free-standing (relaxed) height of the springs (also called the spring free length). Individual spring height should be within 1/16-in. (1.587mm) of the original equipment manufacturer's specification. Line all of them up and position a straight edge on top of them. Any spring that is 1/16-in. (1.587mm) or more shorter than the rest should be replaced. Short springs are often found where exhaust guide clearance has been excessive. Excessive heat from the exhaust weakens the spring. Keep in mind that some cylinder heads use rotators on just the exhaust valves. If the machined spring seats on the cylinder head are all the same height, the exhaust springs will be shorter than the intakes to allow for the thickness of the rotator. In this case the free-standing height of the exhaust and intake springs should be checked separately.

Another spring check is for squareness. A bent spring will exert side pressure on the valve stem. This can cause the guide to wear abnormally or it can result in breakage of the stem tip. Place each spring on a flat surface and hold a square next to it. The spring must sit flush against the square when rotated.

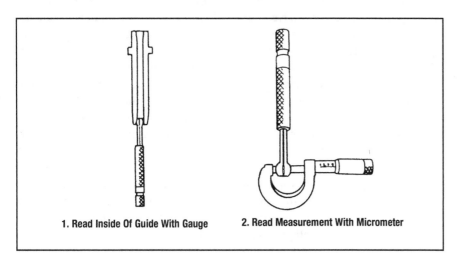

1. Read Inside Of Guide With Gauge   2. Read Measurement With Micrometer

Measuring valve guide inside diameter with a split-ball gauge. The split-ball gauge is then measured with an outside micrometer.

Place the valve spring on a flat surface and check it for squareness with a steel rule or square.

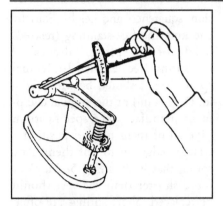

Checking valve spring pressure with a spring tester.

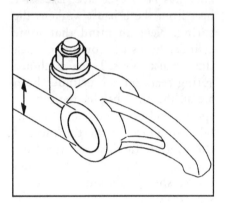

Measuring rocker arm inside diameter. *(Courtesy: GM Corp.)*

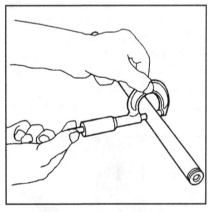

Measuring rocker arm shaft outside diameter. *(Courtesy: GM Corp.)*

If the gap between the top of the spring and the square is more than $1/32$-in. (0.794mm) for each inch of length, the spring is defective.

Check the pressure of the spring. Over time, springs lose tension from exposure to high temperatures and repeated cycling. Weak springs will allow compression loss and cause valves to run hot, shortening their life. Weak springs can also allow valves to float (remain open) at higher rpm, limiting engine speed and risking valve-to-piston contact.

Use a spring tester to check both the open and closed pressure exerted by each spring. Specifications are given for each position. At its installed height, the spring's closed pressure must be within 10% of new specifications. The same rule applies for the open pressure reading when the spring is compressed to its open height.

Valvetrain Components

Carefully check the valve keepers, spring retainers, rocker arms, rocker shafts or balls and studs for wear, cracks, and damage. On OHC cylinder heads, inspect the camshaft, followers and hydraulic lash adjusters, if equipped.

Many experts recommend that spring retainers and keepers be replaced whenever new valves and/or springs are installed, otherwise the retainers and keepers should be reused if they pass visual inspection. Make sure that rotators turn freely by hand without any grinding noise.

Inspect camshaft followers, rocker arms and rocker arm pivots or shafts for wear or damage. On shaft-mounted rocker arm assemblies, disassemble the rocker arms, springs, spacers, shafts, supports, etc. and thoroughly clean all parts. Keep all parts in order so they can be reassembled in their original locations. Measure the diameter of the rocker shafts where the rocker arms pivot and measure the inside diameter of the rocker arms. Compare measurements with specifications and replace any components that are not within tolerance.

Inspect the pushrod ends for wear or damage. Roll each pushrod over a flat surface and check for bending with a feeler gauge. Hollow pushrods that are used for oil delivery must be clean inside.

On OHC cylinder heads, clean

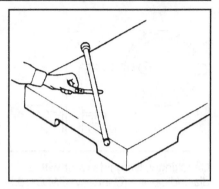

Measuring pushrods for warpage. *(Courtesy: GM Corp.)*

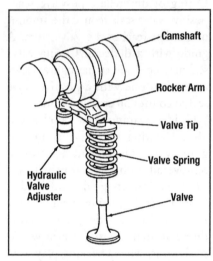

On OHC engines, be sure to inspect the cam follower and camshaft for signs of wear.

the camshaft using solvent, and clean out all oil holes. Visually inspect the cam lobes and bearing journals for excessive wear, rounded lobes, edge wear, scratches, pitting, scoring or galling. If there is any obvious wear or damage, the camshaft must be replaced.

Measure each camshaft lobe height and measure the camshaft journals for out-of-round and taper using a micrometer. Compare measurements with specifications and replace the cam if necessary. If the lobes and journals appear OK, place the front and rear journals in V-blocks and rest a dial indicator on the center journal. Rotate the camshaft to check straightness. If runout exceeds the manufacturer's specifications, replace the camshaft.

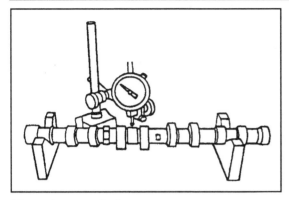

Measuring camshaft runout.
(Courtesy: Ford Motor Co.)

Visually inspect the camshaft bores in the cylinder head for wear and damage. The camshaft bore can be checked using a dial bore gauge or a telescoping gauge and outside micrometer and compared with specifications. If the bores are damaged or clearance is not within specification, the cam bores may be able to be machined to accept a cam with oversize journals.

Position the camshaft in the cylinder head. Move the camshaft to the rear of the head, then install a dial indicator so the indicator foot is resting on the end of the camshaft. Zero the indicator. Move the camshaft forward in the head. Record the indicator reading and compare with specification. If end-play is excessive on applications where a thrust plate is used, replacing the plate may restore the clearance. Some manufacturers recommend replacing the camshaft and rechecking end-play. If end-play still exceeds specification, then the cylinder head may require replacement.

Visually inspect the condition of the hydraulic lash adjuster bores or cam follower bores, as required. Check the fit of each lash adjuster or cam follower in its respective bore. Measure the diameter of the lash adjuster or cam follower and the bore and compare with specifications.

REPAIR

Valves

The valve face and valve stem tip should be reground to a new finish on a valve refacing machine. Many manufacturers specify that the valve be ground to an interference angle of $1/2$ to one degree. For example, if the seat were ground to a 45 degree angle, the valve face would be ground to 44 or 44.5 degrees. Use of an interference angle improves valve seating and helps prevent carbon build-up. Always refer to the manufacturer's specifications for the proper valve face angle and dress the grinding wheel on the valve refacing machine before grinding the valve.

Clamp the valve in the refacing machine chuck and position the valve face just in front of the grinding wheel. Adjust the chuck feed so that when the valve face is moved back and forth, the grinding wheel will clear the valve stem. Start the machine and observe the valve head.

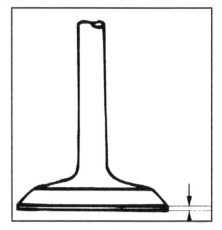

If after machining, the area between the arrows is less than the manufacturer's specifications, the valve must be replaced.

If the valve head appears to wobble as the valve rotates, the valve is bent and must be replaced.

Move the valve back and forth while gradually feeding the valve towards the grinding wheel, until light contact is made. Grind the valve while maintaining light contact until the valve face is smooth. To avoid overheating the valve, make sure the coolant nozzle is directed at the valve while grinding. Grind only what is necessary. Grinding more off

Grinding a valve on a valve refacing machine.

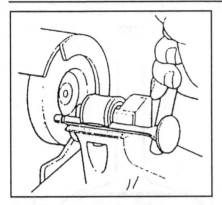

Grinding the valve stem tip.

of the valve face leaves a narrower margin on the top of the valve head. Refer to the manufacturer's specifications for margin thickness.

The tip of the valve stem is ground to restore the surface and also to correct for minor changes in installed height that occur when the seat and valve face are reground. Valve stem height will be checked during assembly. Some manufacturers recommend that the valve stem tips not be ground at all, so be sure to refer to the specific recommendations for the engine in question. Grinding too much from the valve stem tip can also result in the rocker arm or cam follower contacting the keepers or valve spring retainer.

The valve stem tip is ground by clamping the valve in the V-block of the refacing machine and passing it across the grinding wheel. When grinding a valve stem, a 1/32-in. (0.794mm) chamfer is ground around the outside of the tip of the stem. To avoid overheating the stem, direct coolant at the stem tip while grinding.

Warning: Do not use a water-based cooling lubricant when grinding sodium-filled valve stems. If the valve is cracked, the sodium inside can react explosively if it comes into contact with water!

Valve Guides

Options for repairing worn valve guides include knurling, replacement, installing guide liners, and reaming to oversize and using valves with oversized stems.

Knurling

Checking the amount of wear in the guides is the most important step to determine whether or not they can be knurled. Knurling is only an option for guides that are minimally worn. If the guide is worn excessively, knurling may not restore the guide. Knurling decreases the guide I.D. more in the center (unworn area) than at its ends.

The knurling process consists of running a special wheel tool or ridged arbor through the guide. This leaves behind a spiral groove with raised metal on each side. The raised metal reduces the I.D. of the guide. Next, the guide is finished by reaming to its finished size.

Knurling is self-aligning, so the centering of the guide with respect to the valve seat is not lost. Knurling also allows the original valves to be reused. The other primary benefit of knurling is improved valve stem lubrication. The spiral groove retains oil and reduces the chance of the valve stem sticking. The stem-to-guide clearance for a knurled guide can be set on the tight side for this reason. When guides are knurled and clearances are tight, however, positive valve seals are not recommended.

Replacement

Replacing guides is done in both aluminum and cast iron heads. In cast iron heads, guides are often integral and a hole must be bored in the old guide to accept a pressed-in replacement guide.

To replace valve guides in aluminum heads, the heads must be heated to facilitate removal and installation without damaging the head. The guides are then usually driven out with a suitable driver and air hammer. The replacement guides are chilled and lubricated prior to installation. Most wet guides are tapered and require sealer to prevent leaks.

Replacement guides are available in a variety of materials besides cast iron. Bronze guides are generally more expensive than cast iron but usually run cooler and provide superior durability. Bronze alloys include phosphor bronze, silicon-aluminum bronze, and manganese bronze.

Guide Liners

Thin tubes called thinwall valve guide liners are often installed to restore worn guides. This repair technique provides the benefits of a bronze guide surface (better lubricity, longer wear, and the ability to handle tighter clearances). Liners can be installed in heads with either integral or replaceable cast iron guides. The process is portable, fast, and sometimes less expensive than installing new guides.

Reaming Oversize

When valves are replaced, less machining time is required. If valves are replaced with those with oversized stems, all that is necessary is to ream the guide to the proper oversize. Stem-to-guide clearance should be in accordance with the engine manufacturer's recommendations.

Valve Seats

The guides must be reconditioned or replaced before cutting, grinding, or replacing valve seats. All seat machining is done with a pilot that centers in the valve guide. If guide work is done after seat work, the guide and seat will no longer be aligned to each other.

A properly finished valve seat must meet several criteria. If a valve is to cool properly, it must have a concentric seat that is square with the guide. The seat-to-valve contact area must be of the correct width and positioned properly on the valve face.

A non-concentric seat will not allow the valve to make full contact.

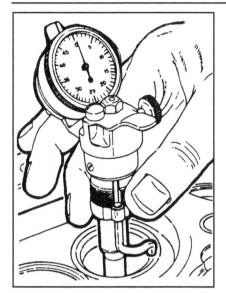

Checking valve seat concentricity using a dial indicator.

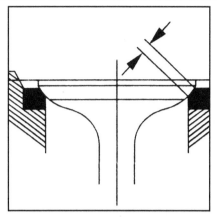

Seat width and where the valve contacts the valve seat are critical for proper sealing and long valve life. *(Courtesy: GM Corp.)*

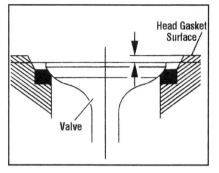

Valve depression is the distance between the valve and the cylinder head gasket surface. *(Courtesy: GM Corp.)*

This results in a poor seal and loss of compression. Poor valve face-to-seat contact will also reduce heat transfer, causing the valve to run hot. This will eventually lead to premature failure. Check seat concentricity with a dial indicator. Concentricity should be within 0.002-in. (0.05mm).

An off-square seat can prevent a valve from seating and holding compression. It can also lead to valve breakage. When a seat is off-center from the axis of the valve guide, every time the valve closes it must flex to conform to the seat. After thousands of such cycles, metal fatigue sets in and stress cracks develop in the valve. The process is accelerated when valve rotators are used. Eventually the valve stem or head snaps. This often results in serious engine damage.

The width of the valve seat is important for good heat transfer, proper sealing and long valve life. A seat that is too narrow can suffer increased wear and will not be able to transfer sufficient heat to the cooling jacket. A seat that is too wide may not provide enough pressure for a tight seal. An excessively wide seat also tends to develop deposits that can prevent the valve from seating. This reduces heat transfer

and lowers compression at idle. Seat width for exhaust valves is generally wider than for intake valves, however always check the manufacturer's specifications.

The point at which the valve and seat mate is also important. Ideally, the valve-to-seat contact area should be about one third of the way down the valve face. The top edge of the contact area should be about 1/64-in. – 1/32-in. below the margin of the valve. This leaves an area of the valve face between the margin and top of the seat contact area that overhangs into the combustion chamber.

When the area of contact is too high on the valve face (too close to the margin), the valve is too far into the head. This increases installed height, reduces valve spring tension, upsets valvetrain geometry, and restricts free breathing. Another valve positioning problem is when the area of contact is too low on the face (too far from the margin). As the engine warms up and the valve expands, the contact point moves down the valve face away from the margin. The valve may lose partial contact with the seat, causing it to lose compression and run hot.

When refinishing diesel engine valve seats, it is important to observe the valve protrusion/depres-sion specifica-

tion. If a valve is too deep in the head, try substituting a new valve. If this does not correct the problem then a new seat must be installed. If a valve sits too high, then the seat must be machined deeper into the head.

Valve seats should be replaced if they are badly worn or ground too deep in the head. Replaceable inserts (typically used in aluminum heads) should also be replaced if they are cracked or loose in the head. Heads with integral seats can be machined to accept a replaceable insert.

Seats can be ground with a wet or dry stone, or cut with a carbide cutter. There are advantages to each method. Grinding requires at least three steps for each seat and in the case of dry stones, produces abrasive dust. Stones must be properly dressed to maintain accuracy. Cutting is cleaner and faster, especially when all three angles are cut at once. Cutters are more expensive, however.

To grind a seat, select a wheel about 1/8-in. larger than the seat. The angle of the stone depends on the manufacturer's specifications. A typical seat face angle is 45 degrees, but occasionally 30 degrees is used (most often for intake valves). The grit of the stone depends upon the material the seat is made from. For best results and fast stock removal, use coarse stones on hard seats and a finer general purpose stone for cast iron seats.

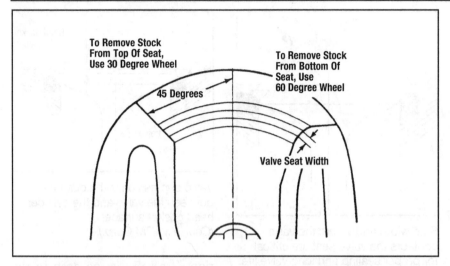

Angles used to locate and narrow a valve seat. *(Courtesy: Ford Motor Co.)*

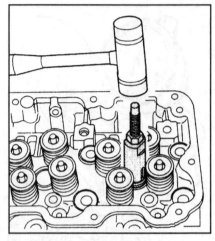

Installing an injector sleeve.
(Courtesy: GM Corp.)

Grind the seat to remove discoloration and pitting. Remove only as much material as required to clean the entire seat and remove all pits in the surface. Dress the wheel frequently (when grinding the face angle in particular). Then switch wheels and use a 30 degree stone (15 degree stone if the face angle is 30 degrees) to cut the top angle on the seat. This will locate it with respect to the valve face.

If the seat is too wide after grinding, narrow it by cutting the throat angle using a 60 degree stone (45 degree stone if the face angle is 30 degrees). Be careful when cutting this angle; removal of too much material from the bottom edge of the seat will call for installation of a new valve seat to correct the problem.

Dykem blue is a dye that some technicians paint on the valve seat. The valve is inserted into the guide, lightly seated, and rotated about 1/8-in. (3.175mm). A continuous blue line should appear all the way around the valve face if the valve and seat are mating properly. Open patches or breaks in the line indicate that the seat is not concentric and the low spots are not making contact.

Some technicians use another type of coloring agent when machining heads. Prussian blue is a paste that is spread on the valve face. The valve is inserted into the guide and its face is pushed into the blue paste to make an imprint. This gives an idea of the height of the valve seat on the valve face.

The procedure for refinishing a valve seat by cutting is essentially the same as for grinding. Carbide cutters are used instead of grinding stones. A seat cutting process popular in high volume machine shops cuts all three angles in a one-step operation. Check concentricity (seat runout) to make sure the seats were cut properly.

Some technicians lap valves after grinding or cutting the seats. An abrasive paste, called lapping compound, is applied to the valve or seat. A rubber suction cup on a wooden or plastic handle is attached to the head of the valve. The valve is worked back and forth against the seat. This process is reassuring in that a very clear pattern becomes apparent on the valve face, showing the valve-to-seat mating area. The fine lapping compound helps the seat and valve to mate exactly with each other, but the valve will expand about 0.015-in. – 0.020-in. (0.381mm – 0.508mm) when hot. This means that the lapped area will no longer match between the valve and the valve seat once the valve is hot. Lapping valve seats was a popular process in the past but it is not necessary if seat refinishing is done correctly.

ASSEMBLY

If any injector sleeves were removed, lubricate and install new O-rings on the new sleeve. Install the sleeve onto the installation tool and apply the specified sealant to the sleeve's lower sealing area. Install the sleeve into the cylinder head, lightly tapping on the tool with a hammer to seat the sleeve. Pressure test the head to ensure the sleeve(s) is sealing.

If the precombustion chambers were removed, reinstall them using new seals or gaskets, according to the manufacturer's instructions.

Wash the head, valves, springs, retainers and keepers thoroughly in clean solvent to prepare for reassembly.

Valve Stem Installed Height And Valve Protrusion/ Depression

Install the valves in the valve guides and measure the installed stem height from the spring seat to the tip of the valve, with the valve fully seated. Refer to the manufacturer's valve stem installed height specifications or, if unavailable, to the dimensions recorded during disassembly. Valve stem height that is not within specifications can change rocker arm geometry and can cause the location of the hydraulic lifter plunger to be too low within the lifter body.

If valve stem installed height is greater than specification, the valve stem tip can be ground to compensate, providing the variance is not too great. However, some valve stem tips are case hardened and should not have more than about 0.010-in. – 0.020-in. (0.254mm – 0.508mm) removed from their surface, and some manufacturers recommend that the tips not be ground at all. Grinding too much from the valve stem tip can also result in the rocker arm or cam follower contacting the keepers or valve spring retainer.

If the proper installed height cannot be obtained by grinding the tip of the stem, the valve is too deep in the head. A small amount of correction can be made with a new valve, which has more metal on its face, enabling it to sit shallower in the head. If a new valve does not bring the valve installed height within specification, a new seat will need to be installed.

Keep in mind that the above must be accomplished while also observing valve protrusion/depres-sion specifications.

Installed Spring Height

Check the installed height of the valve springs. To check the height, lightly lubricate a valve stem, slide the valve into place, and mount the retainer on the stem. Install the keepers without the valve spring for this test. Measure the distance from the machined spring seat on the head to the underside of the retainer and compare it to specifications. Both grinding the valve and grinding the valve seat result in an increase in this dimension. A valve spring insert (shim) can be installed under the spring to restore the original installed height for proper spring tension.

A thin shim is found on alu-

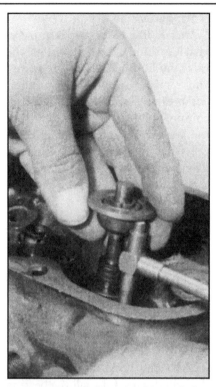

To determine if shimming is needed, a telescoping gauge is expanded between the valve spring seat and the underside of the valve spring retainer. The gauge is then measured with an outside micrometer and the distance compared with the valve spring height specification.

minum heads to protect the softer head surface from damage. There are several thicknesses of valve spring inserts (shims) available. Common sizes for correcting spring height are 0.030-in. (0.762mm) and 0.060-in. (1.524mm). The serrated side of the insert should face the head. These serrations help insulate the spring from the hot cylinder head for longer spring life.

Valve Seals

Valve seals control oil that lubricates the valve stems from seeping into the guides in excessive amounts. There are three types of seals. Positive seals fit tightly around the top of the guide and scrape oil off the valve as it

moves up and down. If the design of the head is such that the guides tend to be flooded with oil (and oil consumption would result), positive type seals may be specified. Positive seals are installed at the factory on almost all OHC engines and are installed on other heads in the aftermarket.

O-ring seals are another type of seal. They fit into the valve stem groove under the keepers and keep oil from traveling down the valve stem. These seals are used with a metal oil deflector that covers the top coils of the valve spring.

Umbrella seals (also called splash or deflector seals), ride on the valve stems to deflect oil away from the guides. These fit tightly on the valve stem and move up and down with the valve.

Valve guide seals are of several qualities. Appearance is not an indicator of quality. The least expensive seal is effective to only about 250°F (121°C). The best seals are good up to about 440°F (227°C). Valve guide seals are often included in a gasket set. Intake and exhaust seals on the same head are sometimes different. Sometimes seals are color coded. Other times they are of different shapes. Follow the manufacturer's directions as to the type of seal to use on the intake and exhaust

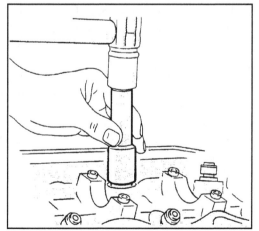

Installing positive valve stem seals.
(Courtesy: Chrysler LLC)

valves. A 250°F (121°C) seal used on an exhaust valve would be an unfortunate error.

When positive valve seals are installed on a head that was not designed for them, the top of the guide boss area must be machined with a special cutter. This is a common modification on high performance engines. On these applications, the valve lift should be calculated before machining, to make sure enough material is removed from the guide boss to prevent the bottom of the valve spring retainer from contacting the valve seal at maximum lift.

When installing positive valve seals, apply a light coat of oil on the valve stem and guide boss. Use a protective cap or sleeve over the valve stem to protect the seal as it is slid onto the valve. A special installation tool is then usually placed over the seal and the seal is tapped into place on the guide boss using a small mallet. Be sure the positive seal seats squarely on the guide boss.

With umbrella or deflector type seals, just push the seal down on the valve stem until it touches the valve guide boss. It will be positioned correctly the first time the valve opens.

O-ring seals must be installed after the spring is compressed. The O-ring typically fits into an extra groove in the valve stem that is just below the keeper grooves. Lubricate it and install it squarely in its groove. Then install the keepers and release the valve spring compressor.

Final Assembly

Before installing the valves in the guides, lubricate the valve stems with assembly lube. Lubricate the springs, rocker arms, rocker shafts or balls and studs, and the cam bores and followers on overhead cam cylinder heads. Spring lubrication on heads with double springs or inner harmonic dampers is especially important. Friction between the inner and outer springs can overheat and weaken the springs when the engine

is first started.

After sliding each valve into place, install a shim if needed. Install the valve guide seal and put the spring and retainer into position. Then compress the spring with a spring compressor just enough to install the keepers. Be careful not to compress the spring too far. This can damage the new valve seal. Grease can be used to hold the keepers in place while releasing the valve spring compressor. Slowly release the spring compressor so there is no chance of misaligning the valve stem seals or disturbing the position of the keepers. Lightly tap on the valve stem tips with a plastic mallet to make sure the keepers are seated on the valve stems and retainers.

On OHC engines, lubricate the journals and install the camshaft in the cylinder head. Install the bearing caps, making sure they are in their proper locations. Torque the caps in the proper sequence. If equipped, install the cam followers in their original locations and adjust valve lash, as required.

Reinstall all housings, covers, fittings, adaptors, sensors and studs. Install new core plugs and oil gallery plugs using suitable sealer.

CYLINDER HEAD INSTALLATION

Before installing the cylinder head(s), Make sure the cylinder head and block gasket mating surfaces are clean. The threads on the head bolts and those in the block must also be clean. Use a thread chaser to chase threads in the block and clean the entire head bolt using a wire wheel. Do not reuse a head bolt that is nicked, eroded, or rusted.

Note: Some engines use torque-to-yield head bolts. These bolts are purposely overstretched when tightened and are usually not reused. New head bolts may be provided with the gasket set. Consult the service manual to see if torque-to-yield bolts are used.

Most diesel engine manufacturers provide different thickness head gaskets, the selection of which is determined by the distance the piston head projects above the cylinder deck surface at TDC. The manufacturer will usually specify at what points the top of the piston should be measured. The following is a general procedure for measuring piston projection; however, always follow the instructions for the particular engine you are servicing:

1. Zero the dial indicator to the cylinder deck surface.

2. Place the dial indicator pointer on the piston top at the first measuring point. Make sure the pointer is directly above the piston pin centerline to prevent inaccurate readings from piston rocking.

3. Rotate the engine through TDC and record the maximum reading on the dial indicator.

4. Repeat the procedure with the dial indicator pointer at the second measuring point on the piston.

Calculate the average value of piston projection for each cylinder to obtain the maximum projection value for that bank of cylinders. Compare with the manufacturer's specifications to determine the head gasket that should be used.

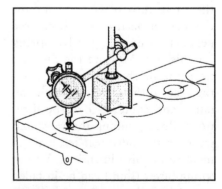

Measuring piston projection/depression to determine head gasket selection.
(Courtesy: GM Corp.)

Note: If the difference between the highest and lowest measured piston head projection is beyond specifications, then piston and/or connecting rod service may be required.

Place the head gasket on the block in the proper direction. Head gaskets are usually marked to indicate which side faces up. Older gaskets used sealer but most modern ones do not.

When installing an OHC cylinder head, be sure that the cam has been rotated until its timing mark is correctly positioned. The number one piston must be positioned at TDC so that the head can be installed. If the cam is not correctly positioned on an interference engine, a valve can be bent when the head bolts are tightened.

The tightening procedure for torque-to-yield bolts, called torque-turn, is different than the procedure for normal head bolts. A torque-to-yield bolt is tightened to a specified torque and then turned an additional amount (like 1/4 turn or 90 degrees). Torquing a bolt into yield purposely overstretches the fastener. This achieves a higher clamping force that is more uniform for each of the fasteners.

Most head bolt specifications are for clean, lightly lubricated threads. Lubricating the threads with other than light weight oil changes the clamping force applied by the bolts at a given torque value. Torque must be reduced for proper loading if an anti-seize or other thread lubricant is used. A shop towel moistened with engine oil can be used to lightly lubricate the threads.

Note: Always refer to the manufacturer's service information, as some new head bolts come pre-lubed. This coating should not be removed and no additional lubricant should be applied.

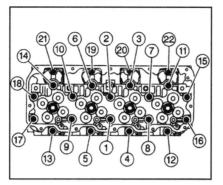

Follow the manufacturer's recommended sequence and steps for tightening head bolts.
(Courtesy: GM Corp.)

Hardened steel washers are placed against aluminum head surfaces. These are also used on some cast iron applications. Sealer is applied to the threads of any fasteners that extend into the cooling jackets.

Tighten head bolts in the sequence and steps specified by the manufacturer. This allows for slight warpage of the head and stresses the block according to its engineering design. For example, the first step might be to torque, in sequence, to 30 ft. lbs. (40.7 Nm), the next to 60 ft. lbs. (81.4 Nm), in sequence, and in the final step, turn each bolt, in sequence, 90 degrees.

If equipped with a timing belt, install the camshaft sprocket(s) and torque the bolt(s) to specification. Align the sprocket timing marks and install the timing belt. If the belt is being reused, observe the mark indicating direction of rotation made during removal. Adjust the tensioner according to the manufacturer's specifications and rotate the engine several times to ensure the timing marks are properly aligned.

If equipped with a timing chain, lubricate the chain, align the timing marks and install the camshaft sprocket(s) and chain. Torque the camshaft sprocket bolt(s) to specification.

Lubricate the pushrod ends and install the pushrods through the guides into the lifters. Lubricate the rocker arm ends and pivot surfaces. If equipped with rocker arm shafts, tighten the shaft bolts gradually and evenly to the proper torque, being careful to align the pushrod ends with the rocker arms as the shaft is drawn down. If equipped with individual rocker arm pivots, align the pushrod with the rocker arm as the nut or bolt is tightened. Torque the bolt or nut or follow the valve adjustment procedure, as required.

After valve adjustment, install the valve cover using new gaskets. Install the fuel injectors and glow plugs and connect the fuel lines and wiring harnesses.

Install the intake and exhaust manifolds and the turbocharger. Connect the ducts and hoses to the turbocharger.

Valve Adjustment

Some engines have a valve lash (clearance) setting that must be set within the range specified by the manufacturer. This compensates for thermal expansion. If the clearance is too tight, the valves will be held open causing compression loss and/or valve burning. If the clearance is too loose, the valvetrain will be noisy and the cam will experience shock loads and premature wear. Engine performance can also be adversely affected by the

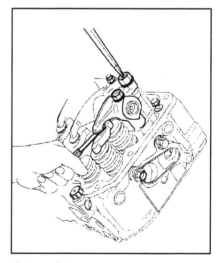

Using a feeler gauge to measure valve clearance (lash).
(Courtesy: GM Corp.)

decreased valve lift and changed duration that results.

To adjust valve lash for one cylinder's cam lobes, rotate the crankshaft so that its piston is at TDC on the compression stroke. This will position the intake and exhaust valve lifters or OHC cam followers on the base circle of their respective cam lobes. With the engine in this position, adjust the clearance with a feeler gauge of the proper thickness.

Note: Some manufacturers may specify that half the valves can be adjusted with the piston in No. 1 cylinder on the compression stroke and the other half with the piston at TDC on the exhaust stroke. The valves that can be adjusted in each position are identified in the service manual.

Adjusting valve lash on pushrod engines calls for inserting a feeler gauge between the tip of the valve stem or valve bridge and the rocker arm. An adjustment nut or screw is turned to change the clearance. Occasionally there is a lock nut.

Some OHC engines use lash pad adjusters. These are shims housed in buckets that ride directly on the camshaft. They are replaced to change valve clearance.

Other OHC engines use rocker arms that have an adjustment feature on one of their outer ends.

Pay attention to whether the valve lash setting recommended by the manufacturer is a hot or cold specification. With a cold specification, the lash setting requires no further adjustment once the engine is warm. A hot setting will have to be readjusted by the installer once the engine is at normal operating temperature.

Hydraulic lifter lash is adjusted by loosening the rocker arm adjusting nut until zero lash is reached. This is when the lifter plunger is extended all of the way in its travel and there is no clearance between the rocker arm and valve stem tip. Loosening the adjustment further would result in valve clearance. From the zero lash point the rocker arm adjustment is given an additional number of turns ($3/4$ to $1 1/2$ turns is typical). The intent is to position the lifter plunger midway in its travel in the lifter body.

Changes in valve stem height resulting from valve and seat grinding or excessive cylinder head or block deck resurfacing can cause a pushrod to move the plunger lower in the lifter body. Too much increase in stem height causes the lifter plunger to permanently bottom out in its bore.

Notes

Engine Block Diagnosis And Repair

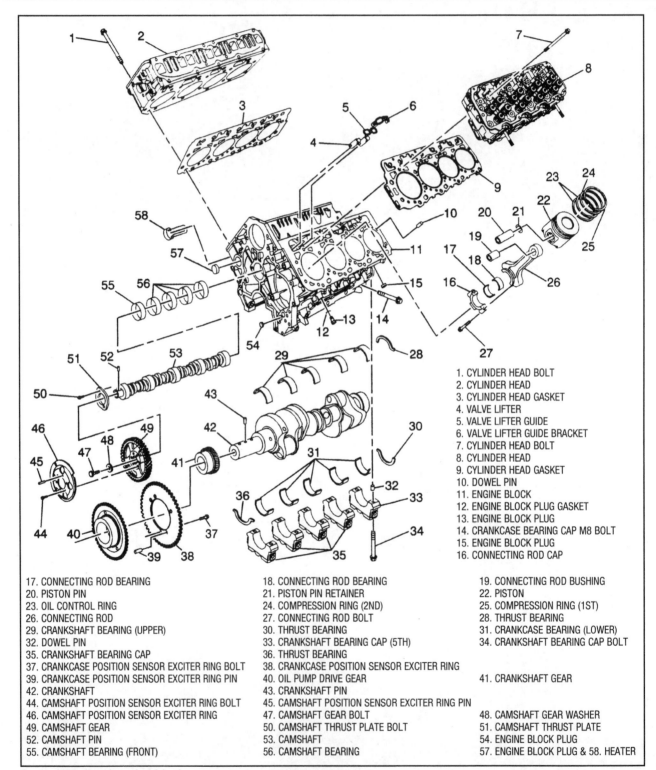

1. CYLINDER HEAD BOLT
2. CYLINDER HEAD
3. CYLINDER HEAD GASKET
4. VALVE LIFTER
5. VALVE LIFTER GUIDE
6. VALVE LIFTER GUIDE BRACKET
7. CYLINDER HEAD BOLT
8. CYLINDER HEAD
9. CYLINDER HEAD GASKET
10. DOWEL PIN
11. ENGINE BLOCK
12. ENGINE BLOCK PLUG GASKET
13. ENGINE BLOCK PLUG
14. CRANKCASE BEARING CAP M8 BOLT
15. ENGINE BLOCK PLUG
16. CONNECTING ROD CAP

17. CONNECTING ROD BEARING	18. CONNECTING ROD BEARING	19. CONNECTING ROD BUSHING
20. PISTON PIN	21. PISTON PIN RETAINER	22. PISTON
23. OIL CONTROL RING	24. COMPRESSION RING (2ND)	25. COMPRESSION RING (1ST)
26. CONNECTING ROD	27. CONNECTING ROD BOLT	28. THRUST BEARING
29. CRANKSHAFT BEARING (UPPER)	30. THRUST BEARING	31. CRANKCASE BEARING (LOWER)
32. DOWEL PIN	33. CRANKSHAFT BEARING CAP (5TH)	34. CRANKSHAFT BEARING CAP BOLT
35. CRANKSHAFT BEARING CAP	36. THRUST BEARING	
37. CRANKCASE POSITION SENSOR EXCITER RING BOLT	38. CRANKCASE POSITION SENSOR EXCITER RING	
39. CRANKCASE POSITION SENSOR EXCITER RING PIN	40. OIL PUMP DRIVE GEAR	41. CRANKSHAFT GEAR
42. CRANKSHAFT	43. CRANKSHAFT PIN	
44. CAMSHAFT POSITION SENSOR EXCITER RING BOLT	45. CAMSHAFT POSITION SENSOR EXCITER RING PIN	
46. CAMSHAFT POSITION SENSOR EXCITER RING	47. CAMSHAFT GEAR BOLT	48. CAMSHAFT GEAR WASHER
49. CAMSHAFT GEAR	50. CAMSHAFT THRUST PLATE BOLT	51. CAMSHAFT THRUST PLATE
52. CAMSHAFT PIN	53. CAMSHAFT	54. ENGINE BLOCK PLUG
55. CAMSHAFT BEARING (FRONT)	56. CAMSHAFT BEARING	57. ENGINE BLOCK PLUG & 58. HEATER

Typical V8 diesel engine block components.   *(Courtesy: GM Corp.)*

ENGINE DISASSEMBLY

Before taking anything apart, carefully inspect the block for obvious damage such as a broken casting, cracks, stripped threads, broken studs, etc. Serious damage like a crack or broken casting may make the block unsuitable for reconditioning, while other kinds of damage will require repairs for which additional time and cost must be added to that which has been allotted for the job.

Identify the locations of all parts, prior to removal, for assembly reference. Photographs, drawings, tags, etc. are methods that can be used for reference. Remove all sensors and external components. These parts cannot be left on the block as they could be damaged during the cleaning and machining process.

While disassembling the engine, note the condition of the various parts. This will be helpful for diagnostic purposes and in deciding which parts require service or replacement. Wear patterns and component failures can indicate the cause of a problem and the steps necessary to prevent it from happening again.

Even when a complete rebuild is performed and most of the major components are to be replaced; it will still be necessary to inspect the old parts as they are removed. For example, an uneven wear pattern on the main bearings can be a result of misalignment in the main crankshaft bores. Machining of the main bearing bores will be necessary to restore proper alignment.

Begin disassembly by draining the oil from the crankcase, noting the presence of any metallic particles that would indicate a major problem. Remove and discard the oil filter.

Carefully remove all electrical components (sensors, sending units, etc.), rubber hoses, emission control components, accessories (alternator, starter) and accessory brackets.

Disconnect the oil and coolant lines to the turbocharger and remove the turbocharger. After removal, cover the turbocharger openings to prevent the entrance of dirt and foreign objects.

Remove the injector lines, injector nozzles, and injection pump. Plug the pump and fuel line connections to prevent the entry of moisture or dirt.

Remove the intake and exhaust manifolds. Inspect the exhaust manifolds for cracks.

Remove the valve cover(s) and the upper valvetrain components while checking for worn or broken parts. Keep all mated parts together. If they are to be reinstalled later they will need to go in the same position. Also, if a part is worn, a cause will have to be determined and a course of action taken to prevent it from happening again. The corresponding part that caused the wear will also have to be carefully inspected.

On OHC (Overhead Cam) engines, remove the water pump, crank pulley and vibration damper. Remove the timing cover and check the timing mark alignment. A belt or chain that has jumped time can result in low compression and valve to piston contact on some engines. Remove the timing belt or chain. Timing belts should not be reused but belt sprockets are usually reused. Visually inspect the belt sprockets for unusual wear. Feel the idler roller bearing used with a timing belt. These are usually replaced with a new belt.

On an OHC engine with a chain drive, the chain guide and tensioner are coated with a layer of synthetic rubber. These parts usually experience wear and are routinely replaced. A master engine kit for these engines usually includes a new timing chain, sprockets, chain guides, and a tensioner. These parts are also available packaged together as a timing set.

Loosen the cylinder head bolts in the recommended sequence or in the reverse order of the torque sequence. Remove the bolts and remove the cylinder head and gasket. Inspect the head gasket and cylinder head and block surfaces carefully. The location of coolant or combustion leaks can often be determined during this inspection. Questionable areas can be scrutinized more carefully while checking warpage. Discard the gasket after inspecting it.

Some diesel engines have head to block sealing rings. Remove these if present.

On pushrod engines, remove the water pump, crankshaft pulley and vibration damper, and timing cover from the front of the engine. Check the timing mark alignment. Timing chains typically stretch in use. Note how much a chain has stretched before removing it.

Turn the crankshaft clockwise to take up slack on the right side of the chain. Mark a reference point on the block at the approximate midpoint of the chain. Measure from this point to the midpoint of the chain. Rotate the crankshaft counterclockwise to take up slack on the left side of the chain. Force the left side of the chain outward with your finger and measure the distance between the reference point and the midpoint of the chain. The timing chain deflection is the difference between the two measurements. Replace the chain and sprockets if deflection exceeds specifications.

Inspect the timing sprockets for visible wear. When they are worn, the chain and both sprockets are replaced in a set. A new timing chain should always be installed on new sprockets.

On an engine with a timing gear drive, a dial indicator can be used to check gear backlash. Backlash should be checked at several points

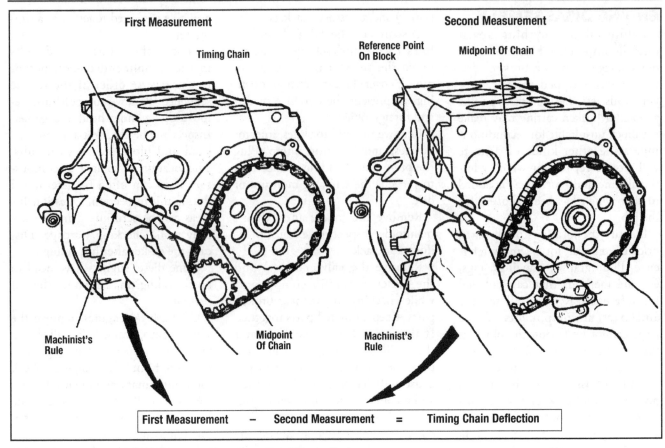

First Measurement   —   Second Measurement   =   Timing Chain Deflection

Measuring timing chain deflection.   *(Courtesy: Ford Motor Co.)*

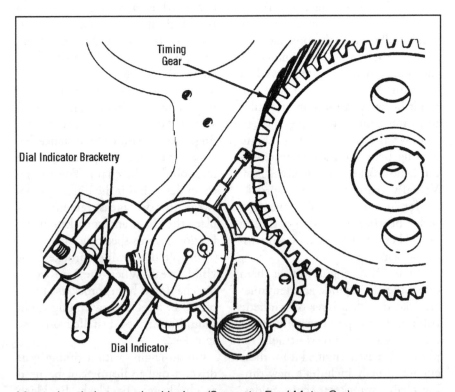

Measuring timing gear backlash.   *(Couresty: Ford Motor Co.)*

around each gear. The timing gears should be replaced if backlash exceeds specifications.

Camshaft end-play can also be checked with a dial indicator. If end-play is excessive the camshaft and/or thrust plate are worn.

Remove the flywheel or flexplate. If the engine is externally balanced, mark the position of the flywheel in relation to the crankshaft prior to removal for assembly reference. This is necessary to maintain proper engine balance.

On a pushrod engine, remove the lifters. If equipped with roller lifters, first remove the necessary guides and hold-downs. If there is a possibility that the cam and lifters will be reused, the lifters must be kept in order so that each one can be put back in the same bore from which it was removed.

Pushrod engines with flat tappet cams usually experience excessive wear to the cam and lifters. Flat tappet lifter cam lobes are tapered and the lifters are convex so that the lifters will spin and dissipate the loads on them. Look for wear on the bottom edges of the cam lobes. One worn lobe is cause for replacement of all of the lifters and the camshaft. New lifters must always be used with a new cam, and vice versa.

Remove the oil pan and gasket and discard the gasket. The oil pump and pickup screen are removed next. Note the presence of any debris in the pickup screen. Oil pump pickup screens are usually replaced. However, if the screen is to be reused, it must be thoroughly cleaned.

Because of extremely high combustion temperatures, most diesel engines are equipped with piston cooling nozzles. These are usually fastened or pressed into the block, and must usually be removed before the pistons and connecting rods can be removed. Inspect the nozzles for damage and clogging.

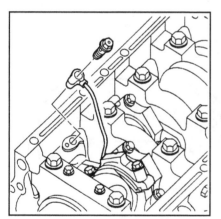

Piston oil cooling nozzle removal. *(Courtesy: GM Corp.)*

Before removing the pistons and connecting rods, look for numbers stamped on the sides of the rods indicating their cylinder number. If there are no numbers, use number stamps to mark the position of each connecting rod according to its cylinder number. Stamp the numbers

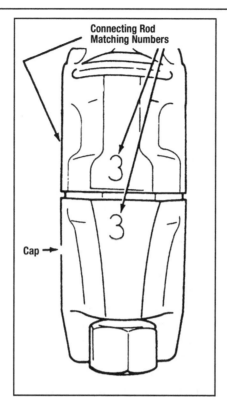

An example of cylinder identification marks stamped on a connecting rod.

on both sides of the big end parting face, so the rod caps will not be mixed up during removal.

Measure and record the piston protrusion with a dial indicator. This is the difference between the piston height and the surface of the block when the piston is at TDC. It will be necessary to reference this information during the machining and/or assembly process.

Before the pistons are removed, check for a ridge at the top of the cylinder bore. This ridge occurs because the piston ring does not travel all the way to the top of the bore, thereby leaving an unused portion of cylinder bore above the limit of ring travel. This ridge will usually be more pronounced on high mileage engines. If the ridge is severe, it must be removed with a ridge reamer before pushing the pistons out the top of the block. When using a ridge reamer, care must be taken to only remove the ridge and not cut into the bore in the ring travel area.

Note: A severe ridge is an indication of excessive cylinder bore wear. Before removing the piston, check the cylinder bore diameter with a bore gauge and compare the measurement with specification. If the bore is excessively worn, the block will be rebored for oversize pistons or the cylinder liners will be replaced, so removing the ridge is not necessary.

Remove the piston and rod assemblies one at a time. Remove the rod bolts or rod bolt nuts, as required, and remove the connecting rod cap. Slip pieces of rubber hose over the rod bolts to keep the bolt threads from damaging the crankshaft during removal. Push each assembly upward and remove from the top of the bore. After the piston and connecting rod assembly is removed from the block, reinstall the rod cap.

Inspect the pistons and connecting rods for cracks, damage and wear patterns that might indicate other problems. Scuffed pistons, for example, might be the result of inadequate lubrication, insufficient piston-to-cylinder clearances and/or overheating. Damaged ring lands and/or holes burned in the top of a piston can be caused by detonation.

On engines with slide fit dry sleeves, the pistons and sleeves can be removed together. A special puller or press is required to remove dry sleeves. Wet sleeves are usually removed easily. Inspect the block counterbore area for erosion, cracks, or other damage that might indicate the need for repairs or reconditioning. Measure the depth of the counterbore from the deck surface at four points around the circumference using a depth micrometer or dial indicator. The depth of the counterbore must be uniform all the way around, and be within the manufacturer's specifications.

During manufacture, each main

bearing cap is finish machined at the same time as its corresponding bore half in the block. On most engines, the cap's position in the block is stamped or cast into the main cap. If no identifying numbers can be seen, before removing any of the main caps, use number stamps to mark their positions in the block. The caps must be reinstalled in their original positions.

Remove the main bearing caps, lift out the crankshaft, and remove the bearings. Mark the back of each bearing with a felt marker for future reference.

Using a suitable driver or puller tool, remove and inspect the camshaft bearings. Note any wear of the camshaft bores that would indicate a need for align honing or align boring. If the center bearing shows more wear than the end bearings, either the camshaft is bent or the block is warped.

Remove the core plugs and oil gallery plugs. Core plugs, also known as freeze plugs, are usually exposed to coolant and can corrode from the inside. A core plug may look fine on the outside but in reality be paper thin from corrosion, so to be safe all core plugs should be replaced. Core plugs can be removed using a punch to twist the plug in its hole so it can be pulled or pried out. They can also be removed by knocking a hole through them with a chisel and prying them out. Be careful not to damage a cylinder by forcing a core plug into the coolant jacket. A cylinder can easily be distorted.

Relief valves, oil gallery restrictors and gallery plugs must be removed to allow thorough cleaning of the oil galleries. If any gallery plugs are left in place, dirt and sludge could remain in the block and the wet sludge could also attract abrasives from the cleaning process. The combination of dirt and abrasives can be carried throughout the engine by the oil when the engine is restarted, with disastrous consequences. Plug type gallery plugs can be removed in the same manner as core plugs. Stubborn threaded oil gallery plugs can be heated with a torch and quenched with paraffin wax or in extreme cases, drilled and the remainder removed with a screw extractor.

Any studs should be removed on an as-required basis. If the studs interfere with allowing a part to be reconditioned, then they should be removed. However, some studs may be difficult to remove without breaking them and attempts to remove them may cause more problems than leaving them in place would.

Spread the main and rod bearings out in the same positions as they were previously installed in the block. Note any unusual wear patterns. Check to see if the center main bearings show more wear than the ones toward either end of the crankshaft. This could indicate that the crankshaft is bent. It will have to be straightened or replaced. If the main bearing bores of the block are misaligned due to block distortion, the upper or lower bearing halves will show wear. The centermost bearing will usually show the most wear. This will require align honing or boring of the main bearing bores.

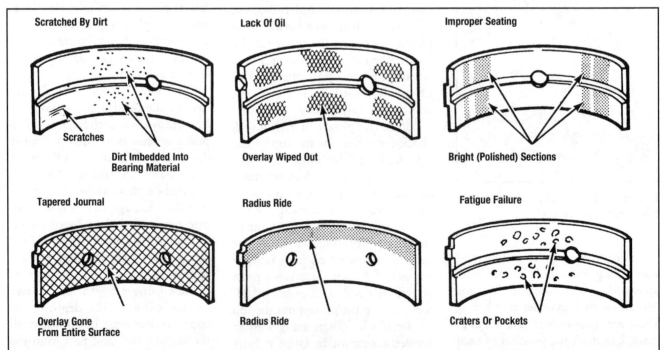

Reading bearings after the engine has been disassembled can help you diagnose engine problems that need repairs.

If only the upper front bearing is worn, too tight of a belt adjustment is indicated.

If the engine had a knock, the rod bearing(s) farthest from the oil pump might show the most wear. This would indicate an oil supply problem.

Oil supply problems can result from:

• A loose or leaky oil pump pickup tube
  • Restricted pickup screen
  • Worn oil pump
  • Excessive main bearing clearance
  • Low oil level
  • Too much oil in the crankcase.

If there is too much oil in the crankcase, the spinning crankshaft can churn the oil into foam. The foam is drawn into the oil pump and a lack of crucial lubrication results.

When a single rod bearing shows excessive wear but the rest are fine, several things could be the cause:

• An obstruction in the crankshaft oil passage(s), which supply the bearing
  • Out-of-round rod bore
  • Stretched rod bolts
  • Loose or improperly torqued rod nuts
  • Twisted or bent rod
  • Out-of-round or rough connecting rod journal
  • Misassembly, including incorrect bearing crush fit, incorrect oil clearance, installation of a wrong-sized bearing, or dirt behind the bearing back.

Burned bearings and/or discolored crank journals are signs of inadequate lubrication. Possible causes include clogged oil passages, internal oil leaks, a weak or broken oil pump, improperly installed pickup tube, engine overheating, an oil relief valve stuck in the open position or low oil level due to leaks or neglect.

Particles embedded in the bearings or badly scored bearings are due to oil contamination. Contamination can result from infrequent oil and filter changes, oil bypassing a clogged filter, or metal debris from damaged components elsewhere in the engine.

CLEANING

After the engine has been disassembled, the cylinder block, crankshaft, and related parts must be thoroughly cleaned before inspection and machining. Sludge, carbon deposits, grease, dirt, scale and other debris are removed. The selected cleaning technique must also clean hidden areas of the block such as oil passages and water jackets.

The most common techniques for cast iron cleaning used to be soaking the block and other parts in a hot tank filled with a solution of caustic soda and hot water, or placing the parts in a jet clean cabinet where they would be cleaned by high pressure jets of caustic solution while rotating on a turntable. Due to environmental concerns, however, thermal cleaning has become a popular alternative. With this method, cast iron parts are placed in a high temperature bake oven or pyrolytic oven set at about 750°F (399°C), and the oven burns out the grease and other contaminants. The remaining ash and scale is then removed by washing or by shot blasting. After shot blasting, the part is tumbled in a tumbler to remove leftover shot.

CAUTION: It is extremely important that no shot blast media be left in the block where it could find its way into the oil system. The abrasive could then be carried throughout the engine by the oil when the engine is restarted, with disastrous consequences.

Aluminum parts can be cleaned chemically; however, caustic solutions are too strong for cleaning aluminum parts. A detergent based or aluminum safe chemical must be used to chemically clean aluminum. If aluminum parts are thermal cleaned, a lower temperature setting, about 450°F (232°C), must be used. Steel shot is too abrasive to use on soft aluminum. An alternative is to use aluminum shot, crushed walnut shells or plastic media. Glass beading can also be used. If the pistons are cleaned with glass beads, only remove the carbon from the top of the pistons and do not glass bead the ring grooves. Wrap masking tape around the ring band and skirt, to protect them, prior to glass beading.

Small parts are typically cleaned in cleaning solvent (cold tank) or chlorinated hydrocarbon (carburetor cleaner). A media tumbler is another option for cleaning small parts like bolts and valvetrain components.

Always disassemble the pistons from the pins and rods if the pistons are to be soaked in a chemical cleaner. Pressed fit pins are removed in a press, with suitable fixtures to properly support the piston. The pins in full floating pistons are retained with clips located in the piston pin bore. These clips are discarded after removal and should not be reused. Prior to disassembly, be sure to record the piston-to-rod orientation for assembly reference.

Bead blasting with glass, aluminum, or soft media can also be used to clean small parts and aluminum castings. As with steel shot cleaning, it is very important that cleaning media does not remain inside the engine. Glass beads are especially prone to sticking to wet surfaces inside oil galleries.

INSPECTION

Crack Inspection

After the block and other parts have been cleaned, they should be inspected for cracks. Components like the connecting rods and crankshaft may appear to be perfectly sound, but microscopic fatigue cracks invisible to the naked eye can grow and expand after parts are returned to service. They can eventually result in a part failure. Crack inspection of the crankshaft, connecting rods, main caps, block and heads can be done using fluorescent dyes and/or magnetic crack detection equipment. Blocks can also be pressure tested.

NOTE: When an engine has a broken crankshaft, check the vibration damper (harmonic balancer). A problem with the damper can often create stress loads that lead to crank breakage.

Magnetic crack detection can only be done on ferrous (iron and steel) parts. Wet magnetic particle inspection is normally used to check crankshafts, camshafts and rods. Dry magnetic particle inspection is used to check blocks.

Magnetic particle detection is a fast and easy way to find hairline cracks in cast iron blocks. The magnetic field created by the tester attracts iron powder applied to the block. A secondary magnetic field is created at the location of a crack. Additional powder accumulates around this field, outlining the crack. This technique will not reveal a crack that is parallel to the magnetic field. A second magnetic check is made by turning the tester 90 degrees. This can catch any cracks that might have been missed on the first try. It is difficult to find internal cracks in water jackets with this technique.

Dye penetrants must be used on the pistons and aluminum castings since they are not magnetic. Dye is sprayed on the surface and allowed to dry. Then the excess is wiped from the surface. A developer is sprayed on to make the cracks visible. A black light can be used with some dyes for greater visibility.

Pressure testing can also be used

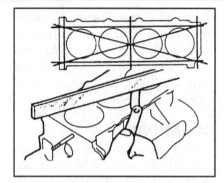

Check the deck surface of the block for warpage with a straightedge at these positions.

to check for cracks or leaks in the block. It is a crack detection method that is good at revealing hard-to-see internal leaks. After plugging all the external openings of the water jackets, the block is lightly pressurized (usually less than 30 psi) with air. A soapy water solution is sprayed on the block to check for leaks. Bubbles highlight leaks.

Cracked blocks are not necessarily replaced. A cracked cylinder can often be successfully repaired by installing a sleeve. Cracks or holes in external water jackets and deck surfaces are tougher to fix. They require welding, gluing or pinning.

Cylinder Block Warpage Inspection

The deck surface of the cylinder block must be clean and flat if the head gasket is to seal properly. A blown head gasket or a buildup of carbon on the deck surface is an indication that the deck surface is uneven. Check for warpage with a straightedge and feeler gauge and compare with the manufacturer's specifications.

On some blocks, warpage beyond specification can be corrected by grinding or milling; however this may be impossible to do and also maintain the specified piston-to-cylinder head clearance. Replacement may be the only alternative if the block is beyond tolerance and some manufacturers require it.

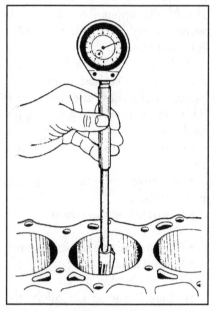

Checking cylinder bore dimensions with a dial bore gauge.

Cylinder Bores

Cylinder bores wear in two ways, taper and out-of-round. Tapered cylinders are worn more at the top, where ring loading is the greatest. Cylinders can be out-of-round as a result of the motion of the piston rocking on its wrist pin.

Visually inspect the cylinder bores for nicks, scratches, scoring or scuffing. Measure the cylinder bore using a dial bore gauge. Measure for wear, taper and out-of-roundness. Refer to the manufacturer's specifications for

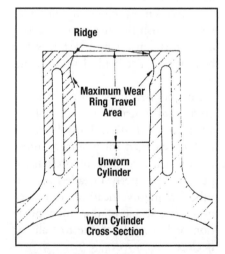

Cylinders develop the most wear at the top where ring loading is the greatest.

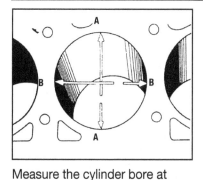

Measure the cylinder bore at both points A (perpendicular to the crankshaft) and B (parallel to the crankshaft) to determine bore wear and roundness. Measurements should be taken at both the top and bottom of the cylinder to check for taper wear.

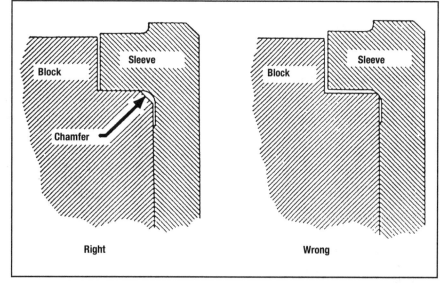

Right   **Wrong**

If the counterbore in the block has to be machined to accept an oversized sleeve, the outer edge should be chamfered to eliminate possible stress loading against the sleeve flange.

bore size to set the gauge or zero the gauge on an unworn portion of the cylinder. Any movement from zero on the gauge represents cylinder bore wear.

Measure the cylinder bore at the lowest point of piston ring travel, then gradually move the gauge to the uppermost point of ring travel. Measure at points perpendicular to and parallel to the crankshaft (90 degrees apart). The difference in the upper and lower measurements is the cylinder bore taper; the difference in the 90-degree apart measurements is the cylinder bore out-of-roundness.

Compare your measurements with the manufacturer's specifications. If cylinder bore wear is within specification, then honing is all that will be necessary to prepare

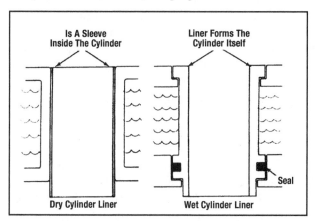

Dry and wet cylinder sleeves.
(Courtesy: John Deere & Co.)

the cylinder wall surface for new rings. However, if wear is beyond specification, the cylinders will have to be bored, honed and new pistons installed or new cylinder sleeves installed. Consult the engine and/or piston manufacturers for available oversizes.

Cylinder Sleeves

Some engines have dry cylinder sleeves or liners that are either slide-fit or pressed-fit in the block. They are called dry sleeves because coolant does not contact the outside of the sleeve. Both types can be replaced if the sleeves are worn, but require the use of special pullers or a press. Sleeves may also be used to repair bad cylinders that are cracked or worn in regular integral liner blocks.

Wet sleeves are so called because they are exposed to coolant. They have soft metal rings at the top, and rubber rings at the bottom

to seal the sleeves in the block. Wet sleeves can usually be replaced without special pullers or a press.

Inspect the cylinder sleeve counterbore for cracks and distortions. The counterbore area should not display rough or abrasive areas that might damage the sleeve or its seal upon installation.

Main Bearing And Camshaft Bearing Bores

Camshaft and crankshaft bores should be checked for alignment and distortion. Bore diameter can be checked using a bore gauge and alignment checked using a straightedge and feeler gauge. Compare measurements with specifications.

If beyond specifications, some blocks can be align honed or align bored. Refer to the manufacturer's recommendations. When cam bores are machined larger, oversized bearings are installed.

Crankshaft

Remove any gears or woodruff keys that may remain on the crankshaft. Clean the crankshaft thoroughly with solvent to permit a thorough inspection. Use pipe cleaning brushes to ensure that all

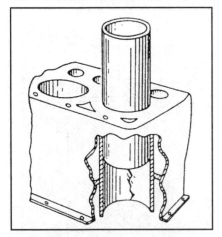

Cracked or damaged cylinder blocks with integral cylinder bores can often be salvaged by boring out the damaged cylinder and installing a repair sleeve.

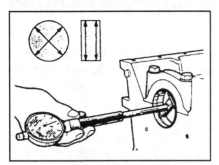

Checking crankshaft main bearing bore diameter.

oil holes and passages in the crankshaft are open and free of sludge. Some crankshafts have oil gallery plugs and these should be removed. If the plugs are difficult to remove, they can be heated and quenched with wax to ease removal.

Check the journals and thrust faces for scoring, nicks, burrs or any form of roughness. If any journals are discolored (blue or black) this indicates overheating, due to a failed bearing. The metallurgy of a crankshaft can be changed when it overheats and the crankshaft will have been weakened; it will have to be replaced or heat treated as part of a repair.

If the crankshaft is from a manual transmission vehicle, check the condition and fit of the transmission pilot bearing. Also check the crankshaft snout, flange, and rear main

Using a straightedge and feeler gauge to check main bearing bore alignment.

seal and thrust areas for damage. Damaged seal and thrust areas can be repaired by building them up with weld and regrinding. Repair sleeves are also available for repairing grooved seal areas.

A crankshaft journal that looks acceptable to the naked eye might still be out-of-round, tapered, or worn. Measure the crank journal diameter with a micrometer at either bottom or top dead center, and again at 90 degrees in either direction. Rod journals typically experience the most wear at TDC so comparing diameters at the two different positions should reveal any out-of-roundness. The traditional rule-of-thumb for journal variation says up to 0.001-in. (0.025mm) is acceptable, but many of today's engines cannot tolerate more than 0.0002-in. - 0.0005-in. (0.0051mm – 0.0127mm) of out-of-roundness. Be sure to check specifications.

Bearing journals can experience taper wear (one end worn more than the other), barrel wear (ends worn more than the center) or hourglass wear (center worn more than the ends). Measure the journal diameter at the center and both ends. The journal diameter itself should be within 0.001-in. (0.025mm) of its original dimensions, or within 0.001-in. (0.025mm) of standard regrind dimensions for proper oil clearances with a replacement bearing.

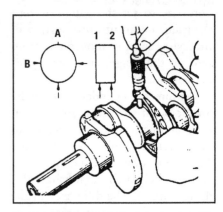

Measure the crankshaft journals with a micrometer.

An easy way to tell that a journal has been previously reground is to look for machinist markings stamped on the crank. A number 10, 20, or 30 stamped near a journal tells you the journal has already been machined undersize. Of course, if there is any question, measuring will give you the actual dimension. Further regrinding may be out of the question, depending on how badly the crank is worn. Replacement bearings are available for most crankshafts machined up to 0.030-in. (0.762mm) undersize. In addition, if the crankshaft is still at standard size, worn uniformly and still useable, bearing shell sets of 0.001-in. (0.025mm), 0.002-in. (0.051mm), and 0.003-in. (0.076mm) over standard size are sometimes available to correct excessive bearing clearance.

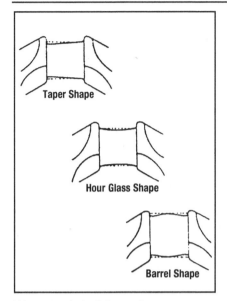

Worn crankshaft journals.

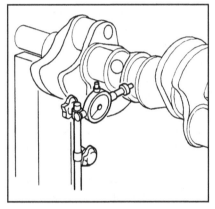

Measuring crankshaft runout with a dial indicator. *(Courtesy: GM Corp.)*

Some manufacturers use select fit bearings during the manufacturing process. In this case there may be markings on the cylinder block and crankshaft, which can be interpreted using a chart to see which bearing grade should be used. If, after inspection, it is determined that the crankshaft can remain at standard size, these select fit bearings may allow the desired bearing clearance to be attained. However, clearance should always be verified by measuring.

A bent crankshaft can be diagnosed by inspecting the main bearings for wear during disassembly. It can also be diagnosed by placing the crankshaft in V-blocks or a turning fixture and

rotating it while watching for wobble at the center main journal with a dial indicator. If runout exceeds limits, the crank will need to be straightened or replaced.

If the journals are free from flaws, and wear, taper, out-of-roundness and runout are within specification, the crankshaft journals can be polished and the crankshaft returned to service. However, if the crankshaft fails to meet these criteria, it will have to be reground 0.010-in. (0.254mm), 0.020-in. (0.508mm) or 0.030-in. (0.762mm) undersize. Most journals will clean up at 0.010-in. (0.254mm) undersize. If it takes more than 0.030-in. (0.762mm) to restore the journals, the crank may have to be replaced or built up by welding metal onto the journals. After grinding, the machinist will chamfer the oil holes to promote good oil flow to the bearings, and then polish the journals with a fine grit emery belt.

Camshaft And Lifters

Clean the camshaft using solvent, and clean out all oil holes. Visually inspect cam lobes, bearing journals and accessory drive gear (if equipped) for excessive wear, rounded lobes, edge wear, scratches, pitting, scoring or galling. If there is any obvious wear or damage, the camshaft must be replaced.

Measure each camshaft lobe height and measure the camshaft journals for out-of-round and taper using a micrometer. Compare measurements with specifications and replace the cam if necessary. If the lobes and journals appear OK, place the front and rear journals in V-blocks and rest a dial indicator on the center journal. Rotate the camshaft to check straightness. If runout exceeds the manufacturer's specifications, replace the camshaft.

Remove any gum and varnish from the lifters using solvent. Inspect the face of flat-tappet lifters for pitting, excessive wear or con-

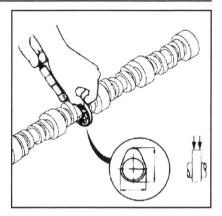

Measuring camshaft lobe lift. *(Courtesy: GM Corp.)*

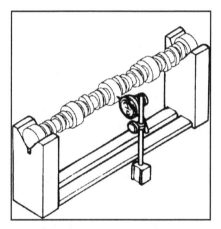

Measuring camshaft runout. *(Courtesy: GM Corp.)*

cave appearance. The face of the lifter should be convex and smooth. If any unusual wear is apparent, inspect the corresponding camshaft lobe. Inspect the lifter body for scuffing and wear and if any are found, inspect the corresponding lifter bore.

Roller lifters must be checked for roller bushing wear and alignment device problems. The bushing shouldn't allow the roller excessive play on the axle pin of the lifter, and the alignment devices should retain the lifter in the bore so that the roller axle centerline stays parallel with the cam lobe centerline. This locking arrangement serves to prevent the lifter from rotating and causing the roller to slide on the lobe of the cam rather than rolling.

Clean the lifter bores in the block.

Any nicks or scratches can be removed with light honing, if necessary. It is essential that the lifters on a flat-tappet cam be able to rotate in their bores. The face on a flat-tappet lifter is convex, the cam lobe is slightly tapered (about 0.0005–0.0007-in.) and the lifter bore is offset to make the lifter rotate during operation. This rotation is essential because it spreads wear over a greater surface area. If the lifter fails to spin it will destroy itself and its cam lobe. It is recommended that if any lifters require replacement, that the camshaft and all lifters be replaced.

Pistons

Clean the pistons and carefully inspect them for wear and damage. Note the condition of the rings. Piston rings can wear in normal use or because of a lack of proper lubrication, or from dirty air or oil. Abrasive wear accounts for most ring failures. Overheating is also a major cause of failed rings.

If the rings are to be replaced, remove the old rings from the pistons with a ring expander. Do not spiral rings off or on. Check the ring lands for wear, cracks or damage. Clean the ring grooves with a ring groove cleaner. Be very careful not to damage the ring grooves.

Do not use the wire wheel on a

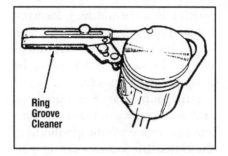

After the rings have been removed, clean and inspect the ring grooves.

grinder or attempt to clean the pistons in a hot tank filled with caustic soda. If pistons are cleaned with a glass bead blaster or in carburetor cleaner (chlorinated hydrocarbon), the connecting rods and wrist pins must be removed first. If the piston is cleaned with glass beads, only remove the carbon from the top of the piston and do not glass bead the ring grooves. Wrap masking tape around the ring band to protect the ring grooves, prior to glass beading.

Note: Do not soak the piston and rod assemblies in solvent as the wrist pin can seize to the piston. Always disassemble the pistons from the pins and rods if the pistons are to be soaked in a chemical cleaner.

Use penetrating dye to check the piston for invisible hairline cracks

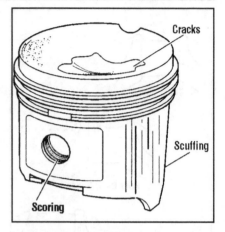

Inspect the piston for cracks, scuffing and scoring. *(Courtesy: GM Corp.)*

around the wrist pin boss, ring lands, crown and skirt areas. Replace any piston found to be cracked.

Note unusual wear patterns. Uniform excessive wear can be caused by dirty oil and/or poor air filtration. Overheating can cause collapsed pistons. Holes or melted spots on the piston indicate a detonation problem. Scuffing or scoring on the thrust side of a piston can be caused by insufficient lubrication. Scuffing or scoring on both sides of the piston can be caused by detonation, overheating or inadequate piston clearance as well as lack of lubrication. Cracked or broken ring lands indicate detonation. A slanted wear pattern on the side of the piston indicates a twisted connecting

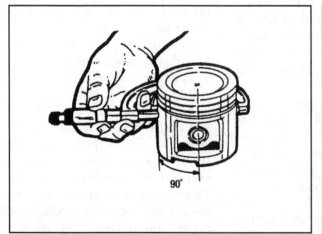

Measuring piston diameter with a micrometer.

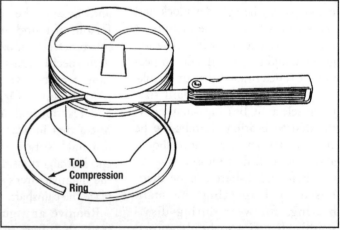

Checking ring side clearance. *(Courtesy: GM Corp.)*

rod. Wear above the wrist pin can be due to a bent connecting rod. Bent and twisted rods can be accompanied by misalignment wear of the connecting rod bearings.

Piston wear can be checked by measuring the diameter of the piston with a micrometer and comparing it to specifications. Pistons are cam ground (slightly oval shaped to allow for thermal expansion). Their largest diameter is at a point about one inch below the oil ring groove, perpendicular to the wrist pin, however, check the manufacturer's specifications for specific measuring locations. If the diameter is smaller than the specified service limits, the piston must be replaced.

Check the ring grooves for wear. Every time the piston changes direction in its up and down travel, the rings are forced against the piston lands. Over time this pounds the lands out of shape. Check the side clearance of a ring by inserting a new ring backward into the land and measuring its clearance to the groove with a feeler gauge. Compare your measurement with specifications. Roll the ring around the circumference of the entire ring groove, while checking for bind. If a groove is damaged or worn excessively, the piston must be replaced.

Wear in the wrist pin area can cause an engine knock as the piston rocks and twists on the ends of the wrist pin. When a pin fits loose in the piston, the piston pin bore and rod small end can be resized to fit an oversize wrist pin.

Once piston inspection has been completed, determine whether or not the pistons will be removed from the connecting rods. If the pistons are to be replaced or connecting rod service is required, the wrist pins and connecting rods must be removed. Pressed fit pins are removed in a press with suitable fixtures to properly support the piston. The pins in full floating pistons are retained with clips located in the piston pin bore. These clips are discarded after removal and should not be reused.

Prior to disassembly, be sure to record the piston-to-rod orientation for assembly reference.

Connecting Rods

Connecting rods can suffer from a variety of problems. Cracked rods should be replaced. Worn piston pin bushings can be replaced and out-of-round bearing bores can be remachined. Bent or twisted rods can be straightened but are most commonly replaced.

Inspect the old connecting rod bearings for uneven wear that could indicate that a rod is bent or twisted. Check connecting rod straightness on a rod alignment fixture.

The connecting rod big end bore concentricity must be within 0.001-in. (0.025mm). This is checked on a gauge that reads to 0.0001-in. (0.0025mm) and compared to the manufacturer's specifications. Rods that do not meet specification are resized on a rod reconditioning machine. The rod bolts are removed and the rod and cap

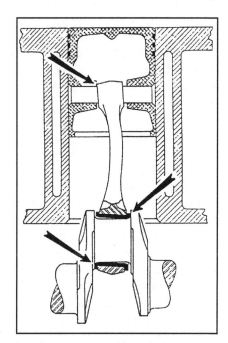

Load areas caused by a bent connecting rod.

ground on a cap grinding machine. The minimum amount of material is removed, usually no more than 0.003 in. (0.076mm). The rod is then reassembled and the big end bore honed to size.

There is one exception to the above and that is for the 'cracked' powdered metal connecting rods that are appearing in many newer engines. During the manufacturing process, the rod caps on these rods are separated from the rest of the rod by fracturing rather than machining, hence the name. The resulting irregular mating surface makes

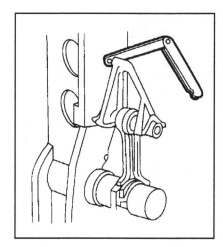

Checking a connecting rod for bend on a rod alignment fixture.
(Courtesy: Ford Motor Co.)

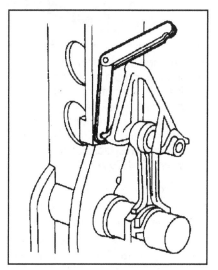

Checking a connecting rod for twist on a rod alignment fixture.
(Courtesy: Ford Motor Co.)

Measuring connecting rod big end bore diameter.

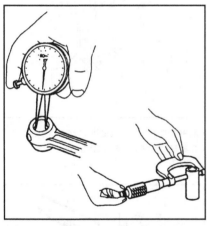

Measure the inside diameter of the connecting rod pin bore and the outside diameter of the wrist pin. On press-fit pins, there must be a specified amount of interference. With full floating pins, the clearance must be within specifications. *(Courtesy: GM Corp.)*

for a stronger bond between the two pieces when they are bolted together.

Because of this design feature, the rod and cap of a 'cracked' rod cannot be ground. Some aftermarket manufacturers have addressed this problem by making rod bearings with oversize outside diameters for some applications. The big end of

the rod can then be honed oversize and the rod reused.

Pressed fit pins must have the right amount of interference in the connecting rod or they can come out and damage the cylinder wall. When the wrist pin is pressed into the rod, the pin bore is usually 0.001-in. (0.025mm) smaller than the pin. If the small end bore is not within specification, the small end bore and the corresponding piston bore can be honed and an oversize wrist pin installed.

When the piston uses full floating pins, bushings are usually installed in the small end bore. If a bushing is damaged or the bore is not within specification, the old bushing is driven out and replaced. The new bushing is then honed to provide the proper clearance to the wrist pin.

Ideally, a new rod should be matched as closely as possible to the weight of the original to maintain engine balance. This is not as critical in a low rpm, light-duty engine as it is in a high rpm or heavy-duty engine. It is more critical in V-type engines than it is with in-line engines.

ENGINE PREPARATION FOR ASSEMBLY

When all machine work has been completed, the block should be thoroughly cleaned and the piston and connecting rods assembled. All component parts should be cleaned, laid out and prepared for assembly.

Cylinder Block

All threaded holes in the cylinder block should be cleaned and repaired, the block deburred, and thoroughly cleaned with soap and water.

Inspect all threaded holes, clean them with a thread chaser and repair as necessary. Clamping force measured when reading a torque wrench changes with friction. When the threads and the underside of the hex head on the bolt are not clean, friction will increase the torque reading.

Major damage to threaded holes is repaired by drilling out the stripped threads, tapping the hole and installing an insert. Some prewound threaded inserts require special size drills and taps as well as a special installation tool, all of which is usually included in a kit. There are also solid type threaded inserts that use standard size drills and taps and are installed using a screwdriver, which fits into slots on the insert.

Inspect the block for sharp edges and casting burrs and flash, pay-

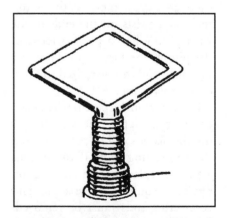

Damaged threads can be repaired by drilling the hole oversize and cutting new threads with a special tap. A prewound insert is then installed with a special tool.

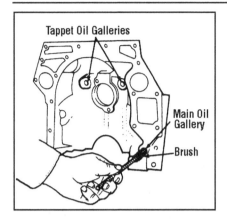

Using a bristle brush to clean an oil gallery. *(Courtesy: Ford Motor Co.)*

carry the abrasives further into the pores of the metal where they can escape later.

All the grit, dirt and machining chips accumulated during the machining process must be removed from the block. A selection of stiff bristle brushes of various diameters should be used to dislodge dirt, grit and chips from all the nooks and crannies in the block, as well as the oil passages and lifter bores. Wash the cylinder bores last, after the rest of the block has been cleaned, to prevent scratching the cylinder wall finish.

Note: Throughout the block washing process, be careful not to let any machined surfaces rust. The cylinder bores especially, will quickly rust after they have been scrubbed clean if a rust inhibitor such as WD-40™ is not quickly applied.

Once the block has been completely cleaned and rinsed, and all machined surfaces have been protected with a rust inhibitor, blow dry the block with compressed air, paying particular attention to the oil galleries. Do not use shop towels for drying. Lint from the towels can accumulate and cause problems.

Camshaft Bearings

The camshaft bearings are the first components to be installed in the prepared and cleaned block. Some engines use different size bearings for some of the bores in the block. Determine the locations of the bearings by comparing their part numbers and positions. This information is usually on one of the tabs of the cardboard carton that the bearings came in.

These bearings are a press fit in the block and must be driven or drawn into place using a suitable installation tool. Universal driving tools have an expander that is turned until it fits into the inside diameter of the bearing. The expander is attached to an exten-

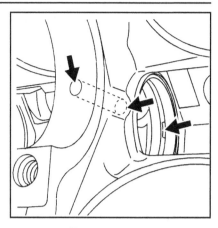

When installing cam bearings, make sure the oil hole in the bearing is aligned with the oil passage from the main bearing bore.
(Courtesy: GM Corp.)

sion that enables all of the bearings in the block to be accessed. A flange on the expander contacts the edge of the bearing and drives it into position when the extension is hit with a hammer. Some tools have solid drivers that are made for the most common size bearings.

Lubricate the outside of the bearings before installing them. Care must be taken to properly align the oil holes in the cam bearings with those in the block so oil can be pumped to the journals. If a hole is partially or totally blocked, it will result in shaft and/or bearing failure.

Core Plugs And Oil Gallery Plugs

After the camshaft bearings are in place, install the rear plug behind the shaft and any cup type oil gallery plugs. Apply the recommended sealer or anaerobic adhesive to the plug to prevent oil leaks. Then stake it in place to aid retention. If an oil gallery plug comes out, all oil pressure to the engine will be lost. This is usually an internal leak (within the timing cover).

Oil gallery plugs on the outside of the engine are most often threaded. Install these next, along with core plugs and wear sleeves. Coat core plugs with sealer or anaerobic ad-

ing special attention to the cam gallery, oil drain passages, main bearing bulkheads and lifter valley. Sharp edges are stress risers that can give cracks a starting point. If not removed, casting burrs and flash could break off later and cause engine damage. Large casting burrs and flash can be carefully chipped off with a hammer and chisel. The rest, along with the sharp edges, can be ground off with a high-speed grinder and carbide cutter.

WARNING: To avoid personal injury, be sure to wear eye protection when deburring and cleaning the block.

Make sure the cam bearing and lifter bores are clean and free of burrs that could cause parts to bind. Lifters on flat tappet cams must be free to spin in the bore; if they cannot turn, the lifter and cam lobe will quickly wear.

Thoroughly wash the block with soap and hot water. Half of all ring failures that occur during break-in can be directly attributed to improperly cleaned cylinder walls. Following the cylinder honing or deglazing process, the cylinder walls must be cleaned with hot, soapy water and a stiff nonmetallic bristle brush. Gasoline, kerosene, or other petroleum solvents cannot wash away abrasive residues. Rather, they hesive and carefully tap them into place. The edge of the plug should be just below the surface of the block and even with the bore chamfer. Put sealer or Teflon tape on threaded gallery plugs to prevent leaks and then install them.

CAUTION: If Teflon tape is used, be absolutely certain that a piece of tape does not extend into the oil gallery. A loose piece could come off and block the flow of oil. Teflon also acts as a thread lubricant. When tightening a tapered pipe plug, do not over tighten it.

Cylinder Sleeves

Cylinder Sleeve Installation

If a block has replaceable cylinder sleeves, they are installed next. First measure the depth of the counterbores in the block to see if shimming is necessary. Shimming is necessary if the block deck surface has been milled and/or the counterbores have been reworked.

After measuring the depth of the counterbores, measure the thickness of the lip or flange on a new cylinder sleeve. Then subtract the depth of the counterbore from the thickness of the cylinder sleeve lip or flange to determine the amount of protrusion above the deck surface.

The tops of both wet and dry sleeves usually project about 0.001-in. to 0.006-in. above the deck surface, but some are flush. Refer to the manufacturer's specifications for the required amount of clearance. Spacer rings can be used to shim up the cylinder sleeves so they will seal properly against the head.

Before installing the sleeves, check the counterbores to be certain they're perfectly clean and free from rust, grease or carbon deposits. On blocks with dry sleeves, the cylinder bores must be clean, smooth and round. Check the inside bore dimensions with a bore gauge, dial

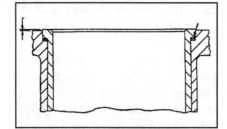

To adjust the installed height of cylinder sleeves, install shims under the flange of the sleeve.

indicator, or inside micrometer at both the top and bottom of each cylinder. Measure also at 90 degrees to check for an out-of-round bore. Proper measurement is critical to ensure a proper dry sleeve fit. If the bore diameter is greater than the OEM dimension, an oversize sleeve will have to be installed.

Measure the outside diameter of the sleeves at the specified location to determine their size. Some dry sleeves require as much as 0.0015-in. of clearance, while others are designed to be installed with up to a 0.001-in. interference fit. Subtract the outside diameter of the sleeves from the inside diameter of the cylinder bores to determine the clearance between the sleeves and bores.

To install loose fitting dry sleeves, insert each one into its bore and push it in as far as it will go. The last inch or so may require the use of a driver. With tight fitting sleeves, it may be necessary to chill the sleeves beforehand for easier installation. In any event, a driver or puller will be needed to install the sleeves in the block.

To install wet sleeves, install new O-rings and/or seals on the cylinder sleeves. Be careful not to nick or twist the O-rings during the installation process. Some sleeves require two or three different O-rings. Be certain they are the correct ones and that they are installed in the correct locations. Once the O-rings are in place, it's a good idea to insert a small pick or blunt screwdriver under each ring and run it all the way around the sleeve to relieve any twist that might

have occurred. This also helps seat the O-rings in their grooves.

The O-rings and lower packing ring area of the block can now be lubricated as required using the specified lubricant (oil, silicone or soap). As the sleeves are inserted into the block, be careful not to damage the O-rings. Gently rotate the sleeves back and forth and then allow them to settle into place under their own weight. Once the O-rings are properly aligned with the chamfers in the block, the cylinder can be pushed the rest of the way in by hand or with the necessary driver.

If the sleeve does not slip into place easily or rises back up after pressure is removed, one or more O-rings are either out-of-position or twisted. The sleeve will have to be pulled back out and the problem corrected. Inspect the O-rings carefully before reinstalling them to make sure they weren't damaged.

Checking Cylinder Sleeve Fit

After all of the sleeves have been installed in the block; check the protrusion height of each to make sure it is within the manufacturer's specified range. Each sleeve should also be within 0.001-in. of the protrusion height of adjacent sleeves for proper sealing. Individual height measurements can be made with a dial indicator or by placing a straightedge along the tops of the sleeves and using a feeler gauge to check clearances.

Use a bore gauge, dial indicator or inside micrometer to check the inside of the sleeves for distortion (out-of-round) in the packing ring area. Misalignment or improper seating between the sleeve's O-ring and the block are highlighted by this check. If the amount of out-of-roundness exceeds the manufacturer's specifications, remove the sleeve and correct the problem.

Crankshaft

The crankshaft should be washed with clean solvent. Run a stiff bristle brush through all the oil passages to make sure they are clean. After the crankshaft has been cleaned, blow it dry with compressed air, paying special attention to the oil passages. Reinstall any woodruff keys and oil gallery plugs that were removed when the engine was disassembled.

Pistons And Connecting Rods

Wash the pistons and connecting rods with clean solvent, dry them and assemble as required. Be sure to properly position the piston and rod prior to assembly, so that they will be facing the proper direction when installed in the engine. Refer to the notes made when the pistons and rods were disassembled.

Most pistons have an arrow, a notch or the letter 'F', for front, to indicate the side that should be toward the front of the engine. Connecting rods are usually oriented with respect to rod numbers, rod bore chamfer or bearing tangs. On some diesel engines, rod orientation is especially critical because the pistons are cooled with oil from squirt holes in the connecting rods instead of cooling nozzles. Always refer to the factory service manual for specifications.

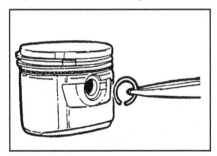

Always position wrist pin clips with the gap facing down.

On pistons with floating wrist pins, lubricate the connecting rod small end and piston bore, and assemble using new pin retainer clips. Some retainer clips will have a rounded edge and a sharp edge.

These clips should always be installed so that the rounded edge is against the pin, leaving the sharp edge to bite into the piston aluminum. The clips should also be positioned with their gaps facing down, so that the full area of the clip is against the groove during combustion.

Pistons with pressed pins can be assembled in either of two ways, by pressing the pin into the connecting rod or by heating the small end of the rod. If the pin is pressed into the connecting rod, the piston must be properly supported using a suitable fixture to prevent distorting or damaging the piston. The press fixture usually includes a stop to properly center the pin in the rod and piston pin bore. Before pressing, the pin, piston bore and connecting rod small end must be well lubricated.

A rod heater heats the small end of the connecting rod to a very high temperature, expanding it and allowing the wrist pin to be pushed through using hand pressure. Protective gloves and a special fixture to properly locate the pin in the rod and piston bore must be used. The process must be performed very quickly, as once the small end of the rod is removed from the heater, it will rapidly cool and grip the wrist pin.

ENGINE ASSEMBLY

NOTE: During engine assembly remember to lubricate bearings and the surfaces of seals with liberal amounts of lubricant. It takes several minutes of engine operation before all areas of the engine become lubricated. This is long enough for unlubricated areas to begin to fail. When engine parts are separated by a film of clean oil, virtually no wear occurs.

Crankshaft

Make sure that the replacement bearing size matches the crankshaft journal diameter. If the crank has been turned 0.010-in., 0.020-in. or

0.030-in. undersize, the bearings must be the appropriate undersize. Check the markings on the back of the bearings and check the diameter of the crankshaft journals with a micrometer before attempting to check bearing fit.

Make sure the bearing saddles in the block and main caps are perfectly clean and dry because even the smallest amount of dirt will decrease bearing clearance. Dirt can also result in deformation in the bearing shell, enough to ruin a bearing.

Install the upper main bearing inserts (the ones with the oil holes in them) in the engine block. Next, install the lower inserts in the main caps. In some bearing sets, lower main bearings will not have lubrication holes in them. In other sets, both the upper and lower bearing halves have holes. Check to see that the oil holes in the upper bearing shells line up with those in the block. Bearing locating lugs must also be correctly positioned in their slots.

When the engine has a split rear main oil seal, install the seal halves in the block and rear main cap. Line up the surfaces where the seal halves meet so that they are above and below the parting half of the main cap. This will ensure that oil cannot leak through.

When the engine uses a one-piece rear main oil seal, it can be installed after the crankshaft and rear main bearing cap have been installed. Some engines have a rear seal housing that is bolted to the back of the block. When the seal fits into a recess in the rear bearing cap, it is often possible to install a full round seal around the crankshaft sealing flange before installing the rear main cap. The seal is held in place while installing the rear main cap. If the cap is already in place, a special installation tool may be used for seal installation.

Main bearing oil clearance can be checked using a dial bore gauge or with Plastigage™. If a dial bore gauge

Measuring crankshaft main bearing oil clearance with a dial bore gauge.

is to be used, the main bearing caps should be installed and the bolts torqued to specification. Measure the crankshaft bearing journal diameter with a micrometer and use the measurement to set the dial bore gauge. Measure the inside diameter of the bearings using the bore gauge; the difference of this measurement and the main journal diameter measurement will be the main bearing oil clearance.

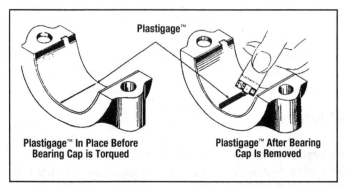

Plastigage™

Plastigage™ In Place Before
Bearing Cap is Torqued

Plastigage™ After Bearing
Cap Is Removed

Checking bearing clearance with Plastigage™.

If bearing clearance is to be checked with Plastigage™, carefully lower the crankshaft onto the upper main bearings. Lay a piece of Plastigage™ lengthwise on the crank journal. Install and torque the main cap to specifications. Be careful not to turn the crankshaft while the Plastigage™ is in position. Remove the main cap and compare the thickness of the crushed piece of Plastigage™ to the gauge on the package to determine

the amount of bearing clearance.

Refer to the manufacturer's recommendations for bearing clearance. A ballpark figure that applies to most engines is 0.001-in. (0.025mm) of clearance for each inch of journal diameter.

After checking bearing clearances, remove the crankshaft. Plastigage™ is easily removed with engine oil because it is soluble in oil. Lubricate the main bearings and crankshaft main journals with assembly lubricant.

Reinstall the crankshaft and main bearing caps. An anaerobic sealer or RTV silicone is sometimes installed on rear main caps to prevent oil leaks. Be careful not to get any under the parting surface of the main cap, as this will increase bearing clearance. Anti-seize compound is used with main cap bolts that are threaded into aluminum blocks.

Lightly tap each main bearing cap with a hammer to seat it in its recess in the block. Then torque the main cap bolts to specifications. If the main bearings

caps are part of a one-piece casting, tighten the bearing cap bolts in the proper sequence. When the engine has upper and lower thrust halves, leave the thrust main until the last. Pry the crankshaft forward and backward to align the thrust halves, before tightening the main cap. This aligns the thrust halves. As each main cap is torqued, turn the crankshaft to see if it binds. If the crankshaft does not rotate freely in the engine block, the main bores may be misaligned, the crankshaft may be bent, or one or more of the main bearings may be too tight. Dirt or debris behind one of the bearing shells can also restrict crankshaft movement.

Check crankshaft end-play. This is done by inserting a feeler gauge between the thrust main bearing flange and crank, or by placing a dial indicator against the end or nose of the crank. End-play can then be measured by pushing the crank fore and aft as far as it will go. Refer to the manufacturer's recommended specifications.

Use a dial indicator to check for crankshaft flange runout. Rotate the crankshaft and compare the minimum and maximum readings to determine the maximum amount of lateral runout.

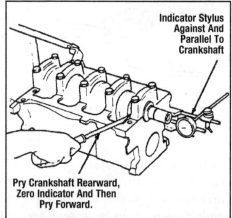

Indicator Stylus
Against And
Parallel To
Crankshaft

Pry Crankshaft Rearward,
Zero Indicator And Then
Pry Forward.

Measuring crankshaft end-play with a dial indicator. (Courtesy: Ford Motor Co.)

Pistons And Connecting Rods

Piston Ring Installation

Place a new piston ring into the cylinder in which it will be installed and measure the ring end gap clearance with a feeler gauge. If the bore is worn, the ring should be positioned in the area of ring travel that is least worn. Square the ring in the cylinder using an inverted piston. The ring end gap should be within the range specified by the manufacturer. As a rule, the minimum end gap will be 0.003-in. – 0.004-in. (0.076mm – 0.102mm) per inch of cylinder diameter. Some manufacturers specify even less.

Excessive end gap can cause blowby. However, an end gap that is too small can also cause problems. If an end gap is too small, as the ring heats up during engine operation, the ring will expand and the ends of the ring can butt together. As the ring continues to expand, the ring face will be forced against the cylinder wall causing rapid wear. If the gap is too small, a rotary ring file is used to carefully trim the ends of a ring to bring it within specification. Use a fine whetstone to deburr the edges of the ring after filing.

After the ring end gaps are set, in-stall the rings on the pistons. Locate the side of the ring that is marked 'up'. This mark is usually a dot, however, refer to the information on the ring packaging for specific instructions. Use a ring expander to install the rings on the piston. Do not over-expand the rings or spiral them on by hand. Doing so can distort the rings, leaving a permanent twist that prevents the rings from seating properly.

Install the oil ring first. The middle compression ring is next, followed by the top compression ring. The position of the rings on the pistons is staggered so the end gaps are at least 60 degrees and preferably 180 degrees apart. This prevents combustion gases from having a direct route to blow by the rings. Follow the recommendations of the manufacturer.

Piston And Connecting Rod Installation

Make sure the connecting rod bearing saddles are clean and dry.

Install the bearing inserts, making sure the locating lugs are correctly positioned in their slots. Some connecting rods have oil squirt holes built into the rod. Make sure the hole in the bearing lines up with the hole in the rod.

Just like the main bearings, connecting rod bearing oil clearance can be checked using a dial bore gauge or with Plastigage™. If a dial bore gauge is to be used, the rod bearing caps should be installed and the bolts torqued to specification. Measure the crankshaft bearing journal diameter with a micrometer and use the measurement to set the dial bore gauge. Measure the inside diameter of the bearings using the bore gauge; the difference of this measurement and the connecting rod journal diameter measurement will be the connecting rod bearing oil clearance. If Plastigage™ is to be used, the bearing clearance is checked after the piston is installed in the bore.

Lightly lubricate the piston, piston rings and cylinder bore. A

Measuring piston ring end gap.

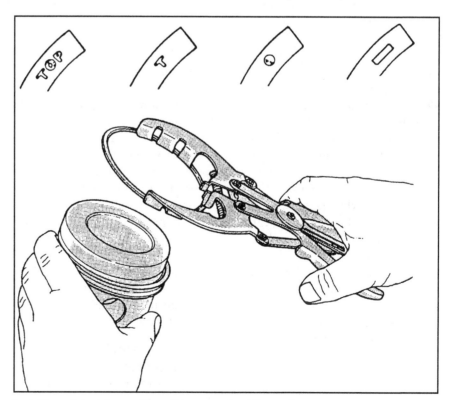

Installing piston rings with a ring expander. Piston rings are usually marked so the correct side can be installed facing up.

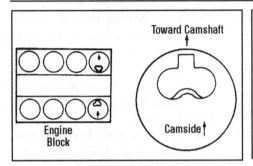

Typical piston orientation.
(Courtesy: Ford Motor Co.)

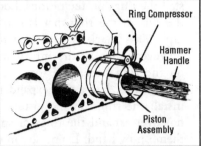

Using a ring compressor to install a piston into the cylinder block.
(Courtesy: Ford Motor Co.)

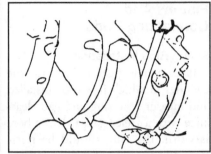

Check connecting rod side clearance with a feeler gauge.

small notch or mark usually indicates which side of the piston faces the front of the engine. The front is usually the end that the vibration damper (harmonic balancer) mounts on, whether the engine is mounted in the usual north/south configuration or transversely (as in many front-wheel drive cars). However, on some engines, the mark may indicate which side of the piston faces toward the camshaft. Always refer to the service manual to make sure.

Before installing the pistons and rods, install rod bolt protectors or pieces of fuel hose over the ends of the rod bolts to protect the crank journals. Position the crankshaft so the rod journal is beneath the cylinder in the bottom dead center position. A ring compressor or tapered sleeve is used to compress the rings into their grooves while the piston is slid into the cylinder. A soft hammer or wooden handle can be used to gently push the piston into place.

If the bearing clearance is being measured with Plastigage™, lay a piece of Plastigage™ lengthwise on the crank journal. Install and torque the rod bearing cap to specifications. Be careful not to turn the crankshaft while the Plastigage™ is in position. Remove the rod cap and compare the thickness of the crushed piece of Plastigage™ to the gauge on the package to determine the amount of bearing clearance.

Remove the Plastigage™ from the crankshaft, then push the piston

and rod assembly back up into the bore just enough to lubricate the upper rod bearing and crankshaft with assembly lube. Pull the rod back onto the crankshaft. Lubricate the lower rod bearing and crankshaft with assembly lube, install the rod bearing cap and torque the nuts to specification.

Check connecting rod side clearance with a feeler gauge. There is seldom a problem with this measurement when the original crankshaft and connecting rods are used. However, if the crank has been welded or replaced, or any rods have been replaced, clearance can be below minimum specification. Clearance that is too tight can result in the rod bearings riding on the journal radius and failing. If clearance is not adequate, the rod can be machined to provide the necessary clearance.

On diesel engines, measure the deck clearance using a dial indicator. Head gaskets with different thicknesses are available for some engines to compensate for changes.

If equipped, install the piston oil cooling nozzles. Make sure each nozzle is aligned properly to accurately direct the oil to the bottom of the piston. Improper alignment can cause insufficient lubrication and engine damage.

Camshaft And Timing Components

Before sliding the camshaft into the block, coat the lobes with a suitable EP (Extreme Pressure) lubri-

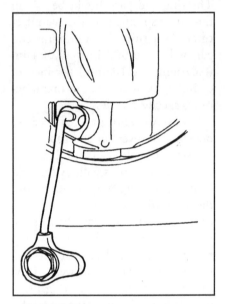

An oil cooling nozzle aligned with an oil inlet hole on the bottom of the piston. *(Courtesy: GM Corp.)*

cant and coat the journals with an assembly lubricant. Be very careful while sliding the cam into the block as the cam lobes can nick or damage the soft cam bearings. Install long bolts into the camshaft gear or sprocket mounting holes or temporarily install the gear or sprocket to provide leverage during installation.

Do not force the cam too far in, as it may push the rear cam plug out. The cam lobes can also be damaged in a careless installation. Rotate the cam to assure that it turns freely. Binding indicates improper clearances, misalignment in the cam bores, or a bent camshaft.

If the camshaft is retained with a thrust plate, check the camshaft

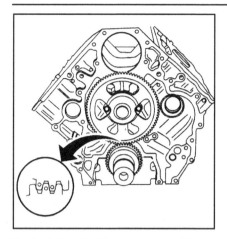

Typical camshaft and crankshaft gear timing marks. *(Courtesy: GM Corp.)*

end-play with a dial indicator after the thrust plate is secured. Position the dial indicator tip against the nose of the cam. Push the cam as far in as it will go and set the gauge to zero. Then pull it as far out as it will go and note the reading on the gauge. On some engines, spacers may be used to achieve the required clearance, while on others the thrust plate or gear may have to be replaced.

Timing gears come as a matched set and must likewise be replaced as a set. On some engines, the camshaft gear must be pressed on to the camshaft. Some timing gears or sprockets slide on to the crankshaft and are retained by the vibration damper, while others must be pressed on or driven on with a suitable tool.

Correctly position the timing marks on the camshaft and crankshaft gears or sprockets. Before installing a timing chain, lubricate it with clean engine oil. Torque the bolt(s) holding the cam gear or sprocket in place to the manufacturer's specifications.

General Gasket Installation

When installing timing covers, oil pans and other covers, never reuse old gaskets, like molded silicone rubber gaskets for instance. These are often found on late model engines because they last longer than cork rubber gaskets, are more flexible, conform better and seal tighter. Oil makes silicone swell, which keeps the gasket tight in use. But because it swells, molded silicone gaskets will usually not fit back in place.

Synthetic rubber gaskets must be installed against a perfectly clean and dry surface. Do not use gasket sealer on any synthetic rubber gaskets. It acts like a lubricant, causing the gasket to slip and leak.

Compression is what prevents a gasket from leaking. A cork/rubber gasket is compressed to about 50% of its original height. With silicone rubber, 30% compression is desirable. Less compression results in a poor seal, while more compression risks splitting the gasket. Unlike cork/rubber, which has many little air pockets in it, silicone is solid and does not compress. It deforms to either side to seal the joint. For that reason, both surfaces and the gasket must be clean and dry. Otherwise the gasket can slip.

Small metal grommets are often used in the gasket bolt holes to prevent the gasket from being over-tightened. The thickness of the grommet is such that the ideal amount of clamping force is achieved when the flange bottoms against the grommet.

Cork/rubber gaskets can be substituted for molded silicone rubber gaskets on some engines. But with a die cast cover the flange design may make it impossible to use anything but an identical replacement.

Here are some gasket installation tips to keep in mind:

• Lip-type oil seals must be lubricated to protect them against damage during initial start-up

• Do not over tighten cover bolts. This can crush or damage the gasket and/or cover flange

• If using RTV silicone instead of a cut or molded gasket to seal a cover or oil pan flange, make sure the flange and engine surfaces are clean, dry and oil free. RTV silicone sealer can only be used on covers with flat flanges, not those with raised lips or beads. Apply a $^1/_8$-in. (3.175mm) to $^3/_{16}$-in. (4.762mm) wide bead of sealer along the length of the cover flange or block surface, going to the inside or all the way around bolt holes. Be careful not to smear the bead of sealer as the cover is being installed

• Do not use excessive amounts of RTV. If too much is used it can squeeze out, break off and clog oil passages, resulting in severe engine damage.

Vibration Damper

The vibration damper, also known as the harmonic balancer, is mounted on the front of the crankshaft. As its name suggests, its function is to dampen the twisting forces (torsional vibration) applied to the crankshaft by the power impulses in a running engine. These power impulses cause the crankshaft to wind and unwind, and without the vibration damper, the shaft would quickly break.

Thus, a defective, loose, or incorrect vibration damper can result in

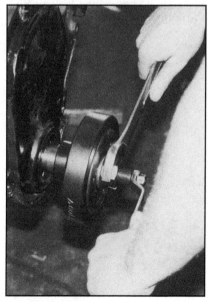

Always use a proper installation tool to install a vibration damper.

a broken crankshaft. Most dampers have an outer weight bonded with rubber to an inner hub. The rubber ring upon which the damper weight is mounted sometimes deteriorates. Some dampers have index marks that can be compared to see if the weight has shifted position.

Viscous dampers are hollow with a heavy ring that floats in a heavy silicone oil. Check these dampers for oil streaks radiating outward. This indicates a loss of fluid. If the damper makes rattling noises, this indicates a dry chamber.

Visually inspect the vibration damper for cracks or other damage. Check for excessive runout using a dial indicator. Some engine manufacturers say the vibration damper should be replaced whenever the engine is overhauled.

Some vibration dampers are a press fit on the crankshaft; however, they should never be hammered on. If the damper is hammered on, not only will the damper be damaged but the crankshaft thrust bearing may be damaged as well. Installation tools are available that thread into the end of the crankshaft. The damper is then started onto the crankshaft; a large bearing and nut are threaded onto the tool and then used to press the damper into position.

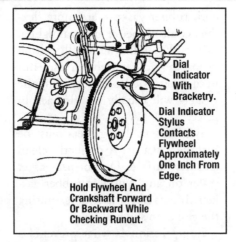

Measuring flywheel runout with a dial indicator. *(Courtesy: Ford Motor Co.)*

Flywheel/Flexplate

Visually inspect the flywheel for wear. Look for cracks, scoring and hot spots (blue or black marks) on the clutch face and missing or damaged teeth on the starter ring gear. Clutch surface damage can usually be corrected by resurfacing on a flywheel grinder. The ring gear can be removed and replaced on some manual transmission flywheels, however when starter teeth are damaged on an automatic transmission flexplate, the flexplate is replaced.

Mount the flywheel on the crankshaft. On externally balanced engines, the flywheel must be correctly indexed when it is mounted on the crankshaft to maintain engine balance (many flywheels have bolt holes that are unevenly spaced

so they can only go on one way). Make sure that the index marks are properly aligned when installing the flywheel. Torque flywheel bolts to specifications in a crisscross pattern in several steps.

Next, check runout on the face of the flywheel with a dial indicator. If runout exceeds specifications, the flywheel may be warped or the crankshaft flange may be bent. Dirt or a burr between the flywheel and crankshaft flange can also cause this problem. Sometimes warpage can be eliminated by resurfacing.

Some vehicles are equipped with a dual mass flywheel for extra vibration dampening and smoother clutch operation, and to reduce shock loading on the transmission. A dual mass flywheel is essentially two flywheels in one housing. The primary flywheel is mounted to the crankshaft and the clutch is mounted on the secondary flywheel. The two flywheels are connected by a series of springs, which provide the extra dampening.

Dual mass flywheels should be checked for the same defects as conventional flywheels, but should also be inspected for broken springs and loose rivets. If the surface is damaged or warped, in most cases a dual mass flywheel cannot be resurfaced. Many manufacturers recommend that the dual mass flywheel be replaced whenever the clutch is replaced.

Notes

Lubrication And Cooling Systems Diagnosis And Repair

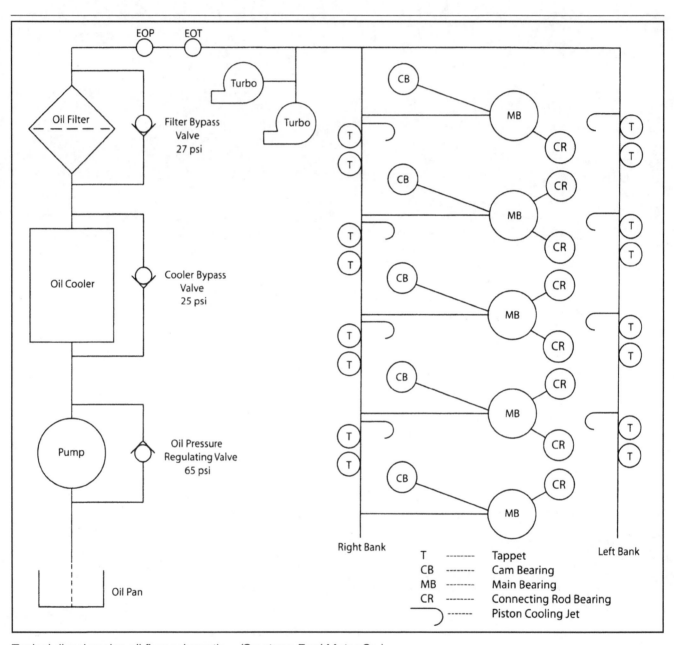

Typical diesel engine oil flow schematic. *(Courtesy: Ford Motor Co.)*

LUBRICATION SYSTEM

The diesel engine lubrication system not only supplies oil to all the necessary internal engine parts, but also usually provides lubrication to the turbocharger. The system begins with a pickup screen and pipe located in the oil pan. Oil is drawn through the screen and pipe by a pump, either located in the pan and driven by the camshaft or located on the front of the engine and driven directly by the crankshaft. From the pump, oil is directed to the oil cooler and filter, and then to oil galleries throughout the engine and the turbocharger.

An oil pressure relief valve is used to prevent overpressurization. If oil pressure exceeds a preset limit, the valve opens and allows pressure to bleed off. Bypass valves are incorporated to permit oil flow if the oil filter and/or oil cooler become clogged. Some systems also include a thermostatic bypass valve that blocks or restricts oil flow to the oil cooler until the oil temperature reaches a certain level.

In addition to the above, vehicles with Hydraulic Electronic Unit Injectors (HEUI) use the crankcase oil to actuate the fuel injectors. Oil is also pumped to a pump reservoir where a separate pump creates a very high oil pressure, which is routed to the fuel injectors through a gallery. The PCM/ECM varies the oil pressure to the fuel injectors according to various sensor inputs.

Oil Pressure

Make sure the engine oil is at the proper level. Remove the oil pressure sending unit and install an accurate oil pressure gauge. Start the engine and observe the oil pressure reading. Refer to the manufacturer's specifications for the temperature and engine speed at which oil pressure should be checked.

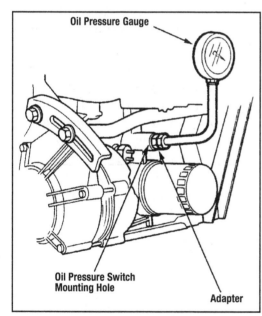

Checking oil pressure with an oil pressure gauge. *(Courtesy: Honda Motor Co.)*

The following are possible causes of lower than specified oil pressure:
• Incorrect oil viscosity or diluted oil
• Clogged oil filter
• Stuck oil pressure relief valve

• Worn oil pump
• Loose or damaged oil pump pickup
• Clogged pickup screen
• Excessive bearing clearance
• Cracked, porous or clogged oil gallery
• Missing oil gallery plug.

If the oil pressure is within specifications, but the oil pressure warning light is on, suspect the switch or circuit wiring. The switch provides a ground, completing the circuit and turning on the light, when the oil pressure is low. When the oil pressure goes above a certain pressure, the switch opens and turns off the light. If the light is still on with the wire to the switch disconnected, there is probably a short to ground in the warning light circuit.

If the indication on a dash oil pressure gauge does not match the tester gauge reading, first determine if the gauge is mechanical or electrically operated. If mechanical, look for leaks at the line and fittings and for kinks in the line. Sometimes the line can become clogged due to sludge in the oil. If the line and connections are sound, the gauge is defective.

To test an electric oil pressure gauge, disconnect the wire from the sending unit and connect a variable resistance between the end of the wire and good ground. Turning the resistance should make the gauge move, if the ignition switch is on. If the gauge does not move, the trouble is in the wiring or the gauge itself. If the gauge passes muster, then the problem must be in the sending unit.

Oil Temperature

Actual oil temperature can be checked by inserting a temperature gauge probe into the oil through the dipstick tube or by using an infrared thermometer aimed at the oil pan or oil filter. Excessive oil tempera-

ture could be caused by a clogged oil cooler or malfunctioning engine cooling system.

Some diesel engines are equipped with an oil temperature sensor. This sensor provides input to the PCM/ECM for cooling fan, glow plug and fuel injection control. On some engines, the PCM/ECM may even protect the engine by shutting it down in response to excessive oil temperature.

A failed sensor will set a DTC and may turn on the MIL. Even if the MIL is not illuminated, check for stored and pending DTCs. Most temperature sensors are thermistors that can be tested for resistance and voltage drop. Refer to the manufacturer's service information for specifications.

Oil Pump

The oil pump is usually replaced as part of an engine overhaul, but it can be disassembled and clearances checked. Camshaft-driven pumps are generally accessed by removing the oil pan. Refer to the manufacturer's service information for crankshaft-driven pump removal, as procedures vary according to design. Some pumps surround the nose of the crankshaft while others are driven by a side gear.

Remove the oil pump cover and seal, if equipped. Remove the gears or rotors from the pump body. Mark the gears prior to removal so that they can be reinstalled with the

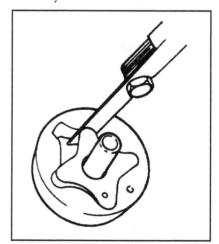

Checking inner and outer rotor tip clearance. *(Courtesy: Ford Motor Co.)*

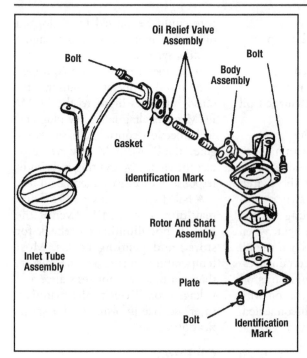

Typical camshaft-driven oil pump exploded view. *(Courtesy: Ford Motor Co.)*

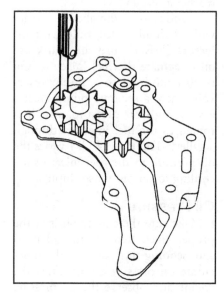

Measuring the clearance between the gear teeth and the oil pump housing.
(Courtesy: GM Corp.)

entire pump, as necessary.

Check the pump cover surface with a straightedge and feeler gauge. Measure the rotor or gear thickness and diameter with a micrometer. Place the rotors or gears in the pump housing and measure the clearance between the two with a feeler gauge. Place a straightedge across the pump housing and measure the gear or rotor end-play with a feeler gauge. Compare your measurements with the manufacturer's specifications.

Measure the relief valve spring's free length or tension and compare to specification. Check the relief valve piston for scoring and for free movement in the bore.

Lubricate the pump housing and gears or rotors with clean engine oil. Install the rotors or gears in the pump housing. Be sure to install gears with the matchmarks aligned. Install the pump cover with a new seal, if equipped, and torque the

bolts to specification. Install the pressure relief valve assembly and retain it with the pin. If necessary,

install a new pickup and screen, making sure it is at the proper angle to fit closely to the bottom of the oil pan.

Oil Pressure Relief Valve

The spring in the oil pressure relief valve provides a force equal to the maximum allowable oil pressure.

same gears meshing. If part of the pump, remove the pressure relief valve pin and the piston and spring. If attached, remove and discard the oil pump pickup.

Clean all parts in solvent. Check the inside of the pump housing, the pump cover and the gears or rotors for nicks, burrs, scoring, damage or excessive wear. Replace parts or the

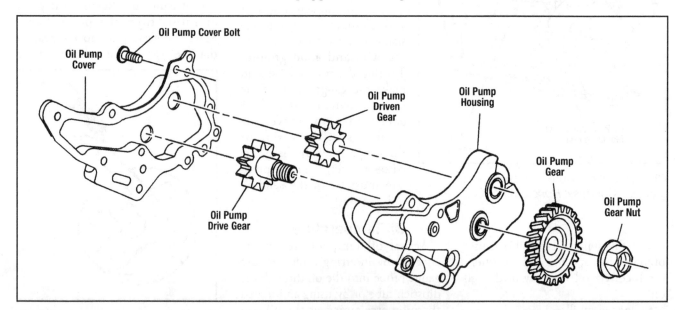

Typical crankshaft-driven oil pump exploded view.   *(Courtesy: GM Corp.)*

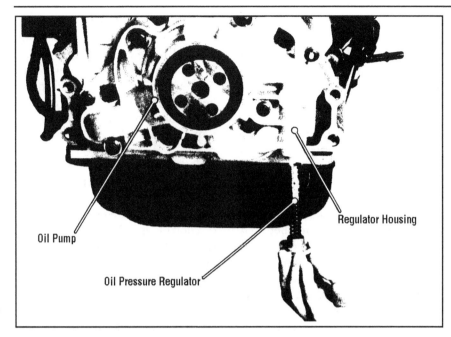

Oil Pump

Regulator Housing

Oil Pressure Regulator

Oil pressure relief valve from a crankshaft-driven oil pump.
(Courtesy: Ford Motor Co.)

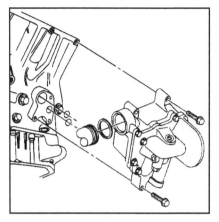

Oil cooler installation.
(Courtesy: GM Corp.)

If oil pressure exceeds this value, the spring pressure is overcome, the relief valve opens and the excess pressure is allowed to bleed off.

The valve is either part of the oil pump or located close to it. Check the spring's free length or tension and compare with specifications. Check the relief valve piston for scoring and for free movement in the bore.

Oil Bypass Valves

The engine will usually have one or more bypass valves that allow oil flow if the oil filter and/or oil cooler become restricted. The valve can be incorporated into the oil cooler or located elsewhere in the system. The oil filter also has an integral bypass valve that opens under either of two conditions.

The filter bypass valve opens when the engine is first started to allow the cold oil, which will not easily pass through the filter, to flow to the engine. When the oil warms up, the bypass valve closes and filtration resumes.

If the filter becomes clogged and the differential pressure across the filter exceeds a certain level, the

valve opens so oil can continue to flow through the engine. However, the oil will now be unfiltered.

Oil Cooler

Diesel engine oil coolers are liquid-cooled, with inlet and outlet ports to circulate coolant. The oil circulates through the oil cooler, and coolant flow within the plates is used to keep the oil at an acceptable operating temperature.

If the oil cooler becomes damaged, corrodes or otherwise fails internally, the engine oil can become contaminated with coolant. Conversely, such a failure can also cause engine oil to enter the cooling system. If the oil cooler is clogged, the oil will flow from the pump through a bypass valve and directly into the oil gallery.

To replace the oil cooler, drain the cooling system and remove any accessories or equipment necessary to gain access to the oil cooler housing. Mark and disconnect the hoses and/or pipes from the cooler. Remove the oil cooler housing bolts and carefully remove the oil cooler assembly.

To install, clean all gasket mat-

ing surfaces and passageways with a suitable cleaner. Install the oil cooler using new gaskets or lubricated O-rings, as required. Install the housing bolts and torque to the manufacturer's specifications. Connect and secure the hoses and/or pipes, and reinstall any components removed to access the oil cooler.

Refill the cooling system, start the engine and check for leaks at the cooler and all lines or hoses to and from the cooler.

CAUTION: Serious engine damage can result if an engine is operated extensively with lubricating oil contaminated with ethylene glycol and water, the usual components of coolant. Sludge, corrosive acids and abrasive contaminants can form through chemical reactions, causing oil flow restrictions and bearing damage. After an oil cooler failure the engine oil must be changed and the engine oil pressure monitored. If the cooling system was contaminated, it should be flushed.

Turbocharger Lubrication

Many turbocharger failures are caused by lubrication problems such as lack of oil flow and foreign material in the oil. The exhaust flow past the turbine wheel creates extremely high temperatures, which creates a harsh operating environment for the turbocharger shaft bearings. Some manufacturers connect coolant lines to the turbocharger to cool the shaft bearings, but others rely on engine oil to lubricate and to cool. With the latter design, it is a good idea to let the engine idle for about a minute before shutting it off, particularly if the vehicle has been run hard, to let oil cool the turbocharger. If the engine is shut off immediately, the oil may burn causing hard carbon particles to form, which in turn will destroy the bearings.

The oil and filter should be changed at regular intervals and the air filter should be inspected regularly to ensure only clean oil goes to the turbocharger. Inspect the routing and integrity of the oil supply and oil drain lines and check for oil leaks.

When a turbocharger is replaced, it should be preoiled prior to installation and the engine should not be revved before the turbo receives oil pressure. A good practice after turbocharger installation is to disable the fuel system so the engine won't start and disconnect the oil drain line. Crank the engine until oil flow is established.

COOLING SYSTEM

In addition to cooling internal engine components, a typical modern diesel cooling system will also supply coolant to an engine oil cooler and on some applications the turbocharger, aftercooler and/or EGR valve.

Coolant Temperature

Actual coolant temperature can be checked by installing a mechanical gauge in place of the switch/sending unit or by using an infrared thermometer aimed at the thermostat housing or upper radiator hose.

If a temperature warning light is on, first verify the actual temperature with the infrared thermometer. On a typical warning system, the switch is open when cold; but if the temperature goes too high, the switch will close and the light will come on. So, if the actual temperature is normal, the switch may

be defective or the wiring may be grounded between the switch and the light. If the light stays on when the switch is disconnected, there is a short to ground; check the wiring. If the light goes out, replace the switch.

If the dash temperature gauge indicates a temperature that varies more than a few degrees from actual, the sending unit or gauge may be faulty. Remove the wire from the sending unit on the engine and connect a variable resistance between the end of the wire and a good ground. With the ignition switch on, rotating the resistance should make the gauge read through the full range. If the gauge does not move, then it is defective or there is a problem in the circuit between the sending unit and gauge. If the gauge moves, replace the sending unit.

All electronically controlled diesel engines are equipped with an Engine Coolant Temperature (ECT) sensor. This sensor provides input to the PCM/ECM for cooling fan, glow plug and fuel injection control. The dash temperature warning light and/or temperature gauge may receive input from this sensor via the PCM/ECM. Always refer to the manufacturer's service information for the system in question.

A failed sensor will set a DTC and may turn on the MIL. Even if the MIL is not illuminated, check for stored and pending DTCs. Most temperature sensors are thermistors that can be tested for resistance and voltage drop. Refer to the manufacturer's service information for specifications.

Cooling System Pressure Testing

Use a hand-held pump with a pressure gauge that is designed for cooling system testing. While the engine is cold, remove the pressure cap from the radiator or expansion tank. Make sure the system is filled to capacity, then attach the tester. Pump it up to the rated system pressure and watch the gauge needle; it

should not drop rapidly. If pressure drops, check for leaks at the radiator and heater hoses, water pump, radiator, intake manifold, sensor fittings, water control valves, oil cooler, heater core and any other components connected to the cooling system. Repair leaks as required and retest.

If you can't spot the leak, it may be internal such as a head gasket, cracked cylinder head or cracked block. Inspect the engine oil for signs of coolant; if it is thick and milky, that's a dead giveaway. Start the engine and watch the tester gauge. If the pressure immediately increases, there could be a head gasket leak, but not into the crankcase. The coolant may be going out the tailpipe, however, which would be indicated by white smoke from the exhaust pipe and a somewhat sweet antifreeze odor in the exhaust.

Use the system tester's cap adapter to check the pressure cap. Pump it up to the cap's rating. It should hold for about 10 seconds and then decrease just a bit. If it drops too much, replace the cap. Pump the cap to exceed its pressure rating. The cap should release pressure; if not it should be replaced.

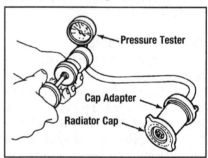

When pressure testing the radiator cap, the proper cap adapter must be used. The cap should be capable of holding the pressure recommended for the vehicle. Pressure test the cooling system at approximately the release pressure of the radiator cap.

Drive Belts, Pulleys And Tensioners

Check the accessory drive belt(s) for evidence of cracking, fraying,

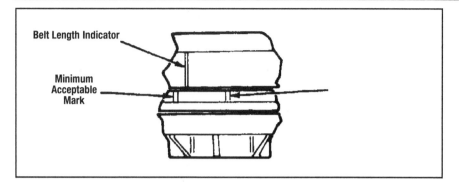

Belt length indicator on an automatic belt tensioner. *(Courtesy: Ford Motor Co.)*

glazing or other damage and replace as necessary.

If the belt is adjustable, belt tension can be checked using the deflection method or by using a belt tension gauge. Locate a point midway between the pulleys on the longest accessible belt span. If using the deflection method, push on the belt with your finger using moderate pressure and measure the belt deflection. If you are using a belt tension gauge, position the gauge and measure the amount of force necessary to deflect the belt. Compare your reading with specifications.

Belt tension should also be checked on vehicles with automatic belt tensioners to make sure the tensioner is functioning properly. Some automatic tensioners are equipped with belt length indicator and minimum and maximum acceptable marks, the theory being that if the correct length belt is installed on the engine and the mark is within range, belt tension is correct.

To adjust V-belt tension, loosen the adjuster pulley, or accessory pivot and adjuster bolts, then use a suitable prybar to move the pulley or accessory until the belt tension is correct. Tighten all fasteners and recheck belt tension.

If belt replacement is necessary, loosen the adjuster pulley or accessory pivot and adjuster bolts, moving the pulley or accessory to eliminate belt tension, and remove the belt. It may be necessary to remove other accessory drive belts to gain access to a particular belt.

Before removing a serpentine V-ribbed belt, make sure there is a belt routing diagram handy or draw one prior to belt removal, to prevent installation problems. Use a socket or wrench to tilt the automatic tensioner away from the belt, and then remove the belt from the pulleys.

After the belt is removed, spin the pulleys to determine if they wobble or if an accessory has any noticeable bearing wear. Inspect the pulleys for chips, nicks, cracks, tool marks, bent sidewalls, severe corrosion or other damage. Check for hard objects such as small stones or sand that may have become imbedded in the bottom of the pulley grooves.

When replacing the belt, inspect all pulleys for improper alignment. Aligned pulleys reduce both pulley and belt wear, and vibration of engine components. If the belt pulleys are severely misaligned, look for improper positioning of an accessory or its corresponding pulley, improper fit of the pulley or shaft, or incorrect components installed.

Install a new belt, making sure it is correctly positioned in its pulley grooves and properly routed. Adjust the belt tension, as required.

Thermostat

The thermostat's function is to allow the engine to come to operating temperature quickly and then maintain a minimum operating temperature. If the thermostat is good, the upper radiator hose should be hot to the touch after the engine has been idling and warm. If the hose is not hot, the thermostat

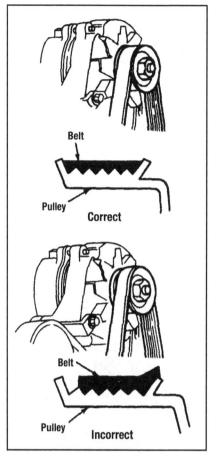

Make sure V-ribbed belts are properly seated in the pulley grooves. One revolution of the engine with the belt incorrectly seated can damage the belt. *(Courtesy: Ford Motor Co.)*

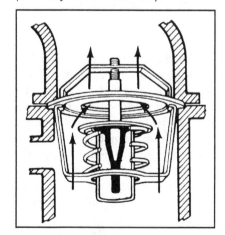

The thermostat is designed to open when the engine coolant reaches a specified temperature.

is most likely stuck open, especially if there has also been a complaint of poor heater performance. If the thermostat were stuck closed, the engine would quickly overheat.

To test thermostat operation, remove the radiator cap while the engine is cold. Put a thermometer in the radiator fill neck and start the engine. Keep an eye on the coolant in the radiator and occasionally feel the upper radiator hose. When the hose gets warm, the coolant should be moving in the radiator. Check the thermometer. If it doesn't go above 150°F (66°C), the thermostat is either stuck open or missing.

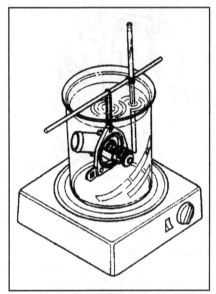

Testing a thermostat.
(Courtesy: Honda Motor Co., Ltd.)

The thermostat can be checked more precisely by removing it from the vehicle. Suspend the thermostat in a container of water, not letting it contact the bottom of the container. Place a thermometer in the container and heat the water. When the thermostat begins to open, check the temperature and compare with the thermostat's opening temperature specification. Remove the thermostat from the water; it should close slowly when exposed to cooler ambient temperature.

To replace the thermostat, drain the cooling system and disconnect the hose from the thermostat housing. Remove the thermostat housing and remove the thermostat. Clean all gasket material from the sealing surfaces and check the surfaces for nicks or burrs.

Properly seat the thermostat in its flange on the engine. Make sure the heat sensing portion of the thermostat is installed so as to expose it to the hot coolant side. Using a new gasket, install the thermostat housing and torque the bolts to specification. Refill the cooling system, start the engine and check for leaks and proper operation.

Water Pump

The water pump employs an impeller fan designed to pump coolant throughout the engine via specially placed water jackets. While some water pumps are mounted directly behind the radiator fan and its pulley, others are mounted independently on the front of the engine. Most water pumps are driven by a belt from the crankshaft, but other methods have been used including gear drive.

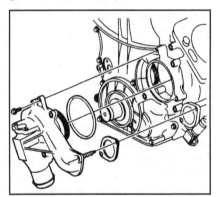

On this V8 diesel engine, the water pump is driven by a gear from the crankshaft. *(Courtesy: GM Corp.)*

Check for a coolant leak from the vent hole at the bottom of the pump shaft housing. It is normal to see some moisture here but if coolant streaks can be seen, then the seal and possibly the bearings are suspect. Check the water pump bearings by grasping the fan or pulley and attempt to move the impeller shaft back and forth. If there is any movement, the water pump bearings are defective. Remove the drive belt and turn the pulley by hand. The pulley should turn smoothly. If there is noise and/or binding, the bearings are faulty. Replace the pump if it leaks or the bearings are defective.

To replace a water pump, drain the cooling system and, if necessary, disconnect the hoses from the pump. Remove the water pump drive belt and pulley. Remove any brackets or other components necessary for water pump removal. Remove the water pump mounting bolts and remove the water pump. Clean all gasket material from the sealing surfaces and check the surfaces for nicks or burrs.

Install the water pump using new gaskets and torque the mounting bolts to specification. Install any brackets or other components that were removed. Install the water pump pulley and the drive belt. Properly tension the belt, as required. Connect the coolant hoses to the water pump. Refill the cooling system, start the engine and check for leaks.

Radiator

Coolant from the engine flows through a series of tubes in the radiator. These tubes are surrounded by a network of fins designed to direct airflow to the tubes. The cooled liquid is then circulated back through the engine in order to maintain proper operating temperature.

Clean the radiator fins of debris, bugs or leaves that may have been drawn in while driving. Sometimes, debris may collect between the radiator and condenser. Make sure all fins are intact, and not bent so as to misdirect airflow. Distorted fins can be straightened using a suitable tool, however, be careful when straightening because the fins are very delicate.

Inspect the radiator for damage and any signs of leakage from the core tubes, radiator tanks and hose collars. Look inside the radiator for large amounts of mineral deposits at the ends of the core tubes, as mineral buildup can cause an internal restriction. If blockage inside the radiator is suspected, an infrared surface thermometer can be used to scan the surface of the radiator when the engine is hot and idling. The radiator should be warmest near the inlet and gradually cool toward the outlet. If there are areas that are considerably cooler than the inlet, then there may be restrictions at those areas.

If visual inspection and/or testing indicate that radiator replacement is required, drain the cooling system and disconnect the hoses and transmission cooler lines, if equipped. Separate the radiator from the fan shroud and electric cooling fan, if equipped, and remove the radiator mounting fasteners. Remove the radiator from the vehicle.

Transfer fittings and/or temperature sending units to the replacement radiator, as required. Position the radiator in the vehicle and tighten the mounting fasteners to specification. Install the shroud and electric cooling fan, if equipped. Connect the radiator hoses and transmission cooler lines, if equipped. Refill the cooling system, start the engine and check for leaks.

Flushing, Filling And Bleeding The Cooling System

Engine overheating can be caused by a clogged cooling system. If you suspect that the system is clogged, drain it and then flush the system using one of the commercially available flushing kits. Flush the system according to the directions supplied with the kit and the vehicle manufacturer's instructions.

All used coolants pick up heavy metals such as lead from the solder used in the assembly of heat exchangers, so drained coolant must either be disposed of properly or recycled.

After flushing, or whenever the cooling system has been drained for service, the system should be refilled with the vehicle manufacturer's specified coolant mixture. Ethylene glycol is the most widely used substance mixed with water to form engine coolant. Ethylene glycol lowers the freezing point of water and raises the boiling point. Not all ethylene glycol antifreeze is the same, however. Most antifreeze consists of about 90% ethylene glycol, with the remaining percentage being additives. The additives prevent corrosion and lubricate pump seals, and it is with the additive packages that antifreeze differs.

The traditional 'green' anti-freeze that has been around for years uses Inorganic Additive Technology (IAT), meaning that the additives used to protect against corrosion are inorganic. The inorganic phosphates and silicates work quickly to apply a corrosion fighting coating in the cooling system, however these additives also deplete quickly, which is why it is necessary to frequently change this type of coolant.

Organic Additive Technology (OAT) antifreeze uses additive packages consisting of organic acids. These coolants don't lay down a coating but rather help preserve the self-protective layers that naturally develop over time on both iron and aluminum. This process uses up additives much more slowly than traditional coolant. The most well known type of OAT antifreeze is GM's Dex-Cool.

HOAT stands for Hybrid Organic Additive Technology. As its name suggests, HOAT antifreeze uses both silicate and organic acid corrosion inhibitors for extended service life.

Do not try to rely on color to identify the type of coolant in the system. Raw coolant is colorless and manufacturers can dye it any color they want. Most experts say that mixing coolant will not cause any damaging chemical reactions and the coolant will still carry away heat and protect against freezing. However, mixing some types will affect the service life. OAT and HOAT are considered long life coolants. If

IAT coolant is mixed with either, the change interval will degrade to that of a shorter life coolant. For optimum system protection, use the type of coolant specified by the vehicle manufacturer.

A mix of 50 percent water/50 percent antifreeze is usually the most effective mixture, but some vehicle manufacturers may specify otherwise. Drain and replace the coolant at the vehicle manufacturer's recommended interval.

The cooling system in some diesel engines is subject to a phenomenon known as cavitation. The vibration that occurs in the cylinder walls during engine operation causes alternating high and low pressure in the coolant against the cylinder wall. This in turn creates voids where air bubbles form, and when these bubbles collapse they form pits in the liner. This pitting can eventually corrode the liner to the point where coolant leaks into engine and combustion gas enters the cooling system.

To combat this type of corrosion, some diesel engine manufacturers recommend that a Supplemental Coolant Additive (SCA) be added to the system periodically. Consult the vehicle service manual to see if such an additive should be used.

When filling the cooling system, follow the manufacturer's recommended procedure for purging air from the system to ensure a complete fill. Some vehicles have bleeder valves to release air trapped in the system. These are usually opened until all air bubbles are expelled and only coolant flows, then tightened. Other vehicles may require that the engine be operated for a period of time at different speeds until the engine reaches a certain temperature, then the engine is shut off and the procedure repeated after topping off the reservoir.

Most all cooling systems in use today are equipped with a coolant reservoir. The radiator cap in the system functions as a two-way check valve: It has a limit that, once ex-

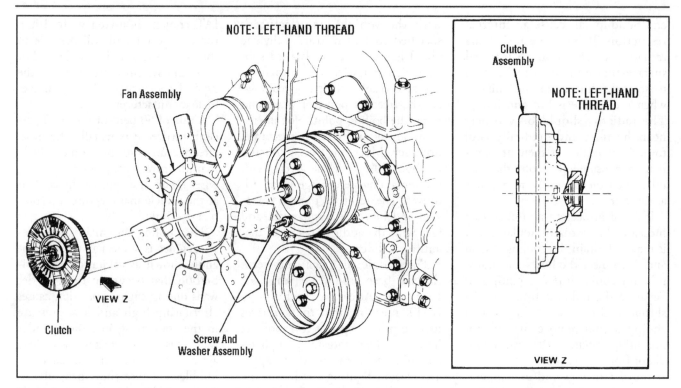

NOTE: LEFT-HAND THREAD

Fan Assembly

VIEW Z

Clutch

Screw And
Washer Assembly

Clutch
Assembly

NOTE: LEFT-HAND
THREAD

VIEW Z

Typical mechanical cooling fan and fan clutch. As noted in the illustration, many have left-handed thread. *(Courtesy: Ford Motor Co.)*

ceeded, allows the coolant to escape from the radiator and into the reservoir. This happens normally as the coolant heats up and expands. As the system cools, it creates a partial vacuum and sucks coolant from the reservoir back into the radiator. It is a closed system where, ideally, no coolant escapes and no air gets into the cooling system. Air in the system contributes to corrosion.

When adding coolant to this type of system, add it to the reservoir. The tank is usually marked with the proper hot and cold fill levels. The overflow tank serves as a receptacle for coolant forced out of the radiator overflow pipe and provides for its return to the system. As the engine cools, the balancing of pressures causes the coolant to siphon back into the radiator.

Cooling Fan

Mechanical Cooling Fan

Most rear-wheel-drive cars and trucks have belt-driven, mechanical fans equipped with a fan clutch. The fan clutch is designed to slip when cold and rotate the fan at certain maximum speeds when hot. Fan clutches improve gas mileage and reduce noise levels.

Inspect the back of the clutch for an oily film, which would indicate that fluid is leaking and replacement is necessary. Turn the fan and clutch assembly by hand; there should be some viscous drag, but it should turn smoothly during a full rotation. Replace the fan clutch if it does not turn smoothly or if it does not turn at all. It should also be replaced if there is no viscous drag when hot or cold.

To test the fan clutch, attach a thermometer or electronic temperature probe to the radiator near the inlet and connect a timing light to the engine. Start the engine and strobe the fan to 'freeze' the blades; note the engine speed. When the engine warms up (check the thermometer), the fan speed should increase and the blades will appear to be moving in the strobe light. As the temperature drops, the fan should slow down. A quick check of fan clutches is to shut down a hot engine, then observe how long it takes for the fan to stop spinning. A properly operating clutch should stop the fan from spinning within two seconds.

Replace the fan clutch if it fails inspection or testing.

Electric Cooling Fan

Many vehicles, especially those with transverse engines, use electric cooling fans. Besides not needing a belt to drive them, electric fans conserve energy since they run only when needed.

When the engine slightly exceeds proper operating temperature, the electric fan should come on. It may cycle on and off as the coolant warms and cools. On most vehicles, the fan also should run whenever the A/C is switched on. (Some vehicles have two fans with one dedicated to the A/C system. Usually both fans are on when the A/C is on.)

On all late-model computer controlled vehicles, fan operation is controlled by the PCM/ECM. The computer commands the fan in response to input from the ECT sensor and A/C pressure sensor. When the engine coolant reaches a certain temperature or the A/C system pressure reaches a certain point, the PCM/ECM energizes a cooling fan relay, which in turn provides battery voltage to the cooling fan motor.

If the cooling fan does not come on, first connect a scan too and check for stored and pending DTCs. Check scan tool data to see if the PCM/ECM is receiving accurate engine coolant temperature information. If not, although an out-of-range sensor should set a trouble code, there may be a problem with the sensor or circuit wiring. If the PCM/ECM is commanding the fan to be on, check for voltage at the fan motor. If there is voltage, the fan motor is defective. If not, the problem could be a blown fuse, faulty relay or a problem in the circuit wiring. Refer to the manufacturer's service information.

Notes

Air Induction And Exhaust Systems Diagnosis And Repair

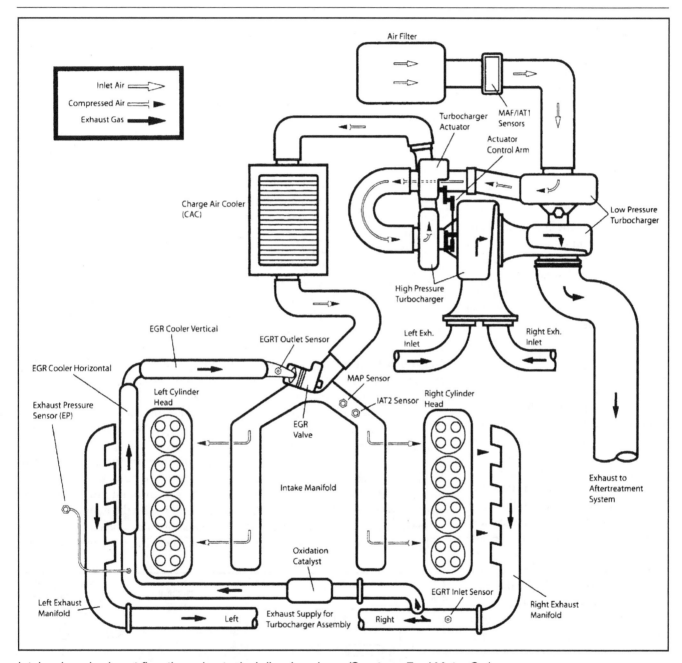

Intake air and exhaust flow through a typical diesel engine. *(Courtesy: Ford Motor Co.)*

AIR INTAKE SYSTEM

The air intake system routes air through the air cleaner and ducting to the turbocharger. From the turbocharger air may pass through a charge air cooler before going to the intake manifold.

Inspect the ducting between the air cleaner housing and turbocharger, looking for cracks, improper connections, missing sections or other damage. Make sure the air cleaner is secured in its housing.

The air cleaner on most diesel en-gines is replaced according to intake restriction specifications. Most diesel air intake systems are equipped with a restriction indicator, usually located on the air filter housing. However, even if the restriction indicator shows that no air cleaner service is

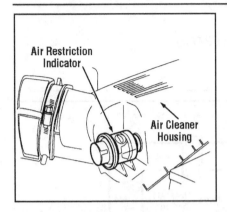

Typical air cleaner restriction indicator mounting.
(Courtesy: Ford Motor Co.)

required, this may not be the case since very often the indicator is not reset when the air cleaner is replaced.

The only way to be certain that intake restriction is within limitations is to measure it with a suitable tool, such as a water manometer. The water manometer is filled with ordinary water. Antifreeze and other additives change the density of the liquid and affect readings. At rest the water is the same height in both tubes and this point is where the manometer scale is set at zero. When a pressure or vacuum is applied to the manometer, the water will rise in one tube and drop in the other tube. Total movement in both tubes is the measured value. For example, if the water dropped one inch in one tube and rose one inch in the other tube, the measured value is two inches of water. The sensitive nature of the water manometer makes it useful for the measurement of intake restriction.

Connect the manometer to a suitable location on the air inlet duct between the air cleaner and the turbocharger. Start the engine and run it at the speed specified by the manufacturer. Record the manometer reading and compare with specifications.

If restriction is greater than specified, inspect the air filter element and also look for plastic bags or other foreign material that may be blocking the air inlet.

TURBOCHARGER

A turbocharger is divided into two sections, the turbine and the compressor. The turbine is attached to the exhaust manifold, where a turbine wheel inside the turbine housing is driven by the exhaust gas pressure and heat energy. The turbine wheel is connected by a shaft to the compressor wheel inside the compressor housing. The spinning of the turbine wheel causes the compressor wheel to spin, drawing in air to the compressor housing where it is compressed and pumped through ducts into the intake manifold. As the speed of the turbine increases, so does the pressure output, or boost, of the compressor.

Boost pressure must be limited to prevent engine damage. Boost is controlled by a wastegate, a valve that opens and allows exhaust gas to bypass the turbine. The wastegate is activated either by a diaphragm or a boost control solenoid. Wastegates are either integral to the turbine housing or are remotely mounted in the exhaust system. If controlled by a diaphragm, when a preset boost limit is reached, the diaphragm moves a rod that opens the wastegate. If controlled by a boost control solenoid, which is operated by the PCM/ECM, the wastegate opens and closes in response to sensor inputs to the PCM/ECM. When the wastegate is opened,

excess exhaust pressure is released from the turbine housing, directed to the exhaust system and expelled into the atmosphere.

One problem with turbochargers is that, when sized for maximum power output, they do not provide boost at low speeds. Conversely, a small turbo that provides good low speed boost will not make enough at high engine speeds. Some manufacturers have solved this problem by using two turbochargers, one that develops boost just off idle and one for maximum power output. Another solution is the Variable Geometry Turbine (VGT) turbocharger.

A VGT turbocharger has adjustable vanes located around the outside of the turbine that open and close according to engine need. At low speeds, the vanes are closed, creating an obstruction that increases the speed of the exhaust against the turbine wheel, making it spin faster. At high engine speeds, the vanes open to allow the turbine wheel to take full advantage of the increased exhaust flow.

VGT turbochargers also help with exhaust gas recirculation. Closing the vanes at low speed increases the backpressure in the exhaust manifold, which is used to drive the exhaust gas through the EGR valve and into the intake manifold.

Vane pitch can be controlled electronically using a stepper, hydrauli-

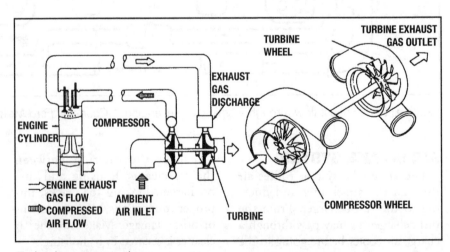

Turbocharger operation.

cally using engine oil or with air pressure.

The turbocharger can be monitored for boost pressure, exhaust backpressure, and compressor inlet and outlet temperatures, depending on the application. Always refer to the service information for the particular vehicle in question.

Diagnosis And Inspection

Symptoms of turbocharger failure include insufficient boost, turbo lag and excessive oil consumption.

Insufficient boost can be caused by a clogged air filter, restriction in the air intake or air leak downstream of the compressor. On the turbine side, it could be caused by exhaust leaks upstream of the turbo or exhaust restrictions downstream, either of which would reduce exhaust gas energy.

Turbo bearing failure, or the rotating assembly rubbing the housing, which can be caused by bearing failure or contact with foreign objects, can also reduce boost. The bearings can fail from normal use, insufficient lubrication, excessive oil temperature or operating practices like not letting the engine idle after it has been run hard, to allow oil to cool the bearings.

If there is turbo lag, indicated by a flat spot during acceleration, and the fuel system is functioning properly, it could be caused by carbon buildup on the compressor wheel and housing. Excessive oil consumption, accompanied by blue smoke, could be caused by failed turbocharger seals.

Listen for unusual noises coming from the turbocharger that could be an indication that the rotating assembly is binding or dragging.

Check for DTCs using a scan tool. If the turbocharger is electronically controlled, a trouble code should set if there is a wastegate control or boost pressure problem.

Inspect the outside of the turbocharger housing for oil leaks, which would indicate seal failure. Remove

the air inlet duct from the turbocharger compressor housing and remove the exhaust pipes from the turbine housing. Disconnect the oil pressure and drain lines. If liquid cooled, drain the cooling system and disconnect the coolant lines. Remove the mounting bolts and remove the compressor from the intake manifold. Cover all openings to prevent the entrance of dirt and foreign objects.

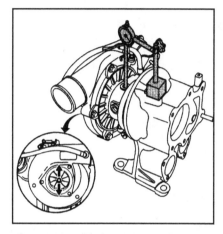

Measuring turbocharger radial play.
(Courtesy: GM Corp.)

Examine the compressor wheel for impact damage and erosion from dirt particles. Check the compressor housing outlet for signs of oil, indicating seal failure. If oil and heavy carbon deposits are found in the turbine housing inlet, they may be

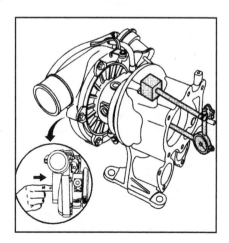

Measuring turbocharger axial play.
(Courtesy: GM Corp.)

signs of an engine problem. Check both the compressor and turbine wheels for signs of rubbing contact with their housings, which would indicate bearing failure. Radial and axial bearing play can be measured with a dial indicator and the results compared with the manufacturer's specifications.

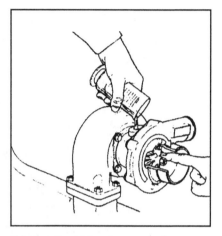

Priming the turbocharger before engine startup.

Some turbochargers can be rebuilt in the field, however this is usually done by a specialized rebuilder. If any defects are found, many manufacturers recommend that the turbocharger be replaced.

When installing the turbocharger, leave the oil pressure and drain lines disconnected. Before starting, prime the turbocharger with clean engine oil, then connect the pressure line. Disable the fuel system and crank the engine until clean oil flows from the drain line. Connect the drain line, start the engine and check for leaks.

CHARGE AIR COOLER

Compressing the engine's intake air with the turbocharger raises its temperature, which is counter to what is needed for the engine to make power. Cooler air provides a denser intake charge to the engine, allowing more air and fuel to be burned, increasing the engine's power output.

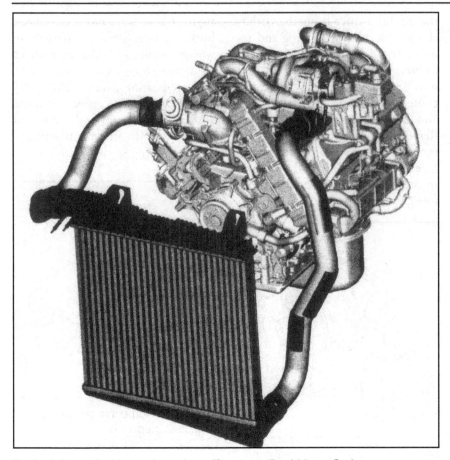

Typical air-to-air charge air cooler. *(Courtesy: Ford Motor Co.)*

To cool the air coming from the turbocharger, many diesel engine vehicles are equipped with a charge air cooler, also called an intercooler. There are air-to-liquid coolers, that use engine coolant, but the most widely used type is the air-to-air cooler. These are usually mounted in front of the radiator.

Anything that blocks airflow through the cooler will decrease its efficiency and raise the intake air temperature. Inspect the charge air cooler for debris, bugs or leaves that may have been drawn in while driving. Make sure all fins are intact, and not bent so as to misdirect airflow. Distorted fins can be straightened using a suitable tool, however, be careful when straightening because the fins are very delicate. Examine the cooler for cracked or distorted duct connections and broken or loose welds. If any defects are found, the charge air cooler must be replaced.

Inspect the ducting from the turbocharger to the cooler and from the cooler to the intake manifold, for cracks, loose connections or other damage and replace parts as necessary.

INTAKE MANIFOLD

The intake manifold on most diesel engines connects the turbocharger to the intake ports in the cylinder head(s). To replace the manifold, drain the cooling system and remove the turbocharger assembly. Disconnect and remove the necessary fuel lines. Remove the intake manifold bolts and remove the intake manifold.

Clean the intake manifold gasket mating surfaces. Inspect the manifold for cracks or other damage. Check the surface that is mounted to the cylinder head for warpage using a straightedge and feeler gauge and compare with the manufacturer's specifications.

Install the intake manifold using a new gasket(s). Apply sealer as recommended by the vehicle and gasket manufacturers. Tighten the intake manifold bolts to the specified torque in the proper sequence. Install the remaining components in the reverse order of removal.

EXHAUST MANIFOLD

The exhaust manifold(s) routes the exhaust gas from the cylinder head exhaust ports to the turbocharger and the rest of the exhaust system. Disconnect the exhaust pipe and turbocharger from the manifold. Remove the mounting bolts and the exhaust manifold.

Carefully examine the exhaust manifold for cracks or other damage. An exhaust manifold heats up and cools down thousands of times during the normal lifespan of a vehicle. Depending on the design of the manifold, some areas of the manifold get hotter than others, particularly those areas that are covered by heat shields. The resulting uneven expansion and contraction that occurs during the heating and cooling cycle can cause cracks and manifold warpage.

Make sure the mating surfaces of the manifold are clean. Examine these surfaces for gouges or other imperfections that could cause an exhaust leak. Check the cylinder head mating surface of the exhaust manifold for warpage using a feeler gauge and straightedge, and compare with the manufacturer's specifications.

If the cylinder head mating sur-

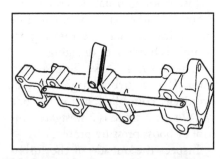

Measuring an exhaust manifold flange for warpage. *(Courtesy: GM Corp.)*

face of the exhaust manifold is marred or warped, it may be able to be corrected through resurfacing. Some engines come from the factory without exhaust manifold gaskets. Gaskets for these applications are generally available in the aftermarket, and using gaskets may be enough to compensate for marring or warpage if it is not severe.

Inspect the exhaust manifold studs for corrosion. Even if the studs did not break when the exhaust pipe was removed, they may be weak enough to break when the exhaust pipe flange nuts are tightened. A damaged stud usually must be drilled out and the hole tapped to restore the threads. If the threads are damaged, a thread repair insert can be installed. Install the new studs in the exhaust manifold.

Install the exhaust manifold to the cylinder head, using new gaskets, as required. Install the attaching bolts/nuts and torque to specification in the proper sequence. Reconnect the exhaust pipe and the turbocharger.

Exhaust Backpressure

Exhaust backpressure can be checked with a manometer. Specifications are critical, not only with regard to a maximum allowable value, but also regarding where the measurement is made. Many manufacturers specify where to take a backpressure measurement, usually a specified number of inches after the turbocharger. When the engine is equipped with an exhaust backpressure sensor, a DMM may be used to measure exhaust backpressure with the proper connections and specifications.

Causes of excessive exhaust backpressure include crimped or collapsed pipes and clogged mufflers or exhaust aftertreatment components.

GLOW PLUG SYSTEM

A diesel engine relies on the heat generated by the compression of air in the cylinders to ignite the fuel. However, when the engine is cold, particularly during cold weather, the engine block acts as a heat sink, quickly dissipating the heat generated by compressing the air. The engine does not start because there is not enough heat to ignite the fuel.

The solution to the problem used by most diesel engine builders is to temporarily introduce heat into the combustion chamber using glow plugs. A typical glow plug has a filament that uses current to quickly heat to temperatures of 1500°F or more. When the ignition key is turned on, a control module or the PCM/ECM energizes a relay that in turn sends power to the glow plugs. The glow plugs remain on while the engine is cranking and then during a short time afterward to keep the engine running while it warms up. Then the control module or PCM/ECM de-energizes the relay and turns off power to the glow plugs. The length of time the glow plugs are on is determined by a timer in the control module and feedback from sensors like the engine coolant and engine oil temperature sensors.

Some systems provide a full 12 volts to the glow plugs, while others use a resistor to limit voltage to 6 volts. Always refer to the vehicle manufacturer's service information when testing the system.

Diagnosis And Testing

If the engine won't start during cold weather or is hard to start during hot weather, but runs normally when it's warmed up, the glow plug system may not be working. Check for voltage at each individual glow plug when the key is turned on. If there is no voltage, use a voltmeter to check the circuit back through the wiring, connections, relay and control module.

The engine may also be hard to start if one or more glow plugs are burned out. The condition of the glow plugs can be checked using an ohmmeter. If resistance is excessive compared with specifications or there is no continuity, the glow plug is defective. Glow plugs can burn out if they get too hot, which can be caused by a defective control module or relay that fails to shut off power to the glow plugs.

Even if the glow plugs check out electrically, they still may not be working properly because of excessive carbon buildup. Remove and clean as necessary.

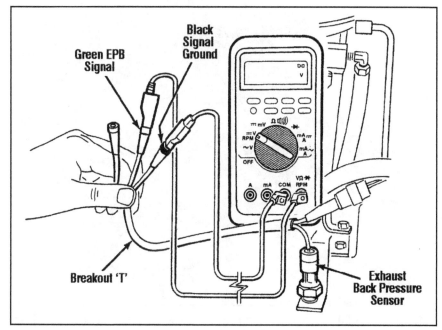

Measuring exhaust backpressure with a digital multimeter. *(Courtesy: Navistar)*

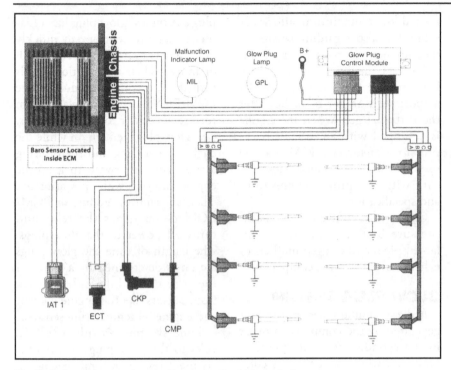

Typical glow plug system. *(Courtesy: Ford Motor Co.)*

EXHAUST GAS RECIRCULATION (EGR) SYSTEM

Most of the air around us is made up of harmless nitrogen. Ordinarily, nitrogen cannot combine with oxygen. However, under very high heat conditions, such as those that occur inside an engine's combustion chamber, where temperatures can exceed 2500°F (1371°C), nitrogen molecules can bond with oxygen molecules and form oxides of nitrogen (NOx). When NOx leaves the tailpipe and is struck by sunlight, photochemical smog is formed.

The EGR system returns a measured amount of exhaust gas to the combustion chamber in order to cool the combustion flame and prevent the formation of NOx. Nitrogen is an inert gas at temperature below 2500°F. If combustion temperatures are kept below this value, NOx will not form. Because the high combustion temperature of a diesel engine gives it the potential to emit more NOx than a comparable spark ignition engine, the application of an EGR system is critical.

Since EGR attempts to control emissions during combustion, the potential to affect performance also exists. EGR must occur at specific times to incur the least detriment to engine performance. EGR is therefore applied to an engine at normal operating temperature during off-idle conditions.

There are a number of differences between a spark ignition EGR system and a diesel EGR system. On a diesel engine, EGR can only take place when the exhaust pressure upstream of the turbocharger, the turbine pressure, is greater than the intake pressure downstream from the turbocharger, the boost pressure. However, under certain operating conditions such as high engine load, where boost pressure is greater than turbine pressure, EGR cannot take place. Diesel engine manufacturers have used several methods to allow EGR even under high engine load conditions. Turbine speed can be increased by means of an exhaust choke valve or by using a VGT turbocharger, or boost pressure can be decreased using an intake throttle valve.

To prevent a loss of air charge density, a cooler is often incorporated on diesel engines to reduce the temperature of the exhaust gases prior to mixing in the intake stream.

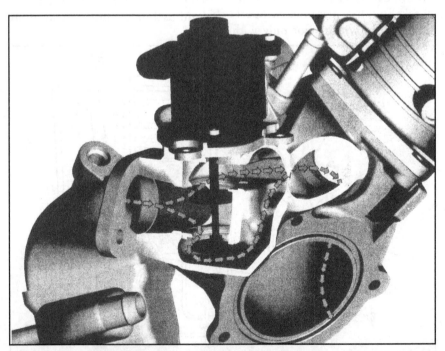

Cutaway view of a manifold showing exhaust flow through an EGR valve. This unit actually has two valves connected on a common shaft. *(Courtesy: Ford Motor Co.)*

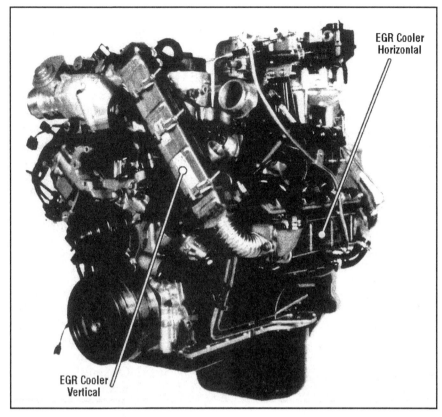

An EGR cooling system utilizing two air-to-coolant heat exchangers.
(Courtesy: Ford Motor Co.)

Engine coolant flows through the EGR cooler and absorbs heat from the exhaust before going to the EGR valve.

The EGR system is controlled by the PCM/ECM, however the methods and systems vary according to manufacturer. Some systems are completely electronic while others are vacuum controlled, with vacuum provided by a pump. An electronic EGR valve is directly controlled by the PCM/ECM using a stepper motor. A vacuum operated EGR valve is controlled using a vacuum control solenoid and vacuum vent solenoid.

The PCM/ECM calculates the required amount of EGR based on inputs from various sensors that provide information on engine load, turbo boost, intake and engine coolant temperature, and vehicle and engine speed. These inputs include:
- The Accelerator Pedal Position (APP) sensor
- The Barometric pressure (BARO) sensor
- The boost sensor
- The Engine Coolant Temperature (ECT) sensor
- The EGR vacuum sensor
- The Intake Air Temperature (IAT) sensor
- The Mass Airflow (MAF) sensor
- The Vehicle Speed Sensor (VSS)
- The engine speed.
- Not all systems will use all the sensors listed here.

The PCM/ECM also relies on a number of feedback sensors. An electronic EGR incorporates an EGR valve position sensor that indicates the amount of valve movement. This is continuously monitored to ensure proper valve position. A vacuum controlled EGR system has an EGR vacuum sensor that monitors the amount of vacuum available to the EGR valve. The PCM/ECM will then make adjustments to the vacuum control system to obtain the vacuum level necessary to attain the desired EGR valve position.

The MAF sensor measures total airflow into the engine. When the EGR valve is open, the MAF rate decreases. The PCM/ECM uses the difference between the closed and open rates to calculate the actual amount of EGR flow into the intake manifold. On some applications, the MAF measurement is compared to a speed-density calculation that is performed using a Manifold Absolute Pressure (MAP) sensor and the engine's rpm signal. The difference between the two measurements is the effective EGR gas flow, and this is compared to what was called for by the PCM/ECM to determine whether a fault exists in the system.

Vehicles with liquid cooled EGR coolers often use temperature sensors to monitor cooler operation, one on the exhaust manifold and one near the EGR valve. The PCM can then monitor the efficiency of the cooler by comparing the difference in temperature readings between the inlet and outlet sensors with the EGR valve open. A failure here would generate a DTC.

Diagnosis And Inspection

Symptoms of EGR failure include lack of power, surging and smoking. A failure in the system should set a DTC and turn on the MIL. Always examine the system wiring and connectors and, on vacuum controlled systems, check for vacuum leaks caused by loose, broken, pinched or missing vacuum hoses.

A common problem with EGR valves is carbon clogging. Excessive carbon deposits can restrict EGR flow and may even cause the valve to stick or operate slowly, hindering effective control. The valve should be cleaned or replaced, however, the EGR passages in the manifold should also be inspected and cleaned. Carbon buildup here can also restrict EGR flow, and if not cleaned, a piece of carbon could break off and cause the replacement

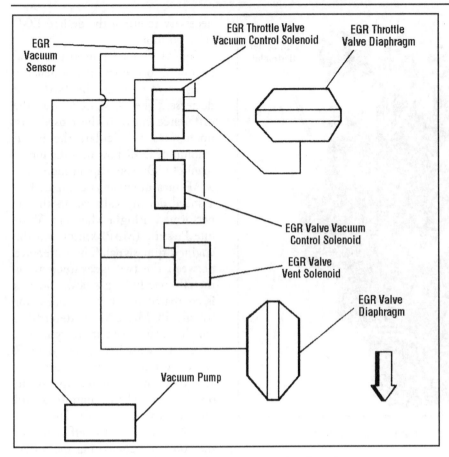

Typical EGR vacuum control system. *(Courtesy: GM Corp.)*

EGR valve to stick open. If carbon buildup is extensive, it may require manifold removal for thorough cleaning.

On some vehicles, a defective EGR cooler can allow coolant to leak into the intake manifold, causing white smoke. However, if there is no smoke the cooler could still be leaking. If the vehicle is using coolant, overheating or blowing coolant out of the reservoir, it could be because the EGR cooler is leaking. If the coolant is leaking into the combustion chamber, then combustion gases are also leaking into the cooling system. These can be detected by placing a vial of a chemical that is sensitive to combustion gases over the coolant reservoir opening while the engine is running. The chemical will change color in the presence of combustion gases. If there is a positive indication of combustion gases, the next task is to determine whether it is the EGR cooler or a blown head gasket, cracked block, etc.

As described earlier, some EGR systems are equipped with a throttle valve. When EGR is desired, the PCM/ECM closes the throttle valve to create a restriction in the air intake, creating a vacuum that allows EGR flow into the intake manifold. This valve can be electrically controlled by the PCM/ECM or on vacuum operated systems, via a throttle valve vacuum solenoid. If this valve fails in the closed position, there will be a permanent restriction and reduced engine power. If it fails in the open position then EGR will not be possible under certain conditions. A failure should set a DTC and turn on the MIL. If the valve is electric, check for voltage and the wiring to the motor. If the valve is vacuum operated, check for vacuum leaks and loose, broken or pinched vacuum hoses. The vacuum control solenoid can be tested with a vacuum pump.

EXHAUST AFTERTREATMENT

Besides NOx, the other great pollutant that results from diesel combustion is particulate matter (soot). Diesel particulate matter is mostly made up of particles that are smaller than 2.5 microns in diameter, and has been identified by both CARB (California Air Resources Board) and the EPA as being a toxic contaminant with the potential to cause cancer and other respiratory illnesses.

Advancing injection timing and reducing EGR flow would increase combustion chamber temperatures and reduce particulate matter emissions. Unfortunately this would also increase NOx emissions.

A device that has been used for some time on diesel engine vehicles to reduce particulate matter is the Diesel Oxidation Catalyst (DOC). The DOC oxidizes Hydro-carbon (HC) and Carbon Monoxide (CO) emissions along with a percentage of particulate matter. However, with increasingly more stringent emissions standards, further particulate matter reduction became necessary. This is accomplished with the Diesel Particulate Filter (DPF).

The DPF is located in the exhaust system after the DOC, and is often incorporated with it. Most DPFs are of the 'wall flow' design. The walls of the filter are porous, which allows gases to flow through freely, but collect the soot in the open channels.

Just as leaded gasoline can damage a catalytic converter, so can the use of high-sulfur fuel damage a DPF. In order for the DPF to operate properly, the sulfur content of the fuel must be kept below 15 parts per million. These requirements are what led the EPA to mandate the use of Ultra Low Sulfur Diesel (ULSD) fuel.

Since the DPF collects soot, if left unchecked it will begin to clog,

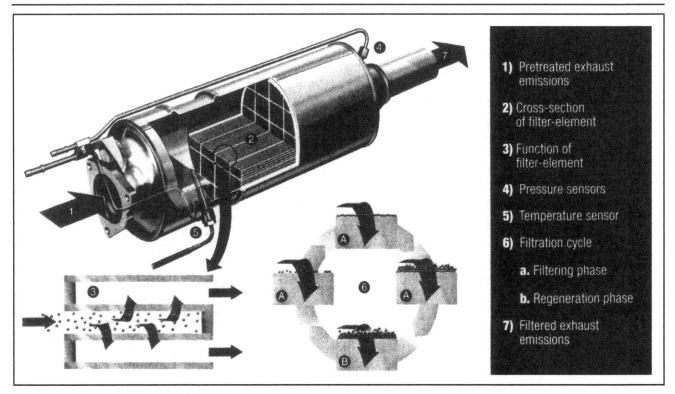

1) Pretreated exhaust emissions

2) Cross-section of filter-element

3) Function of filter-element

4) Pressure sensors

5) Temperature sensor

6) Filtration cycle

   a. Filtering phase

   b. Regeneration phase

7) Filtered exhaust emissions

Cutaway view of a Diesel Particulate Filter (DPF).

increasing exhaust backpressure and reducing engine performance. The DPF is therefore 'regenerated' by igniting the soot and burning it to the point where the filter is cleaned and normal engine operation is restored.

There are various methods used for regeneration, but the most common process used for diesel engine vehicles sold in the U.S. is active regeneration, where fuel is introduced into the exhaust stream ahead of the DOC, which raises the exhaust gas temperature as it oxidizes the excess HC. The increased exhaust gas temperature helps ignite and burn the accumulated particulate matter. This is why the DOC and DPF are usually packaged together, to facilitate regeneration.

Fuel can be metered into the exhaust either by pulsing the fuel injectors during the exhaust stroke or through a fuel vaporizer located in the exhaust system between the engine and the DOC. The vaporizer has a heater that heats the fuel, and is located far enough upstream in

the exhaust system to ensure that the fuel vapors diffuse sufficiently before entering the catalyst.

The PCM/ECM determines when regeneration should be initiated based on input from pressure sensors located at each end of the DPF. The difference between these two measurements is called the pressure drop or pressure differential. The

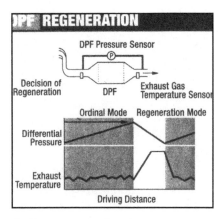

As the pressure drop increases across the filter, regeneration is initiated. This leads to an increase in exhaust temperature that burns off the accumulated soot and lowers backpressure in the exhaust system.

pressure drop increases as the DPF fills up with particulate matter and when a certain threshold is reached, regeneration is initiated.

The regeneration process is monitored by the PCM/ECM using the pressure sensors and by temperature sensors, also located at the DPF inlet and outlet. During regeneration, there should be a rise in temperature and a decrease in pressure across the DPF.

The PCM/ECM also uses the DPF pressure sensors to determine the condition of the DPF. It can compare a normal pressure drop with one that is abnormal. Lower than normal pressure drop could indicate a damaged DPF, whereas a gradual increase in pressure drop values could indicate a DPF that is not completely regenerating; it may have to be removed and manually cleaned.

Diagnosis And Inspection

As indicated, the exhaust aftertreatment process is closely monitored by the PCM/ECM, so any sensor signal that is out of specification will set a DTC and turn on the MIL. The most likely failure for the DPF would be failure to regenerate or for regeneration to fail to completely clean the filter. Either scenario would cause a restriction in the exhaust system. Because the DOC and DPF are in the exhaust system and located under the vehicle, they should of course be inspected for physical damage as well.

Notes

Fuel System Diagnosis And Repair

Typical diesel engine common rail fuel system.   *(Courtesy: GM Corp.)*

The diesel fuel system consists of two subsystems, the low-pressure system and the high-pressure system. The low-pressure system is the fuel delivery system. It pumps the fuel from the fuel tank to the injection pump or to the injectors, and includes the tank, pump, filter(s), water separator, bleeder valve(s) and the necessary fuel lines. A fuel heater is included on some applications.

The high-pressure system varies according to injection type. Common rail systems pressurize a fuel rail with a high-pressure pump. Solenoid-operated electronic injectors are connected to the fuel rail. Electronic Unit Injectors (EUI) are solenoid-actuated, but are pressurized by the camshaft. Hydraulic Electronic Unit Injectors (HEUI)

are also solenoid-actuated, but use high-pressure lube oil to provide injector pressure. Pump-Line-Nozzle (PLN) systems have a high-pressure pump that delivers fuel to nozzles that open according to injection pressure.

Excess fuel not needed by the injectors is returned to the fuel tank by the fuel return line. Sometimes a fuel cooler is included in this line.

WARNING: *Diesel fuel systems develop very high pressures. Personal injury can result if the proper service procedures and precautions are not followed.*

FUEL DELIVERY SYSTEM

An insufficient amount of fuel delivered to the high-pressure side of the fuel system can cause a no-

start condition or a lack of power. Low fuel pressure can be caused by a clogged fuel filter, a defective pressure regulator or a restricted fuel line. Air in the system can cause the engine to stall or misfire.

Inspect the general condition of the fuel system. Look for dented, damaged or corroded lines and leaks. Make sure all connections are secure and all lines are securely mounted so they can't rub against other components.

Check the fuel tank for damage and leaks, and make sure it is securely mounted. Inspect the lines and wiring at the tank, making sure they are properly connected. Make sure the fuel tank neck and cap are secure.

When replacing a fuel line, use only steel tubing, never copper, and make sure the line is properly attached to the frame. Fuel lines and components are connected using various types of fittings, many of which require special tools to disconnect. If specified, always use the special tool to prevent damaging fittings and fuel system components. Many fittings use O-rings, which should never be reused. Always replace O-rings with those specified for fuel system use.

Fuel Pressure Testing

Fuel pressure testing can be used not only to determine the condition of the transfer pump, but also to find flow restrictions. Refer to the manufacturer's service information for pressure specifications and the engine speed at which testing should be performed. To test pump output, disconnect the pump from the fuel tank and provide a separate source of fuel for the pump to draw from. Tee a suitable pressure gauge into the pump outlet and run the engine at the manufacturer's specified rpm. Compare the gauge reading with specifications. Then, reconnect the pump to the fuel tank and repeat the test. If the pressure is now lower, there could be a blockage in the line or the strainer on the fuel tank sending unit could be clogged.

The same testing method can be used for other components in the delivery system, like the fuel filter and fuel/water separator. For example if fuel pressure is measured before and after the fuel filter, and the pressure drop is greater than that of a new filter, then the fuel filter is clogged and must be replaced.

High fuel pressure can be as critical a defect as low fuel pressure. If fuel pressure is too high, the fuel pump pressure relief may open, resulting in low volume. Clogged fuel return components are the first place to look when an engine displays fuel pressure that rises too fast.

Before condemning a fuel pump for low pressure, you must first make sure there is no air in the system. Air can enter the system if the fuel tank runs dry, a filter or other component is changed, or there is a loose connection.

If air is suspected to be in the fuel system, there are usually bleeders located on the filter and injection pump for purging. Crank the engine to build pressure and, working from the tank forward, loosen the bleeder screws until only fuel flows from the opening. Then, tighten the bleeder screws. However, if air is still in the system, there are several ways to find the source.

If the engine starts but dies almost immediately, the air is probably entering close to the injectors or injection pump. Check connections or components that are mounted nearby, like the filter or fuel/water separator. A transparent hose can be installed in line between components where an air leak is suspected; the engine is then run and the fuel observed for the presence of air bubbles.

The fuel line can be disconnected from the tank and the system pressurized with low-pressure air (no more than 15 psi). Then apply soapy water to line connections, filter canisters, fuel/water separators and all other potential leak sources. Various sections of the system can also be disconnected, one end plugged and the other connected a to a vacuum pump. If the line or components won't hold vacuum, there is where the air is being drawn in.

Fuel System Priming

Many diesel primary fuel supply systems feature a hand priming pump and an air bleed to prime the fuel system. The fuel delivery system to the injection pump must be purged of air if the engine runs out of fuel or is taken apart for service.

When restarting the engine after the fuel system has been opened, bleed the fuel delivery system. The priming pump and air bleed often are on the filter housing. After opening a bleeder in the system, hand-pump the primer pump until pure fuel exits the bleeder.

Transfer Pump

The fuel transfer pump, also called the feed or lift pump, supplies fuel to the injection pump or unit injectors. It is usually an electric pump, mounted on the frame rail, and controlled by the PCM/ECM via a relay. However, diaphragm-type mechanical pumps driven off the camshaft are still used in some applications.

To replace a frame-mounted pump, position a drain pan under the fuel pump to catch any spilled fuel. Remove any covers or other components, as necessary, to gain access to the fuel pump. Disconnect all lines and wiring from the fuel pump, remove the fuel pump fasteners and remove the fuel pump from the vehicle.

Place the replacement pump in position and secure it with the fasteners. Connect the lines and wiring, as required. Install any components or covers that were removed. Bleed the fuel system, operate the engine and check for leaks and proper engine operation.

Fuel Filter/Fuel Heater/ Water Separator

On some fuel systems these are separate components, but very often they are combined into one unit. Most water separators have a sensor connected to a WATER IN FUEL light on the dash. The light should come on when the ignition switch is in the ON position to indicate the light and water sensor are functioning, however, if the light remains on when the engine is running, water must be drained from the separator.

The separator should be drained with the engine off, to prevent air from entering the fuel system. Place a container under the separator drain tube. Open the drain valve and allow it to remain open until clear diesel fuel flows from the tube. Close the drain tube, restart the engine and make sure the WATER IN FUEL light is not on.

To replace the fuel filter/fuel heater/water separator, position a drain pan under the unit to catch any spilled fuel. Disconnect the fuel lines and wiring, remove the mounting bracket fasteners and remove the unit from the vehicle.

Place the replacement unit in position and secure it with the fasteners. Connect the lines and wiring, as required. Bleed the fuel system, operate the engine and check for leaks and proper engine operation.

COMMON RAIL FUEL SYSTEM

All the necessary pressure for the fuel injectors is developed by the injection pump on common rail fuel systems. The injection pump is gear driven by the crankshaft and, if on a V8 engine, usually located between the cylinder banks. Pressure is regulated by a control valve located on the pump and controlled by the PCM/ECM. The pump is capable of pumping more fuel than the injectors can use, and this excess fuel is returned to the fuel tank through the fuel return line. On some systems, a transfer pump is not used and the injection pump draws the fuel from the tank.

The injection pump delivers fuel to a tube called a rail. All the fuel injectors are attached to the rail, which acts as a reservoir and stabilizer. Regardless of injector opening, there is always an even supply of fuel at the same pressure available to each injector.

The fuel injectors are solenoid operated and injector timing and rate of injection is controlled by the PCM/ECM. The injectors use a needle-and-seat type valve to control fuel flow, and fuel pressure is fed to both the top and bottom of the needle valve. By bleeding some of the pressure off the top, the pressure on the bottom will push the needle off its seat and fuel will flow through the nozzle holes. Fuel is usually sprayed directly into the combustion chamber on common rail systems.

The newest common rail systems use piezoelectrically actuated injectors. Piezoelectric injectors use crystals arranged in a series called a stack. The crystals change dimension when a voltage is applied, thus the total change of the stack can be used to actuate the pintle of the injector. Piezo injector opening time is much faster than a typical solenoid injector, making them capable of multiple small injections during a single injection event. This allows the engine designer much greater control over performance and emissions control.

Tight fittings and clean fuel are critical to any diesel fuel injection system, but even more critical on common rail injection. The individual injectors develop fuel pressure in unit injection, and injection pumps usually dedicate a high-pressure line to each injector. On a common rail injection system, however, all the injectors are dependent on the fuel pressure in a shared, common rail. A fuel leak at on injector can bleed off enough pressure to prevent engine starting. Injector internal clearances are extremely close, and a small particle of dirt can cause the injector to jam.

Connections between the common rail and the injector can also cause problems. The high-pressure fuel is delivered to the injector by means of an injector supply line and a fuel connector. When the fuel connector nut is tightened, it presses the injector supply line against the injector to form a seal. The injector supply line is then threaded into the fuel connector. If any of these fittings are not torqued to specification, a high-pressure fuel leak will result. In addition, over tightening the connections can cause deformation and once again result in a high-pressure fuel leak. Most leaks of this nature will be inside the cylinder head, and not immediately noticed.

Exploded view of a typical fuel filter/ fuel heater/water separator. (Courtesy: Ford Motor Co.)

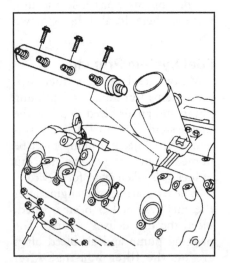

A typical fuel rail assembly. (Courtesy: GM Corp.)

HYDRAULIC ELECTRONIC UNIT

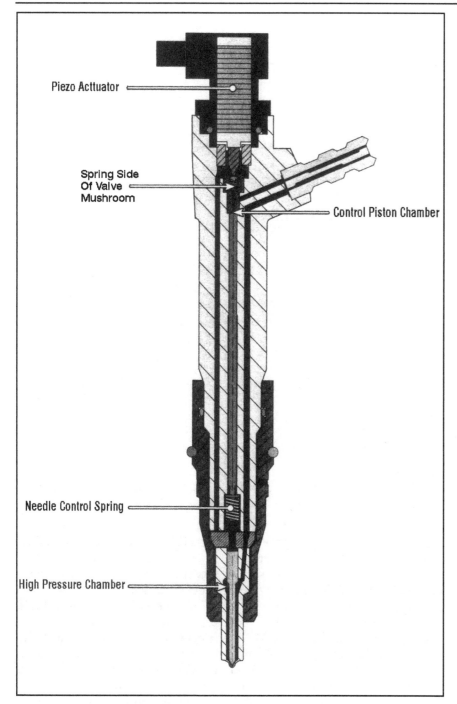

Cross section of a piezo injector.   *(Courtesy: Ford Motor Co.)*

Labels on diagram:
- Piezo Acttuator
- Spring Side Of Valve Mushroom
- Needle Control Spring
- High Pressure Chamber
- Control Piston Chamber

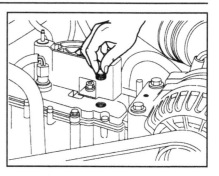

Checking the oil level in the HEUI high-pressure oil reservoir. (Courtesy: Ford Motor Co.)

INJECTOR (HEUI) FUEL SYSTEM

On HEUI systems, fuel is supplied to the fuel filter and then directly to fuel rails in the cylinder heads and the injectors, at approximately 50-70 psi. The injectors are powered by lubricating oil that is pressurized by a pump fed by a separate high-pressure oil reservoir. The oil reservoir is kept supplied by the engine's oil pump.

The pump is gear-driven off the crankshaft. The PCM/ECM controls oil pressure by opening and closing an Injector Pressure Regulator (IPR) valve, mounted on the pump. The pump delivers the oil at pressures up to 3000 psi to rails in the cylinder head via high-pressure hoses.

From the oil rails, the oil is fed to the fuel injector bores through passages machined in the cylinder head. The PCM/ECM commands the injectors using an injector driver module, which supplies power to a solenoid in the injector. The solenoid in turn opens a valve that admits the high-pressure oil to the top of a piston. The oil forces the piston and a plunger against fuel that is trapped in the injector body. Since the fuel end of the plunger is smaller than the oil end, the hydraulic force is multiplied to produce the required fuel injection pressure.

The PCM/ECM controls injection timing and rate of injection with the fuel delivery control signal. Injection pressure and volume are controlled by varying the oil pressure with the Injector Control Pressure (ICP) regulator.

For an HEUI engine to start, naturally there must be enough oil to operate the injectors. Check the engine oil level and examine the oil on the dipstick. If there is not enough oil in the crankcase, the injectors will not operate. If the oil level is higher than it should, then the system was overfilled or fuel is leaking into the crankcase. If there is a substantial amount of fuel in the oil, it will usually have a distinct fuel smell. If the oil is milky, it means there is a coolant leak.

If there is enough oil in the crankcase, next remove the inspection plug and check the level in the high-pressure oil reservoir. If the level is

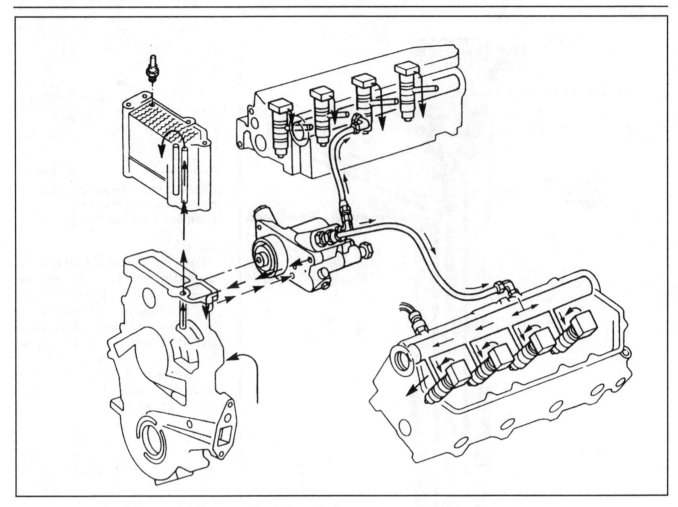

HEUI high-pressure oil system.   *(Courtesy: Ford Motor Co.)*

low, it may be because the engine has not been operated for while, and the oil has drained back to the oil pan. This can make the engine hard to start or it may stall immediately after starting. If this is the case, fill the reservoir to allow the system to prime faster.

Because the HEUI system is so dependent on the engine's lubricating oil, it is important to make sure the oil is changed at regular intervals, kept at the proper level, and that the proper type of oil is used. Using the wrong oil or not changing the oil when necessary can cause aeration in the oil, which can not only cause problems like no-starts, hard starts and erratic idle, but can also damage the injectors. The proper oils have anti-foaming additives that prevent aeration, but these can still break down over time, so

regular oil changes are imperative. Always refer to the manufacturer's service information to make sure that when the oil is changed, the proper grade and weight oil is used for anticipated temperatures.

The Camshaft Position (CMP) sensor provides an engine position and rpm signal to the PCM/ECM. If this sensor is defective, it can cause a no-start, hard start or stalling. A DTC will be set if the PCM/ECM does not receive a signal or if the signal is erratic.

ELECTRONIC UNIT INJECTOR (EUI) FUEL SYSTEM

Electronic unit injectors are similar to hydraulic electronic unit injectors in that all the pressure necessary for injection is created within the fuel injector. However, where

the HEUI system uses oil pressure to create the pressure, the EUI system uses the force provided by the engine's camshaft.

Like the HEUI system, a high-pressure fuel pump is not used. Fuel is delivered to ducts machined into the cylinder head, and the injector is mounted in the cylinder head in the valvetrain area. There it can be pressurized by a rocker arm actuated by a lobe on the camshaft.

The PCM/ECM controls injector timing and duration, but injection can only take place when the injector is pressurized by the camshaft. The PCM/ECM controls the injector by supplying power to a solenoid located on the side of the injector. The solenoid is mounted over the poppet control valve and moves the valve by magnetic attraction with no physical connection to

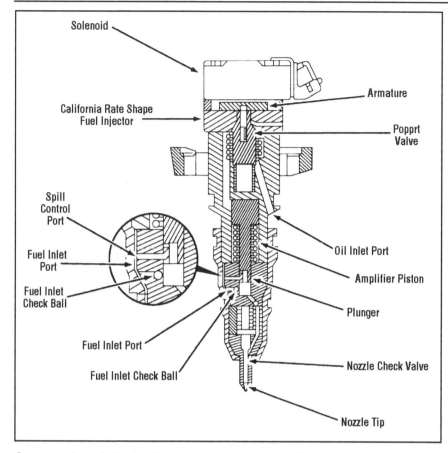

Cross section of a hydraulic electronic unit injector. *(Courtesy: Ford Motor Co.)*

the valve. When fuel injection is not required, the poppet control valve is opened and the fuel pump flows fuel through the injector and out to the fuel tank return. When the solenoid is energized, the poppet control valve closes, trapping a quantity of fuel under the plunger. The plunger compresses the fuel until a specific opening pressure is reached, the injector nozzle needle lifts, and fuel is injected into the combustion chamber.

Although the injection event is controlled by the PCM/ECM, the EUI is still subject to mechanical actuation by the camshaft. Because of this, a lash adjustment between the rocker arm and injector may be necessary. Refer to the manufacturer's service information. Typically, the procedure involves checking injector height with a gauge and adjusting accordingly.

PUMP-LINE-NOZZLE

(PLN) FUEL SYSTEM

In the pump-line-nozzle injection system, the pump creates the high pressure necessary for injection and also controls the injection timing. Fuel is delivered under high pres-

sure through individual fuel lines to injection nozzles located on the cylinder head. Excess fuel is routed from the nozzles and the pump to a return line and back to the fuel tank.

A PLN injection pump operates as follows: Fuel flows into the injection pump inlet through an inlet filter screen. Fuel then flows to the vane-type fuel transfer pump. Excess fuel from the transfer pump is bypassed through the pressure regulator assembly to the suction side.

Fuel under transfer pump pressure flows through the center of the transfer pump rotor, past the rotor retainers into the hydraulic head. It then flows through a connecting passage in the head to the automatic advance and up through a radial passage to the metering valve. The position of the metering valve, controlled by a governor, regulates fuel flow into the radial charging passage that incorporates the head charging ports.

As the rotor revolves, the two rotor inlet passages align with the charging ports in the hydraulic head, allowing fuel to flow into the pumping chamber. With further rotation, the inlet passages move out of alignment and the discharge port of the rotor aligns with one of the

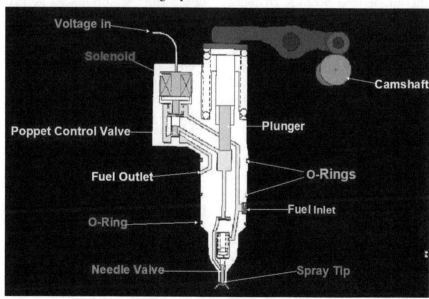

Typical electronic unit injector. *(Courtesy: Detroit Diesel)*

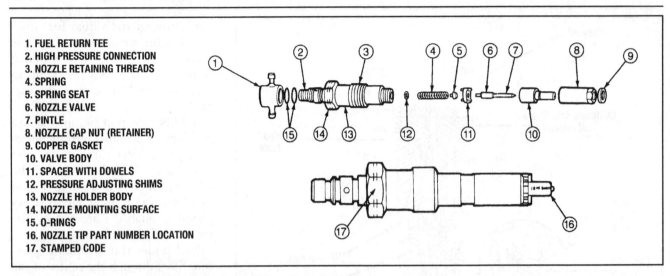

1. FUEL RETURN TEE
2. HIGH PRESSURE CONNECTION
3. NOZZLE RETAINING THREADS
4. SPRING
5. SPRING SEAT
6. NOZZLE VALVE
7. PINTLE
8. NOZZLE CAP NUT (RETAINER)
9. COPPER GASKET
10. VALVE BODY
11. SPACER WITH DOWELS
12. PRESSURE ADJUSTING SHIMS
13. NOZZLE HOLDER BODY
14. NOZZLE MOUNTING SURFACE
15. O-RINGS
16. NOZZLE TIP PART NUMBER LOCATION
17. STAMPED CODE

Exploded view of PLN injection nozzle. *(Courtesy: Ford Motor Co.)*

head outlets. While the discharge port is opened, the rollers contact the cam lobes forcing the plungers together. Fuel trapped between the plungers is then pressurized and delivered to the nozzle.

A typical injection nozzle assembly is retained in the correct position on the cylinder head by a nozzle holder, which also conducts the fuel to the nozzle. The nozzle consists of two parts, the valve body and the nozzle valve, which are lapped together to form a matched set. The nozzle has an extension at its lower end called the pintle.

Fuel passes through ducts in the nozzle to a pressure chamber located just above the spring seat. When the pressure of the fuel acting on the differential area of the valve exceeds a certain spring-load, it lifts the valve from its seat and fuel flows from the nozzle. Fuel is cut off when the nozzle spring seats the valve.

Electronic control of the PLN fuel system is limited to manipulating the injection pump. This usually involves control of the pump's speed/load governor by the PCM/ECM.

HIGH-PRESSURE FUEL SYSTEM DIAGNOSIS AND TESTING

Because so many components are monitored on electronically con-trolled engines, the first step in any diagnosis should be connecting a scan tool and checking for pending and current DTCs and relevant scan tool data.

Inspect the injection pump, fuel lines and injectors for fuel leaks or other damage. Inspect the wiring to the injectors and sensors, looking for broken wires, damaged insulation, and loose or bent connector pins.

Check the fuel pressure at the test port specified by the manufacturer and compare the reading with specifications. Before condemning the pump, make sure that delivery pressure is correct. Also make sure that the PCM/ECM is receiving the camshaft and/or crankshaft position sensor signal.

Fuel injectors can clog, wear and leak. Dirty injectors can lean the air/fuel mixture and cause a rough idle and lack of power. Leaking injectors can richen the air/fuel mixture and cause black smoke.

If the engine is missing on one cylinder, first check the exhaust runners just after engine startup with an infrared thermometer. If an injector has failed, its cylinder will be cooler than the others.

An injector cutout test can also determine a bad cylinder. Perform the cutout test using a suitable scan tool. If a cylinder is disabled for any reason, the PCM/ECM will increase the pulsewidth to the remaining cylinders to maintain engine speed.

When performing a cylinder cutout test, the scan tool will first measure the no cutout pulse-width, and then disable each cylinder and record the pulse-width with that cylinder disabled. The scan tool usually allows the technician the option of performing a manual or an auto test. In addition, the technician can choose to conduct the test at idle or at 1000 rpm. If the cylinder is operable, the PCM/ECM will have to increase pulsewidth to maintain engine speed. When the injector is cutout on a cylinder that is disabled, however, the PCM/ECM will not have to increase pulsewidth to maintain engine speed, and the pulsewidth for that cylinder will match the no cutout pulsewidth.

The cylinder cutout test is in effect a power balance test. When the cylinder with the performance defect is disabled, the PCM/ECM can detect that there was no change in performance and no need to compensate for a performance loss. The cutout test pinpoints the defective cylinder, but it cannot determine why that cylinder is not working. A cylinder with poor compression and a cylinder with a faulty injector will both give the same results on a cylinder balance test, and additional

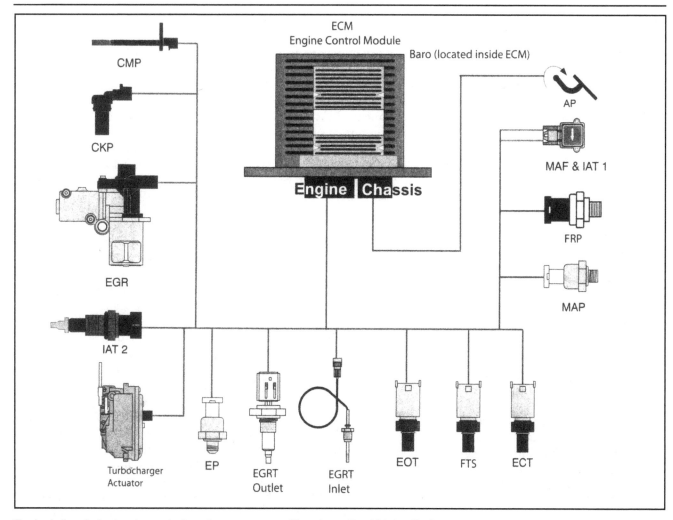

Typical diesel electronic control system sensors.   *(Courtesy: Ford Motor Co.)*

testing will be required.

ENGINE CONTROL SYSTEM DIAGNOSIS AND TESTING

All engine control systems have the same basic format of inputs, the PCM/ECM and outputs, which communicate using electronic circuits. Information is gathered by a wide variety of sensors, using several means. Some sensors vary a resistance to ground for temperature or pressure sensing. Some sensors report movement by a variable resistor. Other sensors vary a frequency output as pressure or airflow changes. All sensors supply the PCM/ECM with information on engine conditions.

Once the PCM/ECM sees what the operating conditions are, it compares what it sees to pre-programmed reference parameters in its EEPROM (Electrically Erasable Programmable Read Only Memory), which it uses to adjust to changing engine conditions. Outputs are voltage commands, such as providing power or ground to circuits, or varying the pulse width of a square wave to control injection.

Diagnosis of the engine control system should be performed in a logical manner. This begins with not automatically assuming that the problem is with the engine control system! Make sure the basic engine and related conventional systems are sound, using inspections and tests like those described elsewhere in this study guide, before getting involved with testing sensors.

Become familiar with the capabilities of the engine control system on the vehicle you are servicing, using available service literature. Check TSBs (Technical Service Bulletins) for information about problems and fixes discovered in the field and not covered in the service manual.

As described in the General Diagnosis section of this study guide, all components and systems that affect a vehicle's emissions output are monitored by the PCM/ECM. If the monitor results indicate a failure, a fault will be recorded in the PCM/ECM's memory. To retrieve any stored and/or pending DTCs and check monitor status, connect a scan tool to the DLC. If a code has turned on the MIL and it is related to a continuous monitor, check and record the freeze frame information. This will give you an idea of the operating conditions that were present when the fault occurred.

Once you have the DTCs that require diagnosis, refer to the appropriate service information to identify the systems and circuits that the DTCs represent. The diagnostic charts will describe the circuit and the fault that the code represents and contain troubleshooting procedures and tests that must be performed, to determine the cause of the malfunction. These tests usually describe various voltage and resistance measurements using a DMM.

If the vehicle exhibits driveability problems but does not set any codes, refer to the symptom-driven diagnostic charts contained in most manufacturers' service manuals.

Intermittent driveability problems are usually more difficult to diagnose and repair. You may have to try to recreate conditions described by the driver to get an intermittent code to reset. Since intermittent problems are often caused by damaged wiring and connectors, tapping and wiggling wiring harnesses and connectors can also get problems to reoccur and reset codes.

Service Precautions

The following precautions should be observed when testing or servicing components and circuits of an electronic engine controls system:

- Never disconnect any electrical connector with the ignition switch ON. This creates high voltage spikes, known as short duration transients, which can permanently ruin delicate circuits
- Some electronic engine control circuits are designed to carry very small amounts of current. For this reason, a high-impedance (over 10 megohms) digital meter must always be used when troubleshooting computer-related circuits
- Always connect the negative lead of a voltmeter first
- • Never use a test light unless specifically instructed to do so

in the manufacturer's diagnostic procedure
- To prevent damage from electrostatic discharge, always touch a known good ground before handling an electronic component. This is especially important after sliding across a seat or walking a distance
- Do not touch the terminals of an electronic component unless it is necessary, as oil from skin can cause corrosion.

Electrical Testing

In order to perform diagnostic tests, a technician must be able to measure voltage, voltage drop, amperage and resistance using a DMM.

Voltage Measurements

If there is a DC/AC switch, make sure it is switched to the DC position. Set the function/ range control to the desired volts position. If the magnitude of the voltage is not known, set the switch to a range that will read the most voltages seen on the vehicle. (Normally, a 20V range will be sufficient). Reduce the range until you have a satisfactory reading. Connect the test leads to the circuit being measured and read the voltage on the display.

Resistance Measurements

Set the function/range control to the desired position. If the magni-

tude of the resistance is not known, set the switch to the highest range, then reduce until a satisfactory reading is obtained. If the resistance being measured is connected to a circuit, turn off the power to the circuit being tested. Turn off the ignition. Connect the test leads to the circuit being measured and read the resistance on the display.

Voltage Drop

Each component in a circuit has some resistance value, and the voltage is reduced as it moves the circuit's resistive loads. The sum of all the voltage drops across a circuit will equal the original amount of applied voltage. Voltage never disappears — it is merely converted into another form of energy by the resistance of the load or wires.

The voltage available at any point depends on the circuit resistance. The higher the resistance, the more voltage is needed to force current through the circuit. Resistance of any type will use some voltage potential, so the use of voltage is lost across any type of resistance.

To measure voltage drop, set the voltmeter switch to the 20-volt position. Connect the voltmeter negative lead to the ground side of the resistance or load to be measured. Connect the positive lead to the positive side of the resistance or load to be measured. Read the voltage

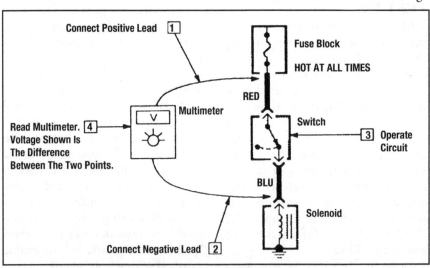

Using a voltmeter to perform a voltage drop test.

drop directly on the 20-volt scale.

A high voltage reading is a sign of too much resistance. Conversely, if the voltage drop is too low, then that condition signifies too little resistance.

Amperage Measurements

An ammeter is connected in series with the circuit, so all the current passing through passes through the ammeter. This means that the fuse must be removed from the circuit, or a connection broken. The ammeter is then inserted into the circuit to replace the fuse or join the two halves of the circuit, observing proper polarity with an analog meter.

Connect the ammeter as you would a voltmeter, with the red or positive probe connected on the battery positive side of the circuit, and the negative lead toward the ground side of the circuit or the battery negative terminal. When working on the voltage side of the load, the negative lead would then be on the load side of the ammeter. If working on the ground side, the positive lead would be on the load side of the ammeter, and the negative lead would then be on the side away from the load.

The ammeter should always be set to the highest range before starting to take a measurement. Then, lower the setting one notch at a time until a usable reading is obtained. If the reading is more than half the scale on an analog ammeter or more than half the digital range on a digital ammeter, don't switch to a lower range. This will protect an analog unit from damage. A digital unit will not be able to give a reading if the amperage measured is out of range.

Engine Control System Sensors

Accelerator Pedal Position (APP) Sensor

Many diesel engine vehicles use a system commonly called 'drive by wire'. In this system there is no physical connection between the accelerator pedal and the engine, but rather sensors are attached to the pedal, which signal its position to the PCM/ECM.

There may be as many as three individual sensors included in one housing, the theory being that having multiple signals for comparison is a safety feature. Typically, as the pedal is depressed, the voltage signal from one sensor should increase at a certain rate, while the remaining two sensors' signals should decrease.

Usually, if one sensor's signal does not agree with the other two, a DTC will be set and the MIL will illuminate, but the vehicle will still operate normally. However, if two signals are lost a code will be set, the MIL will come on and the PCM/ECM will only allow the engine to idle.

Because sensor failure will set a DTC and illuminate the MIL, begin diagnosis by connecting a scan tool to the DLC. However, because the APP is located on the floor of the vehicle, it should first be visually inspected. The sensor, wiring, or connectors could be physically damaged or affected by dirt or corrosion caused by moisture.

Using a voltmeter, move the pedal through its full range of motion and check the output readings of each sensor. Compare with the manufacturer's specifications. If the sensors are OK, check the connectors and wiring back through the circuit.

Camshaft Position (CMP) And Crankshaft Position (CKP) Sensors

The PCM/ECM receives engine rotational position information from these sensors. The PCM/ECM uses the signals to determine correct injection timing. The CMP sensor is located on the front of the engine adjacent to the camshaft. The CKP sensor is usually located on the side of the engine, where it reacts to a trigger wheel on the crankshaft.

Essentially, there are two types of sensors. One is a Hall effect switch and the other is a magnetic reluctance sensor, or PM generator (permanent magnet generator). The easiest way to distinguish the Hall effect switch from magnetic sensors is to remember that the Hall effect switch will have a three-wire harness and control an existing voltage and the reluctance sensors usually have two wires and create a voltage.

When suspecting a camshaft or crankshaft sensor problem, first perform a visual inspection of the wiring harnesses and connectors.

To test a Hall effect switch, set a DMM to the volts setting and check the voltage between the power and ground wires. Take note of this voltage reading.

Connect the DMM between the signal terminal and the ground wire. Rotate the engine with the starter motor by tapping the ignition key. When the engine is rotated, the signal should fluctuate between 0 volts and the system voltage noted in the earlier step. While rotating the engine, check for damaged shutter blades or any indication that the shutter blades are hitting the magnet. You can use a scope to monitor the half wave pulses, which you should see on the output wire. If the hall switch is powered and grounded properly, and the mechanical parts move as intended when the engine is cranked, you should see the pulses. If not, the switch is bad.

To check a magnetic reluctance sensor, disconnect the sensor connector. Using a DMM set to the ohms setting, check resistance across the sensor terminals and compare with the manufacturer's specifications.

EGR Cooler Outlet Temperature Sensor

The EGR cooler outlet temperature sensor is a thermistor sensor. The PCM/ECM uses the sensor's signal to control EGR valve position and throttle position.

Check sensor resistance with an ohmmeter and compare with the manufacturer's specifications.

Engine Coolant Temperature (ECT) Sensor

The PCM/ECM sends the Engine Coolant Temperature (ECT) sensor a voltage and the sensor varies the voltage according to coolant temperature. The ECT sensor is a Negative Temperature Coefficient (NTC) thermistor, meaning that the resistance varies inversely by temperature. When the coolant temperature increases, the resistance of the thermistor decreases and the signal voltage decreases. When the coolant temperature decreases, the resistance of the thermistor increases and the signal voltage increases.

The PCM/ECM uses the coolant temperature information for fuel control, glow plug control, exhaust gas recirculation, and on some applications, cooling fan control.

Using an ohmmeter, measure the resistance between both terminals. Start the engine, and as it warms up check that the values change smoothly. Most manufacturers have temperature/resistance charts in their service information. Compare measurements with these specifications. If the resistance doesn't change or it doesn't match the corresponding temperatures, the sensor is defective.

Engine Oil Temperature (EOT) Sensor

The EOT sensor is a Negative Temperature Coefficient (NTC) thermistor, meaning that the resistance varies inversely by temperature. When the oil temperature increases, the resistance of the thermistor decreases and the signal voltage decreases. When the oil temperature decreases, the resistance of the thermistor increases and the signal voltage increases.

The EOT sensor signal is used by the PCM/ECM to calculate fuel quantity, injection timing and glow plug operation.

Using an ohmmeter, measure the resistance between both terminals. Start the engine, and as it warms up check that the values change smoothly. Most manufacturers have temperature/ resistance charts in their service information. Compare measurements with these specifications. If the resistance doesn't change or it doesn't match the corresponding temperatures, the sensor is defective.

Exhaust Backpressure Sensor

The exhaust backpressure sensor is a 3-wire variable capacitance sensor that is supplied a 5-volt reference signal by the PCM/ECM and returns a linear analog voltage signal that indicates pressure. The PCM/ECM uses the exhaust backpressure signal to control exhaust gas recirculation and on some applications, turbocharger actuation.

Fuel Rail Pressure (FRP) Sensor

The FRP sensor is a 3-wire variable capacitance sensor. The PCM/ECM supplies a 5-volt reference signal to the sensor, which it uses to produce a linear analog voltage signal that indicates the pressure of the fuel in the fuel rail.

The PCM/ECM uses the FRP sensor signal to modulate the injection pump pressure control valve. The fuel rail pressure is adjusted according to load, speed and temperature conditions. The PCM/ECM also uses the FRP signal input for injection timing.

During engine operation, if the PCM/ECM receives an FRP signal that is lower or higher than the value the pressure control valve is trying to attain, the PCM/ECM will set a DTC and illuminate the MIL.

Fuel Temperature Sensor

The fuel temperature sensor is a Negative Temperature Coefficient (NTC) thermistor, meaning that the resistance varies inversely by temperature. When the fuel tempera-ture increases, the resistance of the thermistor decreases and the signal voltage decreases. When the fuel temperature decreases, the resistance of the thermistor increases and the signal voltage increases.

The PCM/ECM uses the fuel temperature information for fuel control.

Using an ohmmeter, measure the resistance between both terminals. Most manufacturers have temperature/resistance charts in their service information. Compare measurements with these specifications. The sensor can be removed and heated with a hair dryer to see how it responds. If the resistance doesn't change or it doesn't match the corresponding temperatures, the sensor is defective.

Injection Control Pressure (ICP) Sensor

The ICP sensor is used on vehicles with HEUI fuel systems. It is a variable capacitor sensor that is supplied a 5-volt reference signal by the PCM/ECM and returns a linear analog voltage signal that indicates pressure. The sensor measures the oil pressure in an injection rail and the PCM/ECM uses the signal to determine injection control pressure. The ICP sensor and the ICP regulator form a closed loop fuel pressure control system.

If the PCM/ECM does not receive an ICP sensor signal, it will set an estimated injection control pressure.

Intake Air Temperature (IAT) Sensor

The IAT sensor is a Negative Temperature Coefficient (NTC) thermistor, meaning that the resistance varies inversely by temperature. When the air temperature increases, the resistance of the thermistor decreases and the signal voltage decreases. When the air temperature decreases, the resistance of the thermistor increases and the signal voltage increases.

Depending on application the

IAT sensor signal is used by the PCM/ECM for idle speed, glow plug and/or exhaust gas recirculation control.

Using an ohmmeter, measure the resistance between both terminals. Most manufacturers have temperature/resistance charts in their service information. Compare measurements with these specifications. The sensor can be removed and heated with a hair dryer to see how it responds. If the resistance doesn't change or it doesn't match the corresponding temperatures, the sensor is defective.

Manifold Absolute Pressure (MAP) Sensor

The MAP sensor is a variable capacitance sensor that is supplied a 5-volt reference signal by the PCM/ECM and returns a voltage signal to the PCM/ECM indicating intake manifold pressure. The sensor voltage increases as pressure increases.

Depending on application, the PCM/ECM uses the MAP sensor signal to calculate EGR duty cycle, fuel delivery and throttle body position. On some applications the signal is used to control smoke by limiting the fuel quantity during acceleration until a specified boost pressure is obtained.

Check the MAP sensor voltage and compare with the manufacturer's specifications.

Mass Air Flow (MAF) Sensor

The MAF sensor uses a hot wire sensing element to measure the amount of air entering the engine. Air passing over the hot wire causes it to cool. The hot wire is maintained at a certain temperature above ambient temperature as measured by a constant cold wire.

The current required to maintain the temperature of the hot wire is proportional to the mass airflow. The MAF sensor outputs a frequency signal to the PCM/ECM proportional to the air mass. The PCM/ECM uses the MAF signal for fuel control and on some

applications for EGR control.

You can test the MAF with a DMM or an oscilloscope. The waveform on an oscilloscope should appear as a series of square waves. The frequency should increase smoothly and proportionately when engine speed and intake airflow is increased. If the frequency is erratic, the MAF or circuit wiring is defective.

PCM/ECM Reprogramming

Over the years, the OEMs (Original Equipment Manufacturers) have found it necessary in many cases to reprogram vehicles' PCM/ECMs with changes to correct various performance problems. These changes are usually detailed in TSBs. On pre-OBD II vehicles, it was common practice to replace a PROM (Program-mable Read Only Memory) or chip to update the PCM/ECM. However, OBD II vehicles do not have replaceable PROMs. OBD II PCM/ECMs have an EEPROM (Electrically Erasable Program-mable Read Only Memory) chip, which can be reprogrammed without removing the unit from the vehicle.

At first, updates could only be installed using a manufacturer-specific tool, but because the U.S. EPA (Environmental Protection Agency) wants the aftermarket to be able to perform emissions-related repairs and they cannot require shops to purchase specific brands of tools, the SAE (Society of Automotive Engineers) and the tool and equipment industry developed communication protocol J2534. This is a translator that allows a PC (Personal Computer) to communicate with the PCM/ECM on all makes and models. The translation software is contained in a pass-through device that connects to the PC and the vehicle's DLC.

Before reprogramming a PCM/ECM, the existing calibration must be identified. This can be done using Mode $09 on a scan tool and then checking a calibration list at

the OEM web site.

The updates and installation programs are available through the OEM web sites. To program a PCM/ECM without using a factory scan tool, you need the software, a PC or laptop computer running the Windows 2000 or later operating system, a high-speed internet connection and the pass-through tool. A high-speed internet connection is essential because the programs are large and would take many hours to download using a dial-up connection. It is also recommended that a stand-alone PC or laptop be used, instead of one that is also used for other jobs in the shop. Other computer processes can interrupt or stop the reprogramming process, which can ruin the PCM/ECM.

Two software packages are needed for programming, the updated PCM/ECM software and the computer program that installs the software on the PCM/ECM. These can usually be downloaded to the PC or laptop before connecting the computer to the pass-through tool, however some manufacturers require a 'live' link between the vehicle and the OEM's server while the PCM/ECM is being updated.

As stated earlier, interrupting reprogramming can cause the process to fail and possibly ruin the PCM/ECM. To avoid this, pop-up blockers, virus protection and firewall software must be turned off. E-mail programs, screensavers and all other automatic processes should be disabled.

Another way that reprogramming can be interrupted is if the vehicle's battery voltage drops. During reprogramming, battery voltage to the PCM/ECM and the pass-through tool gets power from the OBD II connector and must remain constant. The ignition switch must be turned on for part of the process, which may automatically turn on lights or other loads that could cause a significant battery voltage drop. To avoid this, connect a second fully charged battery to the vehicle battery with jumper cables. Do not use a battery charger.

Reprogramming can also be interrupted if something is accidentally turned on, like the vehicle's interior lights. Before starting the job, make sure the key is in the ignition and the driver's window is down. Make sure the security system is turned off.

Once all safeguards against interruption are in place and the software is downloaded into the PC, start the reprogramming application and follow the process step-by-step. Once reprogramming is completed, the PCM/ECM will have to undergo a relearning procedure, which may be as simple as completing a drive cycle, but could also require more reprogramming. Information on relearning procedures is usually available at the OEM web sites.

Prepare yourself for ASE testing with these questions on LIGHT VEHICLE DIESEL ENGINES

NOTE: The following questions are written in the ASE style. They are similar to the kinds of questions that you will see on the ASE test. However, none of these questions will actually appear on the test.

1. A customer brings his vehicle to a technician with a drive-ability complaint. Which of the following should he do first?
   A. Check for diagnostic trouble codes.
   B. Visually inspect the engine.
   C. Road test the vehicle.
   D. Interview the customer.

2. After road testing the vehicle, the technician determines that the customer has a valid driveability complaint. After connecting his scan tool to the diagnostic link connector, what information should he look for to see if reprogramming the PCM/ECM could fix the problem?
   A. diagnostic trouble codes
   B. calibration number
   C. freeze frame data
   D. monitor status

3. When checking monitor status with a scan tool, a technician finds a monitor that is shown as being 'incomplete'. This means that _____.
   A. The monitor is not used on this vehicle.
   B. There is a failure in the system being monitored.
   C. The drive cycle criteria has not been met and the monitor isn't finished.
   D. There is a fault recorded in the PCM/ECM's memory.

4. All of the following can cause white smoke from a diesel's exhaust EXCEPT:
   A. leaking injectors
   B. dirty injectors
   C. bad glow plugs
   D. lean air/fuel mixture

5. A diesel engine has a deep knocking noise that goes away when the clutch pedal is depressed. Technician A says that worn main bearings could be the cause. Technician B says that excessive crankshaft end-play could be the cause. Who is right?
   A. Technician A only
   B. Technician B only
   C. Both A and B
   D. Neither A or B

6. A diesel engine vehicle with a HEUI (Hydraulic Electronic Unit Injector) fuel system starts and idles fine, but will not develop normal power. Which of the following could be the cause?
   A. no CMP (Camshaft Position Sensor) signal
   B. defective glow plug control module
   C. low injector oil pressure
   D. insufficient turbo boost

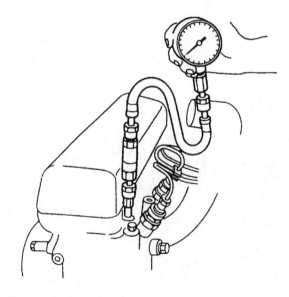

7. The results from the test shown above are below specification in two adjacent cylinders. Technician A says the head gasket may be blown. Technician B says the block may be cracked. Who is right?
   A. Technician A only
   B. Technician B only
   C. Both A and B
   D. Neither A or B

8. On a cold winter morning, a diesel engine vehicle will not start. All of the following are possible causes EXCEPT:
   A. using Number 1 grade diesel fuel
   B. using the wrong viscosity engine oil
   C. weak battery
   D. excessive starter current draw

9. When the starter current draw is checked on a diesel engine vehicle, the reading is greater than specifications. Which of the following could be the cause?
   A. an open in the starter circuit
   B. a decrease in circuit voltage
   C. decreased circuit resistance
   D. excessive circuit resistance

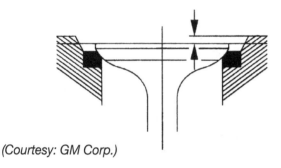

(Courtesy: GM Corp.)

10. The valve and seat in the illustration shown above were machined, and then the distance between the arrows was measured using a depth gauge. The measurement was 0.0814 inches., however, the manufacturer's service limit is 0.0787 inches. Which of the following should the technician do next?
   A. reface the valve
   B. machine the seat
   C. replace the valve
   D. replace the seat

11. Which of the following should be used to find an injector sleeve that is leaking coolant?
   A. magnetic particle detection
   B. dye penetrant
   C. pressure testing
   D. vacuum testing

12.
   1. 0.0118-in., 0.0120-in.
   2. 0.0126-in., 0.0130-in.
   3. 0.0106-in., 0.0108-in
   4. 0.0132-in., 0.0126-in.

Gasket Grade	Projection Value	Gasket Thickness
A	0.0088 – 0.0107 in.	0.0354 – 0.0394 in.
B	0.0108 – 0.0127 in.	0.0374 – 0.0413 in.
C	0.0128 – 0.0147 in.	0.0394 – 0.0433 in.
D	0.0148 – 0.0167 in.	0.0414 – 0.0453 in.

A cylinder head is being installed on a 4-cyl. diesel engine. The measurements next to the numbers 1 – 4 shown above were obtained when the technician measured the piston protrusion in each cylinder. Based on these measurements and the cylinder head gasket grade chart shown above, which gasket should the technician use?
   A. gasket grade A
   B. gasket grade B
   C. gasket grade C
   D. gasket grade D

13. Resurfacing the cylinder head gasket surface of a diesel cylinder head will affect all of the following dimensions **EXCEPT**:
   A. valve stem installed height
   B. valve protrusion/depression
   C. injector tip protrusion
   D. piston protrusion

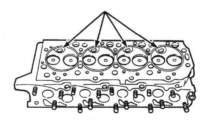

14. All of the following are true statements regarding the cylinder head components indicated by the arrows in the illustration above, **EXCEPT**:
   A. They may require removal when the head is cleaned.
   B. They may require removal if the head is resurfaced.
   C. They are either pressed in or threaded into the head.
   D. They must be replaced if they are cracked.

Prepare yourself for ASE testing with these questions on
LIGHT VEHICLE DIESEL ENGINES

15. Technician A says a dual mass flywheel must be replaced if the clutch surface is cracked, scored or excessively worn. Technician B says a dual mass flywheel must be replaced if the teeth on the ring gear are worn or damaged. Who is right?
    A. Technician A only
    B. Technician B only
    C. Both A and B
    D. Neither A or B

16. A diesel engine with wet cylinder sleeves is being disassembled. What should the technician do concerning the sleeves?
    A. Remove the sleeves using a puller.
    B. Leave the sleeves in the block.
    C. Measure the depth of the counterbore with a bore gauge.
    D. Inspect the counterbore area for erosion, cracks or other damage.

17. A rubber-bonded vibration damper is being inspected. The damper should be replaced if any of the following conditions exist EXCEPT:
    A. excessive runout
    B. oil streaks radiating outward
    C. cracks or other damage to the bonding ring
    D. The outer weight has shifted in relation to the hub.

18. A diesel engine with piston oil cooling nozzles is being rebuilt. Technician A says the nozzles should be removed and inspected during disassembly. Technician B says they must be aligned during installation. Who is right?
    A. Technician A only
    B. Technician B only
    C. Both A and B
    D. Neither A or B

19. When installing a wet cylinder sleeve, which of the following should the technician do if the sleeve height is not within specifications?
    A. Replace the sleeve.
    B. Install new O-rings or seals.
    C. Install a shim at the bottom of the sleeve.
    D. Install a shim under the flange of the sleeve.

20. The oil pressure warning light remains on when a diesel engine is running. What should the technician do next?
    A. Check the oil pressure with an accurate oil pressure gauge.
    B. Test the oil pressure warning light circuit.
    C. Replace the oil pressure switch.
    D. Check the engine oil level.

21. An oil bypass valve will open under all of the following conditions EXCEPT:
    A. when the engine is cold
    B. when engine oil pressure is excessive
    C. if the oil filter is clogged
    D. if the oil cooler is clogged

22. There is a milky gray sludge in the radiator of a diesel engine vehicle and the engine oil is milky. All of the following could be the cause EXCEPT:
    A. defective oil cooler
    B. blown head gasket
    C. defective water pump bearings
    D. cracked cylinder head

23. A technician partially drains a diesel engine vehicle's cooling system to replace an upper radiator hose. After the repair, he tops off the cooling system with a 50/50 mix of IAT (Inorganic Technology) antifreeze and water. However, the owner's manual states that the vehicle requires HOAT (Hybrid Organic Additive Technology) antifreeze. Technician A says the vehicle could now overheat and not have enough freeze protection. Technician B says the coolant must be changed sooner. Who is right?
    A. Technician A only
    B. Technician B only
    C. Both A and B
    D. Neither A or B

24. When an oil pump is disassembled, the oil pressure relief valve piston is found to be scored and will not move easily in its bore. If this piston were to be reused, Technician A says it would cause excessive oil pressure. Technician B says it would cause low or no oil pressure. Who is right?
    A. Technician A only
    B. Technician B only
    C. Both A and B
    D. Neither A or B

Prepare yourself for ASE testing with these questions on
LIGHT VEHICLE DIESEL ENGINES

25. A radiator is being scanned with an infrared thermometer while the engine is running. The radiator is warmest near the inlet and cool toward the outlet, but there are also areas that are considerably cooler than the inlet. This could be caused by:
   A. bugs
   B. leaves
   C. debris
   D. mineral buildup

26. A diesel engine is leaking oil and when tested, is found to have excessive crankcase pressure. Technician A says the excessive crankcase pressure could be caused by worn rings. Technician B says it could be caused by a restricted crankcase breather tube. Who is right?
   A. Technician A only
   B. Technician B only
   C. Both A and B
   D. Neither A or B

27. All of the following can cause black smoke from a diesel's exhaust EXCEPT:
   A. dirty air filter
   B. leaking injectors
   C. restricted charge air cooler
   D. low fuel pressure

28. A diesel engine vehicle's air intake system is being inspected. Technician A says the air filter appears dirty and should be replaced. Technician B says the air filter should be replaced based on intake restriction specifications. Who is right?
   A. Technician A only
   B. Technician B only
   C. Both A and B
   D. Neither A or B

29. All of the following could cause insufficient boost from a turbocharger EXCEPT:
   A. an exhaust leak downstream from the turbine
   B. a hole in the charge air cooler
   C. a clogged air filter
   D. debris in the air inlet

30. A diesel engine vehicle is using excessive amounts of oil and has blue smoke coming from the exhaust. There is also abnormal noise coming from the turbocharger and oil stains around the turbocharger housing. Which of the following is the MOST Likely cause?
   A. worn piston rings
   B. worn valve guides
   C. worn turbocharger seals
   D. clogged air filter

31. A vehicle with a diesel engine has experienced repeated glow plug failure. Technician A says the cause could be a defective glow plug relay. Technician B says the condition could be due to a faulty control module. Who is right?
   A. Technician A only
   B. Technician B only
   C. Both A and B
   D. Neither A or B

32. On a diesel engine vehicle with a vacuum controlled EGR valve, the PCM/ECM detects a lower than desired EGR vacuum sensor signal and a higher than expected MAF (Mass Air Flow) rate. The PCM/ECM sets a DTC for EGR Open Position Performance. All of the following could be the cause EXCEPT:
   A. vacuum leaks in the EGR control system vacuum lines
   B. restrictions in the EGR control system vacuum lines
   C. defective EGR valve vacuum control solenoid
   D. defective EGR throttle valve

33. The PCM/ECM on a diesel engine vehicle has detected insufficient EGR flow and set a DTC. The EGR valve is electronically controlled and the engine has a sensor that detects manifold temperature. With the key on, engine off, the technician commands the EGR valve while monitoring the EGR valve position sensor parameters. Based on this test, the technician determines that the EGR valve can respond to commands. However, when the EGR valve is commanded while driving on the highway at a steady cruise, there is no increase in manifold air temperature. Which of the following could be the cause?
   A. restricted air intake
   B. clogged intake manifold EGR passages
   C. insufficient boost pressure
   D. defective EGR valve

Prepare yourself for ASE testing with these questions on
LIGHT VEHICLE DIESEL ENGINES

34. A diesel engine vehicle is overheating, using coolant and blowing coolant out of the reservoir. Technician A says the cooling system should be pressure tested to determine the problem. Technician B says the coolant should be tested for the presence of combustion gases. Who is right?
   A. Technician A only
   B. Technician B only
   C. Both A and B
   D. Neither A or B

35. The strategy used by most manufacturers of light-duty diesel engine vehicles sold in the U.S. to remove the soot collected by the Diesel Particulate Filter (DPF) is called _____ regeneration.
   A. active
   B. passive
   C. manual
   D. occasional

36. When the regeneration process is being monitored by the PCM/ECM, which of the following conditions is it looking for?
   A. a rise in temperature and a rise in pressure
   B. a rise in temperature and a decrease in pressure
   C. a decrease in temperature and a rise in pressure
   D. a decrease in temperature and a decrease in pressure

37. Over a period of time, the PCM/ECM sees a gradual increase in pressure drop values. This means that the DPF_____.
   A. must be replaced
   B. has become contaminated
   C. must be removed and cleaned
   D. is missing

38. A diesel engine starts but will not stay running. Technician A suspects air in the system. Technician B says air in the system can be found using a clear hose installed at the return side of the injection pump. Who is right?
   A. Technician A only
   B. Technician B only
   C. Both A and B
   D. Neither A or B

39. A diesel engine vehicle has higher than specified fuel pressure at idle. Technician A says a clogged fuel return could be the cause. Technician B says that a faulty fuel pump could be the cause. Who is right?
   A. Technician A only
   B. Technician B only
   C. Both A and B
   D. Neither A or B

40. Low fuel volume can be caused by a defective fuel pump or:
   A. a defective fuel pump relay
   B. a clogged fuel filter
   C. a defective injector driver
   D. defective fuel injectors

41. A high mileage vehicle with an electronically controlled common rail diesel engine and a manual transmission will not start. When it was last driven, the customer said it was running rough and making a knocking sound that went away when the clutch pedal was depressed. Technician A says the cause of the no-start could be a leaking injector. Technician B says the cause could be a problem with the Crankshaft Position (CKP) sensor. Who is right?
   A. Technician A only
   B. Technician B only
   C. Both A and B
   D. Neither A or B

42. During an injector cutout test, there is very little engine speed change when the injector in cylinder number 6 is turned off. Technician A says to replace the injector on cylinder number 6. Technician B says to perform a compression test on cylinder number 6. Who is right?
   A. Technician A only
   B. Technician B only
   C. Both A and B
   D. Neither A or B

43. A high mileage vehicle with a HEUI diesel engine won't start. While cranking, the fuel pressure is 60 psi and the injector oil pressure is less than 500 psi. All of the following could be the cause EXCEPT:
   A. a defective CMP sensor
   B. a leak in the high-pressure oil system
   C. excessive engine bearing clearance
   D. defective fuel pump

Prepare yourself for ASE testing with these questions on
LIGHT VEHICLE DIESEL ENGINES

44. Technician A says in an Electronic Unit Injector (EUI) fuel system, the injection pressure is created by the force provided by the engine's camshaft, but the quantity of fuel injected is controlled by the PCM/ECM powering the injector solenoid. Technician B says in a Pump-Line-Nozzle fuel system, the injection pump creates the high pressure necessary for injection and also controls the injection timing. Who is right?

    A. Technician A only
    B. Technician B only
    C. Both A and B
    D. Neither A or B

45. Which of the following sensors would the PCM/ECM monitor for an individual cylinder problem?

    A. MAF sensor
    B. IAT sensor
    C. CKP sensor
    D. ICP sensor

46. Which of the following tools can be used to check for a misfire?

    A. voltmeter
    B. pressure tester
    C. vacuum tester
    D. infrared thermometer

47. An ECT sensor is being tested. Technician A says that the resistance should be checked on an NTC (Negative Temperature Coefficient) sensor. Technician B says that the voltage drop across the sensor should be checked on this type of sensor. Who is right?

    A. Technician A only
    B. Technician B only
    C. Both A and B
    D. Neither A or B

48. To test a MAF sensor, a technician should check:

    A. resistance
    B. voltage drop
    C. current draw
    D. frequency output

Sensor	0 Pedal Travel	100% Pedal Travel
APP 1	0.9 volts	2.1 volts
APP 2	4.1 volts	2.9 volts
APP 3	3.9 volts	3.2 volts

49. The table shown above represents voltage specifications for an Accelerator Pedal Position (APP) sensor. However, when the vehicle's sensor output is checked with a voltmeter, only APP 3 performs according to specification. Based on this the PCM/ECM should _____.

    A. set a DTC, turn on the MIL and allow normal operation
    B. set a DTC, turn on the MIL and let the engine idle only
    C. not let the vehicle start
    D. set a DTC, turn on the MIL but not allow speeds over 25 mph

50. The PCM/ECM on a diesel engine vehicle must be reprogrammed with a new software calibration to solve a driveability complaint. Technician A says a stand-alone PC should be used. Technician B says the PC in the shop used for diagnostic information and internet access can be used. Who is right?

    A. Technician A only
    B. Technician B only
    C. Both A and B
    D. Neither A or B

Answers to Study-Guide Test Questions

1. The correct answer is D. It makes no sense to do any of the other things before finding out as much detail about the customer's complaint. Then take the vehicle for a road test. In some cases, a driveability complaint may turn out to be nothing more than a customer's unrealistic expectation of their vehicle's performance capabilities, particularly if their vehicle is new and unfamiliar to them.

2. The correct answer is B. Very often, driveability complaints can be resolved by 'reflashing' the PCM/ECM. The technician should check TSBs, which will list the old and new calibration numbers. He can then compare this information with the calibration number found by the scan tool to see if reprogramming is necessary.

3. The correct answer is C. Monitors shown as 'not ready' or 'incomplete' means that either the drive cycle criteria have not been met and the monitor isn't finished or a related monitor has recorded a fault. Answer A is wrong because if the monitor were not used on that particular vehicle, 'NA' or 'not available' would be displayed. Answers B and D are wrong because only a monitor that has run to completion can indicate a failure, and only when a failure has occurred will a fault be recorded in the PCM/ECM's memory. For some faults, the PCM/ ECM will set a DTC and turn on the MIL (Malfunction Indicator Light) or CHECK ENGINE light. However, for most DTCs the PCM/ECM must see the same fault occur during two 'trips'. A trip is a completed drive cycle. After the first trip, the fault is recorded as 'pending'. Once the PCM/ECM sees the same fault the next time the monitor runs, the PCM will turn on the MIL. If the same fault is not seen during the next monitor, the pending code will be cleared.

4. The correct answer is A. Leaky injectors would richen the air/fuel mixture and cause black smoke. All of the other answers are possible causes of white smoke from a diesel's exhaust. A lean condition can cause white smoke and dirty injectors can cause a lean condition. White smoke can also occur when there is not enough heat to burn the fuel, such as would occur during a cold start with bad glow plugs. The unburned fuel particles go out the exhaust and appear as white smoke.

5. The correct answer is B. Crankshaft end-play noise occurs when there is excessive clearance between the crankshaft thrust bearing and the machined faces of the crankshaft thrust journal, allowing the crankshaft to move back and forth. When crankshaft end-play is excessive, the engine may make a deep knocking sound that is usually most obvious at idle but diminishes when a load is placed on the crankshaft, such as when the clutch is disengaged on a manual transmission vehicle. Technician A is wrong because, if the knock was caused by excessive main bearing clearance, it would not go away when the clutch pedal was depressed.

6. The correct answer is D. Insufficient turbo boost could cause a lack of power and could in turn be caused by a clogged air filter or other air intake restriction, air leaks downstream from the compressor, damage to the compressor from dirt or lubrication failure, or wastegate malfunction. If the PCM/ECM did not receive a CMP signal or if the minimum injector oil pressure specification were below the level at which the injectors would be enabled, the engine would not even start.

7. The correct answer is C, both technicians are right. A cylinder compression test is shown in the illustration. When compression is low in two adjacent cylinders, the head gasket may be blown or the block cracked between those two cylinders.

8. The correct answer is A. There are different grades and ratings for diesel fuel. Number 2 grade is the standard fuel and is used during the summer months. All diesel fuels have what are called 'cloud' and 'pour' points. The cloud point refers to the temperature at which the fuel begins to thicken and 'cloud'. The pour point is the temperature at which the fuel will no longer flow. Using Number 1 grade fuel, which has a lower pour point, or a mixture of grade's 1 and 2, in the colder, winter months can aid starting. All of the other answers are possible causes of slow cranking and not starting.

9. The correct answer is C. Decreased circuit resistance will cause excessive current draw. The decreased resistance could be caused by a short circuit in the starter motor.

10. The correct answer is C. The distance between the arrows is the valve depression measurement. It is critical that this dimension be maintained within specifications; if the valve extends too far into the combustion chamber it could contact a piston and if the valve is sunk too far in the head it will impede the combustion process. A new valve should have more meat on the valve face and a larger margin than a used one that has been refaced. This added thickness may be enough to bring the measurement within specification. The technician should install the new valve and measure. Answer D, replacing the valve seat, would also serve to reduce the measurement, but trying a new valve first is less expensive and far less labor intensive. Answers A and B are wrong because refacing the valve or machining the seat would only make the situation worse by increasing the measurement.

11. The correct answer is C. Vacuum testing is a quick way to determine if a head is cracked or porous, but it will not indicate the source of the leak. To find a leaking injector sleeve, the head should be pressure tested. Answers A and B are wrong because they are methods of crack detection.

12. The correct answer is C. The piston-to-cylinder head clearance specification must be maintained to ensure the piston does not contact the cylinder head or valves. To ensure this clearance, the piston protrusion must be measured and the head gasket selected accordingly. Piston protrusion measurements from each cylinder should be averaged, and then the highest averaged measurement used to determine the head gasket that should be used. The highest piston is in cylinder No. 4, where the averaged height of the piston is 0.0129 inches. Therefore, gasket grade C should be used.

13. The correct answer is A. Valve stem installed height will not be affected by resurfacing a cylinder head. Valve protrusion/depression will be affected because resurfacing will change the distance between the valve and the cylinder head gasket surface. Injector tip protrusion will be increased if the cylinder head is resurfaced and must be adjusted using shim gaskets or by replacing the injector sleeve. Piston protrusion will be indirectly affected in that the actual protrusion dimension will not be affected. However, the manufacturer recommends the appropriate head gasket thickness based on the assumption that the cylinder head is at factory specifications. Resurfacing will reduce the clearance between the piston crown and the roof of the combustion chamber and the valves.

14. The correct answer is D. The components indicated in the illustration are precombustion chambers. A certain amount of cracking in the precombustion chambers is generally acceptable; however always refer to the manufacturer's service information. All of the other answers are true statements regarding precombustion chambers.

15. The correct answer is A. If the clutch surface of a dual mass flywheel is damaged or warped, in most cases it cannot be resurfaced. However, the ring gear can be removed and replaced on some flywheels. The old ring gear is heated evenly with a torch and then removed with a hammer and punch. The replacement ring gear is also heated, being careful not to get it so hot that it turns blue or red, and then installed using a hammer and brass punch.

16. The correct answer is D. Answer A is wrong because only dry sleeves require a puller; wet sleeves can be pulled out by hand. Answer B is wrong because the sleeve seals can be damaged during the block cleaning process. Answer C is wrong because the counterbore depth is measured with a depth micrometer or dial indicator.

17. The correct answer is B. Oil streaks radiating outward could be a sign that a viscous damper was leaking fluid and should be replaced. However, the same streaks on a rubber-bonded damper would indicate a leaking crankshaft seal. In this case the seal should be replaced and, if the seal contact area on the damper flange is grooved, a wear sleeve installed. All of the other answers are defects that would require vibration damper replacement.

18. The correct answer is C, both technicians are right. Because of extremely high combustion temperatures, most diesel engines are equipped with piston cooling nozzles. These are usually fastened or pressed into the block, and must usually be removed before the pistons and connecting rods can be removed. Inspect the nozzles for damage and clogging, and clean or replace as necessary. When installing the nozzles, make sure each one is aligned properly to accurately direct the oil to the bottom of the piston. Improper alignment can cause insufficient lubrication and engine damage.

Answers to Study-Guide Test Questions

19. The correct answer is D. To ensure proper sealing, sleeves must be installed so the protrusion is within the manufacturer's specifications. The sleeve height is adjusted by installing a shim under the sleeve flange. Answer A is wrong because replacement is not necessary to correct protrusion. Answer C is wrong because the shim is not placed at the bottom of the sleeve. Answer B is wrong because the O-rings or seals are installed to seal the coolant passages and have no affect on sleeve height.

20. The correct answer is D. It makes little sense to do anything else before making sure there is enough oil in the engine. Once that is established, then check the oil pressure with an accurate gauge to see if it really is low enough to turn on the light. If the oil pressure is normal, then test the warning light circuit. The switch should only be replaced if testing indicates that it is the part of the circuit that is defective.

21. The correct answer is B. If oil pressure exceeds a preset limit, an oil pressure relief valve will open and allow pressure to bleed off. Bypass valves permit oil flow to the engine if the oil filter and/or oil cooler become clogged. An oil filter bypass valve opens when the engine is first started to allow the cold oil, which will not easily pass through the filter, to flow to the engine. When the oil warms up, the bypass valve closes and filtration resumes.

22. The correct answer is C. These symptoms indicate engine oil has contaminated the cooling system and coolant has combined with the engine oil. This can only happen when a component fails that affects both systems. The most obvious and the first place to look is the engine oil cooler. The oil circulates through the oil cooler, and coolant flow within the plates is used to keep the oil at an acceptable operating temperature. If the oil cooler becomes damaged, corrodes or otherwise fails internally, the engine oil can become contaminated with coolant and oil can enter the cooling system. A blown head gasket or cracked cylinder head can expose oil and coolant passages to one another and cause the same migration. Defective water pump bearings could be noisy, cause a coolant leak or cause the engine to overheat if the impeller failed, but they could not cause the symptoms indicated because the bearings are not connected to the engine lubrication system.

23. The correct answer is B. The additives used in IAT antifreeze to protect against corrosion are inorganic. However, these additives deplete quickly, which is why it is necessary to frequently change this type of coolant. HOAT antifreeze uses both silicate and organic acid corrosion inhibitors for extended service life. Most experts say that mixing coolant will not cause any damaging chemical reactions and the coolant will still carry away heat and protect against freezing. However, mixing some types will affect the service life. OAT (Organic Additive Technology) and HOAT are considered long life coolants. If IAT coolant is mixed with either, the change interval will degrade to that of a shorter life coolant. Therefore, Technician B is right. Also, when the coolant is changed the system should be flushed to ensure that only one type of antifreeze is then in the system.

24. The correct answer is C, both technicians are right. A scored oil pressure relief valve piston can stick in the bore, and depending on how it stuck, it could cause either condition. If it stuck in the closed position, excessive pressure would develop, causing oil leaks and possibly blowing out pressed-in oil gallery plugs or rupturing the oil filter. If the piston stuck in the open position, little or no oil pressure would develop, possibly causing serious engine damage.

25. The correct answer is D. Mineral buildup can cause an internal restriction. If blockage inside the radiator is suspected, an infrared surface thermometer can be used to scan the surface of the radiator when the engine is hot and idling. The radiator should be warmest near the inlet and gradually cool toward the outlet. If there are areas that are considerably cooler than the inlet, then there may be restrictions at those areas. Bugs, leaves and other debris could cause an obstruction on the outside of the radiator, but because this would be restricting the air instead of the coolant, those areas would most likely be warmer.

26. The correct answer is C, both technicians are right. Excessive crankcase pressure can be due to blowby caused by worn rings and cylinder walls and/or excessive piston-to-cylinder wall clearance. It can also be caused by a clogged breather tube. Usually, fresh air enters through the breather and then the air, along with the crankcase vapors, is routed to the intake duct, before the turbocharger, where it can mix with the incoming air and be burned in the engine. However, when the engine is under load there may be more crankcase gases than the system can handle and some

Answers to Study-Guide Test Questions

may escape back through the breather. Over time, this can clog the breather filter and cause excessive crankcase pressure, which can in turn cause oil leaks.

27. The correct answer is D. Low fuel pressure would cause a lean condition and would be indicated by white smoke. Black smoke is an indication of a rich running engine, and can be caused by either excessive fuel or insufficient air. Leaking injectors would provide excessive fuel, while a dirty air filter or a clogged charge air cooler would restrict airflow.

28. The correct answer is B. Air filters should be replaced solely on the basis of intake restriction specifications and not on visible condition. Restriction must be checked to ensure that air can flow freely through the induction system. Most diesel air intake systems are equipped with a restriction indicator, usually located on the air filter housing, however this should not be relied upon since it may not have been reset the last time the filter was replaced. The only way to be certain that intake restriction is within limitations is to measure it with a suitable tool, such as a water manometer.

29. The correct answer is A. A lack of boost pressure can be caused by a reduction in airflow entering the compressor or a loss of compressed air between the turbocharger and intake manifold, or by exhaust leaks upstream of the turbine or exhaust restrictions downstream, either of which would reduce exhaust gas energy. A hole in the charge air cooler would allow boost pressure to escape, reducing boost pressure, so answer B is wrong. A clogged air filter and debris in the air intake would both restrict airflow into the turbocharger and reduce boost pressure, so answers C and D are wrong. An exhaust leak downstream from the turbine would not reduce turbine speed, so boost pressure would not be affected. Therefore, answer A is right.

30. The correct answer is C. Blue smoke is caused by oil in the combustion process. A clogged air filter would cause a rich mixture and result in black smoke, so answer D is wrong. Worn valve guides, worn piston rings and defective turbocharger seals would all increase the amount of oil in the combustion process and cause blue smoke, but the turbocharger symptoms indicate that the turbocharger seals are most likely the cause of the smoke and increased oil consumption. Worn bearings can result in turbocharger seal failure

and would cause the rotating assembly to contact the turbo housing, causing noise and vibration.

31. The correct answer is C, both technicians are right. Glow plugs can burn out if they get too hot, which can happen if they are left on for too long. A relay that is stuck on or a control module with a faulty timer can cause glow plugs to remain on, overheat and burn out. If the relay or control module is not replaced, the replacement glow plugs will also burn out.

32. The correct answer is D. The PCM/ECM uses the MAF sensor to calculate the amount of exhaust gas that is consumed by the engine. When the EGR valve is opened, the MAF rate will decrease. When the PCM/ECM commands the EGR valve to open, the EGR throttle valve is commanded closed, creating a restriction in the air intake to produce a vacuum that allows EGR flow into the intake manifold. If the throttle valve were at fault and not closing, the MAF rate would be higher, but in this case the PCM/ECM has also detected a lower than desired EGR vacuum sensor signal. This is interpreted by the PCM/ECM as a vacuum problem that is causing the EGR valve to not open enough, which would also cause a high MAF rate. Answers A, B and C are all potential problems in the vacuum system; therefore answer D is right.

33. The correct answer is B. The indication that there is no increase in manifold air temperature means that there is no EGR flow. Answers A and C are wrong because, if anything, these defects would aid EGR flow. Answer D is wrong because it has been established that the EGR valve is able to respond to commands. Carbon buildup in the intake manifold EGR passages can restrict EGR flow, and if extensive, it may require manifold removal for a thorough cleaning. The carbon buildup can be due to extended idling and using poor quality fuel.

34. The correct answer is B. If the vehicle is using coolant, overheating or blowing coolant out of the reservoir, it could be because the EGR cooler is leaking. Pressure testing will probably show that there is a leak, but because the leak is internal, the test will not show the location. If the coolant is leaking into the combustion chamber, then combustion gases are also leaking into the cooling system. These can be detected by placing a vial of a chemical that is sensitive to combustion gases over the coolant reservoir opening while the engine is running. The chemical will change color in

Answers to Study-Guide Test Questions

the presence of combustion gases. If there is a positive indication of combustion gases, the next task is to determine whether it is the EGR cooler or a blown head gasket, cracked block, etc.

35. The correct answer is A. Passive regeneration is a strategy where increased exhaust backpressure, caused by the increase in soot, leads to an increase in temperature and the soot eventually ignites on its own. However, this strategy only works if the engine is under a constant heavy load and the exhaust temperature remains high. Most light-duty diesel engine vehicles are not operated this way and, in fact, spend much of their time idling or at low load, so this strategy is impractical. Therefore, answer B is wrong. Manual initiation of regeneration may be possible by a technician using a scan tool, but it is not a strategy for regeneration during normal vehicle operation, so answer C is wrong. There is no such thing as an occasional regeneration strategy so answer D is wrong. Active regeneration is initiated by the PCM/ECM on light-duty diesel engine vehicles when regeneration is required and only under certain conditions. The system monitors itself and provides feedback to the computer.

36. The correct answer is B. The regeneration process is monitored by the PCM/ECM using pressure sensors and temperature sensors, located at the DPF inlet and outlet. During regeneration, there should be a rise in temperature and a decrease in pressure across the DPF. This confirms that the regeneration process is working properly.

37. The correct answer is C. A gradual increase in pressure drop values after regeneration means that ash is collecting in the filter. The DPF must then be removed and manually cleaned. Replacement is not usually required and some manufacturers have exchange programs where a cleaned used DPF can be installed in place of one that is filled. A missing DPF would be indicated by a lower overall pressure drop.

38. The correct answer is C, both technicians are right. Dieing after starting, rough running, missing and white smoke in the exhaust are all symptoms of air in the fuel, so Technician A is right. To find out if air is the problem, a clear hose can be installed in the fuel return system. Crank the engine and observe the fuel in the hose. If bubbles can be seen, air is entering somewhere on the inlet side of the system. Technician B is also right.

39. The correct answer is A. A clogged return is like testing a fuel pump against a closed valve, and pressure will be higher than normal. A worn or faulty pump usually causes low pressure, and even a clogged pressure relief would not cause high pressure until higher rpm.

40. The correct answer is B. Defective fuel injectors will not affect fuel pump volume, and a fuel pump relay can only turn a fuel pump on or off. The injector drivers will affect injector operation. A clogged fuel filter will cause a restriction and have an effect on fuel pump volume.

41. The correct answer is C, both technicians are right. The cause of the rough running could have been a faulty injector. On a common rail injection system, all the injectors are dependent on the fuel pressure in a shared, common rail. If that injector is leaking, it could bleed off enough pressure to prevent engine starting, so Technician A is right. The cause of the knocking noise that went away when the clutch pedal was depressed is probably excessive crankshaft end-play, especially considering that this a well used vehicle. Excessive crankshaft end-play can cause the CKP sensor reluctor wheel to move out of alignment with the CKP sensor, causing a no-start. Therefore, Technician B is also right.

42. The correct answer is B. A cylinder cutout test is nothing more than a power balance test. While the injector could be the cause of the dead cylinder, general cylinder condition must first be verified since engine condition can cause the same defect in spite of a good fuel injector.

43. The correct answer is D. The fuel pump is generating enough pressure for the engine to start, so that is not the problem. However, less than 500 psi in the high-pressure oil system is not enough to enable the injectors. A failed CMP pressure could hold pressure below the threshold for starting. A leak in the high-pressure oil system could bleed off pressure and prevent starting. Finally, excessive bearing clearances could prevent the low-pressure oil system from developing enough pressure to supply the high-pressure system, starving it of oil.

44. The correct answer is C, both technicians are right. Electronic unit injectors are similar to hydraulic electronic unit injectors in that all the pressure neces-

Answers to Study-Guide Test Questions

sary for injection is created within the fuel injector. However, where the HEUI system uses oil pressure to create the pressure, the EUI system uses the force provided by the engine's camshaft. The PCM/ECM controls injector timing and duration, but injection can only take place when the injector is pressurized by the camshaft. The PCM/ECM controls the injector by supplying power to a solenoid located on the side of the injector. In the Pump-Line-Nozzle injection system, the pump creates the high pressure necessary for injection and also controls the injection timing. Fuel is delivered under high pressure through individual fuel lines to injection nozzles located on the cylinder head.

45. The correct answer is C. The PCM/ECM monitors changes in crankshaft speed using input from the Crankshaft Position (CKP) sensor. The computer adjusts the fuel delivery to each cylinder in order to minimize crankshaft speed changes. The PCM/ECM will set a DTC when it identifies a cylinder or cylinders requiring an excess amount of fuel in order to maintain the correct crankshaft speed.

46. The correct answer is D. If the engine is missing, first check the exhaust runners just after engine startup with an infrared thermometer. If an injector has failed, its cylinder will be cooler than the others.

47. The correct answer is C, both technicians are right. Resistance varies inversely with temperature on an NTC sensor. The sensor's function is usually checked by measuring the resistance between the sensor terminals. Most manufacturers publish resistance/temperature tables, but in general the resistance should be approximately 3000 ohms at room temperature (70°F, or 21°C). Start the engine, and as it warms up check that the values change smoothly. If the resistance value doesn't change, the sensor is probably defective. The sensor can also be checked by measuring voltage drop. More voltage is dropped across the sensor when it is cold, and less when hot. With the sensor installed, backprobe the sensor terminals with a voltmeter connected across the sensor terminals. Compare the voltage readings at various temperatures with the manufacturer's voltage/temperature table. The voltage drop can also be seen using a scan tool.

48. The correct answer is D. The MAF sensor uses a hot wire sensing element to measure the amount of air entering the engine. Air passing over the hot wire causes it to cool. The hot wire is maintained at a certain temperature above ambient temperature as measured by a constant cold wire. The current required to maintain the temperature of the hot wire is proportional to the mass airflow. The MAF sensor outputs a frequency signal to the PCM/ECM proportional to the air mass. The sensor can be tested with a DMM or an oscilloscope. The DMM should be set to read the frequency of DC voltage. Connect the meter and record the readings as the engine speed is gradually increased. When plotted on a graph, the results from a properly functioning sensor should show a smooth and gradual increase in relation to engine speed. The waveform on a scope should appear as a series of square waves. The frequency should increase smoothly and proportionately when engine speed and intake airflow is increased. If the frequency is erratic, the MAF or circuit wiring is defective.

49. The correct answer is B. Many diesel engine vehicles use a system commonly called 'drive by wire'. In this system there is no physical connection between the accelerator pedal and the engine, but rather sensors are attached to the pedal, which signal its position to the PCM/ECM. There may be as many as three individual sensors included in one housing. Typically, as the pedal is depressed, the voltage signal from one sensor should increase at a certain rate, while the remaining two sensors' signals should decrease. Usually, if one sensor's signal does not agree with the other two, a DTC will be set and the MIL will illuminate, but the vehicle will still operate normally. However, if two signals are lost a code will be set, the MIL will come on and the PCM/ECM will only allow the engine to idle.

50. The correct answer is A. Interrupting reprogramming can cause the process to fail and possibly ruin the PCM/ECM. To avoid this, a stand-alone PC or laptop should be used, instead of one that is also used for other jobs in the shop. Other computer processes can interrupt or stop the reprogramming process. If the shop computer must be used, pop-up blockers, virus protection and firewall software must be turned off and email programs, screensavers and all other automatic processes should be disabled.

Glossary of Terms

--a--

abrasion - rubbing away or wearing of a part.

abrasive cleaning - cleaning that requires physical abrasion (e.g., glass bead blasting, wire brushing).

accelerator pedal position (APP) sensor - a sensor or sensors that signals the accelerator pedal position to the PCM/ECM. Used in so-called 'drive-by-wire' systems where there is no physical connection between the accelerator pedal and the engine.

actuator - any device controlled by the PCM/ECM, such as an injector or relay. Most actuators are controlled by low-side (ground) drivers in the PCM/ECM.

air duct - a tube, channel or other tubular structure used to carry air to a specific location.

air gap - space or gap between motor and generator armatures and field shoes.

air restriction indicator - also known as a filter minder, it is usually located on the air cleaner housing. A part of the indicator changes color when air filter replacement is necessary. After filter replacement, the indicator is reset.

align boring - a machining method that realigns bearing bores to center and makes the bores round.

alignment - an adjustment to bring into a line.

alloy - a mixture of different metals (e.g., solder, an alloy consisting of lead and tin).

alternating current (AC) - electrical current that flows in one direction, from positive to negative, and then reverses direction, from negative to positive.

alternator - a belt driven device that provides electrical current for the vehicle's charging system.

aluminum - a lightweight metal used often for cylinder heads and other parts.

ambient temperature - the temperature of the air surrounding an object.

American Petroleum Institute (API) - U.S. trade association for the oil and natural gas industry; advocates and negotiates with governmental, legal and regulatory agencies, researches economic, toxilogical and environmental effects, and establishes and certifies industry standards. Mostly known in the automotive service industry for establishing the specifications motor oils must meet.

ammeter - instrument used to measure electrical current flow in a circuit.

amperage - the amount of electrical current flowing in a circuit.

antifreeze - usually ethylene glycol, but sometimes propylene glycol, based liquid that is mixed with water to form coolant. Also contains various corrosion inhibitor packages depending on the manufacturer.

--b--

battery - a device that produces electricity through electrochemical action.

battery acid - the sulfuric acid solution used as the electrolyte in a battery.

battery cell - the part of a storage battery made from two dissimilar metals and an acid solution. A cell stores chemical energy to be used later as electrical energy.

bearing - part that supports and reduces friction between a stationary and moving part or two moving parts.

bearing cap - the lower half of the bearing saddle. It is removable, as in main cap or rod cap.

bearing clearance - the space between a bearing and its corresponding component's loaded surface. Bearing clearances are commonly provided to allow lubrication between the parts.

bearing crush - the bearing is slightly larger at its parting lines so that when the two halves of the bearing are tightened together, the bearing seats firmly in its bore. This keeps the bearing from rotating.

bearing lining - the bearing surface area of a bearing, it is usually made up of an alloy of several metals, including lead.

Glossary of Terms

bearing race - machined circular surface of a bearing against which the roller or ball bearings ride.

bearing spread - the condition in which the distance across the outside parting edges of the bearing insert is slightly greater than the diameter of the housing bore.

blowby - the unburned fuel and products of combustion that leak past the piston rings and into the crankcase at the last part of the combustion stroke.

boost pressure - term used when a turbocharger increases the air pressure entering an engine above atmospheric pressure

bore - a cylindrical hole.

bore gauge - a precision measuring instrument used to measure the diameter of a bore.

boss - the part of a piston that fits around its pin.

bottom dead center (BDC) - when the piston is at its lower limit in the cylinder bore.

break-in - a slow wearing-in process between two mating part surfaces.

--c--

California Air Resources Board (CARB) - a regulatory agency in the state of California that conducts research, monitors air quality, sets health based air quality standards and sets and enforces emission standards for motor vehicles, fuels and consumer products.

camshaft - a shaft with eccentric lobes that control the opening of the intake and exhaust valves.

camshaft bearing - a bearing that supports the camshaft journal. On some engines it is full round and pressed in place. On some OHC engines the camshaft bearing is made up of two shells like a connecting rod bearing.

camshaft follower - on OHC engines the equivalent of a rocker arm.

camshaft journal - the bearing area of a camshaft.

camshaft lobe - the eccentric on a camshaft that acts on lifters or followers and in turn, other valvetrain components as the camshaft is rotated, to open the intake and exhaust valves.

camshaft position (CMP) sensor - a hall-effect sensor that provides engine speed and position information to the PCM/ECM.

camshaft sprocket - the sprocket on a camshaft that is turned by a chain or belt from the crankshaft. The camshaft sprocket has twice as many teeth as the crankshaft sprocket.

carbon - a hard or soft nonmetallic element that forms in an engine's combustion chamber when oil is burned.

carbon dioxide (CO$_2$) - a colorless, odorless, noncombustible gas, heavier than air; can be compressed into a super-cold solid known as dry ice; changes from solid to vapor at -78.5˚C.

carbon monoxide (CO) - a colorless, odorless gas, which is highly poisonous. CO is produced by incomplete combustion. It is absorbed by the bloodstream 400 times faster than oxygen.

Celsius - the basis of the metric system of temperature measurement in which water's boiling point is 100ºC and its freezing point is 0ºC.

cetane - the measurement of the combustion quality of diesel fuel. The cetane number represents the fuel's ignition delay, the time period between the start of injection and the start of combustion. A fuel with a higher cetane rating has a shorter ignition delay period than a one with a lower rating.

charge air cooler - also known as an intercooler or aftercooler; a device that cools the air coming from the turbocharger before it enters the engine. There are air-to-liquid coolers, that use engine coolant, but the most widely used type is the air-to-air cooler.

chemical cleaning - relies primarily on chemical action to remove dirt, grease, scale, paint or rust.

cloud point - the temperature at which diesel fuel begins to thicken and 'cloud'.

cold cranking amps (CCA) - the amount of cranking amperes that a battery can deliver in 30 seconds at 0˚F (−18˚C).

combustion - the burning of the air/fuel mixture.

combustion chamber - enclosure formed by a pocket in the cylinder head and the top of the piston, where the

Glossary of Terms

fuel is injected and ignites with the compressed air. The volume of the cylinder above the piston when the piston is at TDC.

common rail fuel system - a diesel fuel injection system that uses a high-pressure injection pump, which pumps fuel to a tube called a rail. All the fuel injectors on one cylinder bank are attached to this common rail, from whence the system gets its name. The fuel injectors are solenoid operated and injector timing and rate of injection is controlled by the PCM/ECM.

comparator gauge - a metal card with sample patches of various surface textures to visually compare with a milled or ground surface.

compression - in a solid material, compression is the opposite of tension. In a gas, compression causes the gas to be confined in a smaller area, raising its temperature and pressure.

compression ratio - ratio of the volume in the cylinder above the piston when the piston is at bottom dead center to the volume in the cylinder above the piston when the piston is at top dead center.

compression rings - usually the top two rings on a piston, they form a seal between the piston and cylinder wall to compress the air/fuel mixture in the cylinder.

compression stroke - the second stroke of the 4-stroke engine cycle, in which the piston moves from bottom dead center and the intake valve is closed, trapping and compressing the air in the cylinder.

conductor - a material that provides a path for the flow of electrical current or heat.

connecting rod - a rod that connects the crankshaft to the piston and enables the reciprocating motion of the piston to turn the crankshaft.

connecting rod bearings - the plain bearing shells located in the big end of the connecting rod that support the connecting rod and piston on the crankshaft.

connecting rod cap - the removable part of the big end of the connecting rod.

continuity - the condition that exists in a working electrical circuit. A circuit that is unbroken, not open.

coolant - mixture of water and antifreeze that circulates through the engine to help maintain proper temperatures.

cooling fan - a mechanically or electrically driven propeller that draws air through the radiator.

cooling system - the system used to remove excess heat from an engine and transfer it to the atmosphere. Includes the radiator, cooling fan, hoses, water pump, thermostat and engine coolant passages.

core - in automotive terminology, the main part of a heat exchanger, such as a radiator, evaporator or heater. Usually made of tubes, surrounded by cooling fins, used to transfer heat from the coolant to the air.

core plugs - plugs that fill holes in a block or head left from the casting process. Also called freeze, welsh or expansion plugs.

corrode - gradual loss from a metal surface from chemical action.

corrosion - the eating into or wearing away of a substance gradually by rusting or chemical action.

corrosivity - the characteristic of a material that enables it to dissolve metals and other materials or burn the skin.

counterbore - to enlarge a hole to a given depth.

countersink - to cut or form a depression to allow the head of a screw to go below the surface.

counterweight - weights that are part of a crankshaft casting or forging. They counterbalance the weight of the connecting rods and journals to reduce vibration.

crankcase - the lower part of an engine block that houses the crankshaft.

crankshaft - a lower engine part with main and rod bearing journals. It converts reciprocating motion to rotary motion.

crankshaft position (CKP) sensor - a hall-effect sensor that provides crankshaft speed and position information to the PCM/ECM.

current - the flow or rate of flow of an electric charge through a conductor or medium between two points having a different potential, expressed in amperes.

cylinder - a round hole in the engine block for the piston.

cylinder bore - a cylindrical hole.

cylinder head - the casting that contains the valves and valve springs, and covers the top of the cylinders.

cylinder leakage test - an engine diagnostic test where the piston in the cylinder to be tested is brought to top dead center (TDC) on the compression stroke and compressed air is pumped into the cylinder through the injector or glow plug hole. Where the air leaks out shows the location of the compression leak. A leakage tester will compare the air leaking out of the cylinder to the amount of air being put into it, expressed as a percentage.

cylinder power balance test - an engine diagnostic test used to compare the power output of all the engine's cylinders. Also known as a power contribution test.

cylinder sleeve - a replacement iron liner that fits into a cylinder bore. It can be either wet or dry. The outside diameter of wet sleeves contacts the coolant.

cylinder walls - the walls of the cylinder bore.

--d--

diagnostic link connector (DLC) - a means through which information about the state of the vehicle control system can be extracted with a scan tool. This information includes actual readouts on each sensor's input circuit and some actuator signals. It also includes any trouble codes stored. Before OBD II, each OEM had a unique data link connector and called it by a different name. With the advent of OBD II, the DLC became standardized as a 16-pin connector to which the scan tool could be connected to read data and sometimes control outputs of the PCM/ECM.

diagnostic trouble code (DTC) - a code that represents and can be used to identify a malfunction in a computer control system.

diesel oxidation catalyst (DOC) - a catalyst located in the exhaust system of late-model electronically controlled diesel engine vehicles that oxidizes Hydrocarbon (HC) and Carbon Monoxide (CO) molecules in the exhaust gases. Often combined with the Diesel Particulate Filter (DPF) for regeneration purposes.

diesel particulate filter (DPF) - a filter located in the exhaust system of late-model electronically controlled diesel engine vehicles. The filter allows exhaust gases to flow, but collects the particulate matter, or 'soot'. The DPF is monitored by the PCM/ECM via temperature and pressure sensors located at the inlet and outlet. An increase in pressure between the inlet and outlet sensors means that the DPF is filling up with soot and must be 'regenerated'. Regeneration is accomplished by raising the exhaust gas temperature. Exhaust gas temperature is raised by the Diesel Oxidation Catalyst (DOC), which is often packaged with the DPF, and sometimes by introducing fuel into the exhaust stream ahead of the DOC. The increased exhaust temperature burns off the accumulated soot and lowers backpressure in the exhaust system. The temperature sensors provide feedback to the PCM/ECM on the regeneration process.

diode - a simple semiconductor device that permits flow of electricity in one direction but not the other.

discharge - the flow of current from a battery; to remove the refrigerant from an air conditioning system.

driveability - the degree to which a vehicle operates properly, including starting, running smoothly, accelerating and delivering reasonable fuel mileage.

dry sleeve - a sleeve, that when installed in a cylinder block, does not come into contact with coolant.

duration - the length of time that a valve remains open, measured in crankshaft degrees.

dye penetrant - a method of crack detection. Dye is sprayed on the surface and allowed to dry. Then the excess is wiped from the surface. A developer is sprayed on to make the cracks visible. A black light can be used with some dyes for greater visibility.

dykem blue - a dye that is painted on a valve seat in order to determine seat concentricity. The valve is inserted into the guide, lightly seated, and rotated about 1/8-in. (3.175mm). A continuous blue line should appear all the way around the valve face if the valve and seat are mating properly. Open patches or breaks in the line indicate that the seat is not concentric and the low spots are not making contact.

--e--

EEPROM - an acronym for Electrically Erasable Programmable Read Only Memory; a type of computer memory that can be reprogrammed.

electrolysis - chemical and electrical decomposition process that can damage metals such as brass, copper and aluminum in the cooling system.

electrolyte - a material whose atoms become ionized (electrically charged) in solution. In automobiles, the battery electrolyte is a mixture of sulfuric acid and water.

electronic unit injector (EUI) - a type of diesel fuel injector where all the pressure necessary for injection is created within the injector with the force provided by the engine's camshaft. The PCM/ECM controls injector timing and duration, but injection can only take place when the injector is pressurized by the camshaft. The PCM/ECM controls the injector by supplying power to a solenoid located on the side of the injector.

embedability - the ability of the bearing lining material to absorb dirt.

enable criteria - a specific set of conditions that must be met in order for the PCM/ECM to run an OBD II monitor.

end-play - the amount of axial or end-to-end movement in a shaft due to clearance in the bearings.

energy - the ability to do work.

engine - a device that converts heat energy into mechanical energy.

engine block - the casting made up of cylinders and the crankcase.

engine control module (ECM) - the electronic computer that controls engine operation. ECM is synonymous with ECA and ECU. It is less powerful than the PCM (Powertrain Control Module) or VCM (Vehicle Control Module) in that it controls only engine operation.

engine coolant temperature (ECT) sensor - a sensor that works by a negative coefficient thermistor, which loses resistance as its temperature goes up (just like the intake air temperature sensor). When the computer applies its 5-volt reference signal to the sensor, this voltage is reduced through a ground circuit by an amount corresponding to the temperature of the engine coolant.

engine displacement - calculated by multiplying the number of cylinders in the engine with the bore diameter and the length of the stroke.

engine oil temperature (EOT) sensor - a sensor that works by a negative coefficient thermistor, which loses resistance as its temperature goes up (just like the engine coolant temperature sensor). When the computer applies its 5-volt reference signal to the sensor, this voltage is reduced through a ground circuit by an amount corresponding to the temperature of the engine oil.

Environmental Protection Agency (EPA) - U.S. agency that ensures that Federal environmental laws are implemented and effectively enforced.

exhaust backpressure sensor - a 3-wire variable capacitance sensor that is supplied a 5-volt reference signal by the PCM/ECM and returns a linear analog voltage signal that indicates pressure. The PCM/ECM uses the exhaust backpressure signal to control exhaust gas recirculation and on some applications, turbocharger actuation.

exhaust gas recirculation (EGR) cooler - a device that cools the exhaust before it enters the EGR valve, to prevent a loss of air charge density. Engine coolant flows through the EGR cooler and absorbs heat from the exhaust before going to the EGR valve.

exhaust gas recirculation (EGR) cooler outlet temperature sensor - a sensor that provides an input top the PCM/ECM, which uses the sensor's signal to control EGR valve position and throttle valve position.

exhaust gas recirculation (EGR) system - helps prevent the formation of oxides of nitrogen (NOx) by recirculating a certain amount of exhaust as an inert gas through the intake manifold to keep the peak combustion temperatures below what would form those chemical compounds. The computer determines when and how much exhaust to recirculate based on information from all its other sensors. It then actuates the EGR solenoid, which operates an electronic circuit to actually work the EGR valve. The computer uses a duty-cycle (percentage of on-time) signal to activate the solenoid.

exhaust gas recirculation (EGR) throttle valve - when EGR is desired, the PCM/ECM closes the throttle valve to create a restriction in the air intake, creating a vacuum that allows EGR flow into the intake manifold.

exhaust gas recirculation (EGR) valve - component in the EGR system, used to meter a controlled amount of exhaust gas into the intake air stream.

exhaust manifold - the part of the exhaust system that is fastened to the cylinder head.

exhaust pipe - the pipe between the exhaust manifold and muffler.

exhaust port - the passage or opening in a four stroke cylinder head for the exhaust valve.

exhaust stroke - the final stroke in a 4-stroke cycle engine during which the exhaust valve is open and the intake valve is closed, exhausting the combusted gases.

exhaust valves - poppet valves in the cylinder head that control the flow of exhaust from the engine.

expansion - to make greater in size; in mechanical terms, the expanding in volume of gas in a cylinder of an internal combustion engine after explosion.

--f--

Fahrenheit - a scale of temperature measurement with the boiling point of water at 212°F and the freezing point at 32°F.

fan - a mechanically or electrically driven propeller that draws or pushes air through the radiator, condenser, heater core or evaporator core.

fan clutch - a device attached to a mechanically driven cooling fan that allows the fan to freewheel when the engine is cold or the vehicle is driven at speed.

fan shroud - an enclosure that routes air through the radiator cooling fins.

feeler gauge - thin metal strip manufactured in precise thickness and used to measure clearance between parts; usually part of a set.

field coil - a wire coil on an alternator rotor or starter motor frame; a field coil produces a magnetic field when energized.

filter - a screen or filter element that can be made to filter specified sizes of particles from air or liquid.

flexplate - a steel wheel mounted to the end of the crankshaft, the teeth around its circumference provide an engagement for the starter, and it provides the mounting points for the torque converter of an automatic transmission/transaxle.

flywheel - a cast iron or steel wheel mounted to the end of the crankshaft; helps to smooth the engine's power delivery, the teeth around its circumference provide an engagement for the starter, and it provides the mounting points for the pressure plate and friction surface for the clutch disc.

foot pound - a unit of measurement for torque. One foot pound is the torque obtained by a force of one pound applied to a wrench handle that is 12 inches long; a unit of energy required to raise a weight of one pound, a distance of one foot.

force - a pushing effort measured in pounds; the form of energy that puts an object at rest into motion or changes the motion of a moving object.

four stroke cycle engine - an engine, either gasoline or diesel that uses four strokes: intake, compression, power and exhaust. A firing impulse occurs every two turns of the crankshaft. When this engine is a gasoline engine it is also called an Otto cycle engine after its inventor. A diesel engine is called a Diesel cycle engine for the same reason.

freeze frame data - a snapshot of information recorded by an OBD II PCM/ECM the moment it recognizes an emissions-related failure. Freeze Frame data is recorded for the first failure only, and may be overwritten by a different failure with a higher priority.

fuel injector - device that receives metered fuel and is activated either electrically or mechanically to spray the fuel under relatively high pressure into the engine.

fuel pump - a mechanical or electronic device that draws fuel from the fuel tank and sends it to the injection pump or injectors.

fuel rail - a manifold used to connect the fuel injectors to the injection pump in a common rail injection system.

fuel rail pressure (FRP) sensor - a 3-wire variable capacitance sensor. The PCM/ECM supplies a 5-volt reference signal to the sensor, which it uses to produce a linear analog voltage signal that indicates the pressure of the fuel in the fuel rail.

fuel temperature sensor - a sensor that works by a negative coefficient thermistor, which loses resistance as its temperature goes up (just like the engine coolant temperature sensor). When the computer applies its 5-volt reference signal to the sensor, this voltage is reduced through a ground circuit by an amount corresponding to the temperature of the fuel.

fuel/water separator - device used in a diesel fuel system to remove water, which can damage fuel system components like pumps and injectors. Contains a chemically-treated filter media that repels water, which then settles to the bottom of the housing where it can be drained according to the manufacturer's recommended service intervals.

--*g*--

glow plug - electrical component containing a high-resistance heating coil, which projects into the combustion chamber and aids cold starting. Glow plugs can reach temperatures of over 1500°F within a few seconds. On time is determined by glow plug controllers based on a timer and ambient, oil and/or coolant temperature.

ground - a connecting body whose electrical potential is zero to which an electrical circuit can be connected.

ground circuit - that part of the circuit that is connected electrically to the negative terminal of the battery. Every electric circuit has a power and ground side. Most computer actuations consist of completing the ground side of an actuator's circuit; this protects the computer from short circuits. Resistance in a ground circuit will reduce the current through it and cause deterioration in the function of the circuit.

GVWR - The Gross Vehicle Weight Rating indicates the maximum allowable vehicle weight when loaded with driver, passengers and cargo.

--*h*--

harmonic balancer - a device that reduces the torsional or twisting vibration that occurs along the length of the crankshaft in multiple cylinder engines. It is also called a vibration damper.

harmonic vibration - periodic motion or vibration along a straight line. The severity depends on the frequency or amplitude.

harmonics - potentially damaging vibration in the crankshaft or valve springs.

hone - abrasive tool for correcting small irregularities or differences in diameter in a cylinder, such as an engine cylinder or brake caliper; to enlarge or smooth a bore with a rotating tool containing an abrasive material.

housing bore - the machined bore in a block or head where a bearing will be installed.

hydraulic electronic unit injector (HEUI) - a type of diesel fuel injector that uses high-pressure crankcase oil to develop the fuel pressure in the injector necessary for injection. A high-pressure pump delivers crankcase oil to the injectors, each of which is equipped with a solenoid. The PCM/ECM commands the solenoid to open a valve that admits the high-pressure oil to the top of a piston. The oil forces the piston and a plunger against fuel that is trapped in the injector body. Since the fuel end of the plunger is smaller than the oil end, the hydraulic force is multiplied to produce the required fuel injection pressure.

hydraulic valve lifter - an automatic lash adjusting device that provides a rigid connection between the camshaft and valve, while absorbing the shock of motion. A hydraulic valve lifter differs from the solid type in that it uses oil to absorb the shock that results from movement of the valvetrain.

hydrocarbons (HC) - solid particles of fuel present in the exhaust and in crankcase vapors that have not been fully burned.

hydrometer - an instrument used to measure the specific gravity of a solution.

--*i*--

injection control pressure (ICP) sensor - used on vehicles with HEUI fuel systems. It is a variable capacitor sensor that is supplied a 5-volt reference signal by the PCM/ECM and returns a linear analog voltage signal that indicates pressure. The sensor measures the oil pressure in an injection rail and the PCM/ECM uses the signal to determine injection control pressure. The ICP sensor and the ICP regulator form a closed loop fuel pressure control system.

injector - device that receives metered fuel and is activated either electrically or mechanically to spray the fuel under relatively high pressure into the engine.

injector sleeve - a housing that the fuel injector is installed inside of; seals the injector from the coolant passages in the cylinder head and transfers heat from the injector to the coolant.

insert bearing - a bearing made as a self-contained part and then inserted into the bearing housing.

Glossary of Terms

insert guides - valve guides that are a press fit in the cylinder head.

installed spring height - distance from the valve spring seat to the underside of the retainer when it is assembled with keepers and held in place.

installed stem height - distance from the valve spring seat to the stem tip.

intake air temperature (IAT) sensor - a sensor that works by a negative coefficient thermistor, which loses resistance as its temperature goes up (just like the engine coolant temperature sensor). When the computer applies its 5-volt reference signal to the sensor, this voltage is reduced through a ground circuit by an amount corresponding to the temperature of the air.

intake manifold - a part with runners that connects the air intake system to the intake valve ports.

intake port - the passage or opening in a cylinder head that is closed by the intake valve.

intake stroke - first stroke of the 4-stroke engine cycle in which the piston moves away from top dead center and the intake valve opens.

intake valve - also called inlet valve, it closes off the intake port and opens it at the correct time in response to movement from the cam lobe.

integral - made of one piece.

integral guides - valve guides that are part of the cylinder head.

integral seats - valve seats that are part of the cylinder head.

intercooler - device used on some turbocharged engines to cool the compressed air.

--j--

jet clean - a cleaning machine that sprays engine parts with degreasing solution under high pressure. The parts rotate on a carousel during the cleaning process to expose all surfaces to the cleaning spray.

journal - the bearing surface on a shaft.

--k--

keepers - small locks that hold the valve retainer onto the valve stem. Also called split locks.

key - a small block inserted between the shaft and hub to prevent circumferential movement.

keyway - a slot cut into a shaft to accept a key.

knurling - technique used for restoring the inside diameter dimensions of a worn valve guide by plowing tiny furrows through the surface of the metal.

--l--

land - the areas between the grooves of a piston.

lapping - the process of fitting one surface to another by rubbing them together with an abrasive material between the two surfaces.

lash - the amount of clearance between components in a geartrain or valvetrain.

lash adjuster - a device for adjusting valve lash or maintaining zero lash in certain types of OHC engines. The lash adjuster is stationary in the cylinder head, with one end of a cam follower mounted on top of it. The other end of the follower acts on the valve stem when the camshaft lobe, which is positioned over the center of the follower, pushes the follower down.

leakdown test - diagnostic test where the piston in a cylinder is brought to TDC and compressed air is pumped into the cylinder through the injector or glow plug hole. Where the air escapes indicates the defect, i.e. through the exhaust, the exhaust valve is not seating.

lifter - the valvetrain part that rides on the camshaft lobe.

lifter bores - the holes in an engine block that the lifters fit into.

liner - a thin layer, used as a wear surface or a replaceable guide liner or cylinder sleeve.

load - in mechanics, the amount of work performed by an engine; specifically, the external resistance applied to the engine by the machine it is operating. In electrical

A9 - Light Vehicle Diesel Engines

terms, the amount of power delivered by a generator, motor, etc., or carried by a circuit. The work an engine must do, under which it operates more slowly and less efficiently (e.g., driving up a hill, pulling extra weight).

lobe - the eccentric part of the camshaft that moves the lifter.

lock stitch - a crack repair method.

lubrication - the process of introducing a friction reducing substance between moving parts to reduce wear.

--*m*--

magnet - any body that attracts iron or steel.

magnetic field - the areas surrounding the poles of a magnet, which are affected by its forces of attraction or repulsion.

magnetic particle detection - a process, often called magnaflux, which is used with iron or steel parts to detect cracks.

main bearing caps - the removable lower halves of the main bearing bores.

main bearing clearance - the clearance between the main bearing journal and its bearings.

main bearing journal - the central, load-bearing points along the axis of a crankshaft, where the main bearings support the shaft in the block.

main bearings - the plain bearings that support the crankshaft in the engine block.

main bearing saddle bores - the housings that are machined for main bearings.

malfunction indicator light (MIL) - also known as the CHECK ENGINE or SERVICE ENGINE SOON light on many vehicles. The MIL comes on when the ignition is first turned on (to check the bulb) and then goes out once the engine is started, unless a trouble code is stored in the computer. If the MIL is on when the vehicle is running, there has been a malfunction on one of the sensor or actuator circuits monitored by the computer, and a diagnosis will have to be made by retrieving the code.

manifold absolute pressure (MAP) sensor - a variable capacitance sensor that is supplied a 5-volt reference signal by the PCM/ECM and returns a voltage signal to the PCM/ECM indicating intake manifold pressure. The sensor voltage increases as pressure increases.

mass air flow (MAF) sensor - a sensor that measures the mass (weight/density) of the incoming air flowing through a meter. The measurement transmitted to the PCM/ECM is usually either a frequency or a voltage.

microbe - short for microorganism, an organism that is microscopic and usually too small to be seen by the naked eye.

misfire - failure of an explosion to occur in one or more cylinders while the engine is running; can be continuous or intermittent failure.

monitor - the term used for the OBD II diagnostic tests run by the PCM/ECM. Monitors are executed on a continuous or a non-continuous basis, and are used to evaluate the performance of emission-related components and subsystems.

multimeter - a tool that combines the functions of a voltmeter, ohmmeter and ammeter into one diagnostic instrument.

--*n*--

negative temperature coefficient thermistor - a thermistor that loses electrical resistance as it gets warmer. The temperature sensors for the computer control system are negative temperature coefficient thermistors. The effect is to systematically lower the 5-volt reference voltage sent them by the computer, yielding a signal that corresponds to the temperature of the measured source. Typically the ECT and IAT sensors use this principle.

normal wear - the average expected wear when operating under normal conditions.

NOx - see oxides of nitrogen.

--*o*--

OBD II drive cycle - a driving routine that occurs within one key on, key off period, consisting of various vehicle-operating conditions such as idle, acceleration, cruise and deceleration. A complete drive cycle is required to run all of the OBD II monitors.

ohm - a unit of electrical resistance of a circuit in which an electromotive force of one volt maintains a current of one ampere, named after German physicist Georg Ohm.

ohmmeter - an instrument that measures electrical resistance in ohms.

oil bypass valve - a valve that will open and allow oil flow if the oil filter or oil cooler become restricted.

oil clearance - the difference between the inside bearing diameter and the journal's diameter.

oil cooler - a device used to remove heat from the engine or transmission oil. There are oil-to-air coolers and oil coolers that are incorporated into the vehicle's cooling system.

oil gallery - a line that supplies oil to areas of the engine block or cylinder head.

oil groove - a groove machined in the bearing surface that provides a channel for oil flow.

oil pan - the part that encloses the crankcase at the lower end of the block.

oil pressure - the pressure that results from resistance to flow from the oil pump. As the pump turns faster, it produces more flow. A relief valve limits the amount of pressure it can produce.

oil pressure relief valve - relief valve with a spring that provides a force equal to the maximum allowable oil pressure. If oil pressure exceeds this value, the spring pressure is overcome, the relief valve opens and the excess pressure is allowed to bleed off.

oil pump - the pump that circulates lubricating oil throughout the engine, usually driven by the camshaft (by way of the distributor).

oil pump pickup - the screen that filters and keeps debris out of the oil pump.

oil rings - the bottom ring on the pistons, scrapes excess oil from the cylinder walls to keep it from entering and burning in the combustion chamber.

on-board diagnostics (OBD) - a diagnostic software system in the PCM/ECM that monitors computer inputs, outputs, and resultant engine/ transmission operations for failure. OBD I is thought of as any of the systems in use before OBD II, typically 1979 to 1995 systems, although some OEMs started transitioning gasoline engine vehicles to OBD II in 1994 and 1995. OBD II was required by CARB (California Air Resources Board) and EPA (U.S. Environmental Protection Agency) on light-duty (less than 8,500 lb. GVWR) diesel vehicles beginning in 1997. As of 2007, all 8,500-14,000 lb. GVWR diesel vehicles must also be OBD II compliant. OBD II monitors emission control systems for degradation as well as for failures.

open circuit - an electrical circuit that has a break in the wire.

O-ring seal - a sealing ring, usually made of rubber and installed in a groove; a type of valve seal that fits into a valve stem groove under the valve keepers.

out-of-round - refers to an inside or outside diameter that was originally designed to be perfectly round, but instead has varying diameters when measured at different points across its diameter.

overbore - the dimension by which a machined hole is larger than the standard size.

overhead cam (OHC) engine - an engine with the camshaft located in the cylinder head.

overhead valve (OHV) engine - an I-head engine. The intake and exhaust valves are located in the cylinder head.

overlap - the point at TDC where both valves are open at the same time. The intake valve is just beginning to open while the exhaust valve is just finishing closing.

oxidation - the process of combining with oxygen, resulting in rusting or burning. Rust is slow oxidation; fire is rapid oxidation.

oxides of nitrogen (NOx) - various compounds of oxygen and nitrogen that are formed in the cylinders during combustion, and are part of the exhaust gas.

--*p*--

pending DTC - a temporary code recorded by the PCM/ECM. Pending codes are used to identify the first occurrence of a two-trip failure. If the original failure does not recur on the second consecutive trip, the pending DTC will be automatically removed.

piezoelectric injector - a type of electronic unit injector that uses crystals arranged in a series called a stack. The crystals change dimension when a voltage is applied, thus the total change of the stack can be used to actuate the pintle of the injector.

piston - the cylindrical component that is attached to the connecting rod and moves up and down in the cylinder bore. The top of the piston forms the bottom of the combustion chamber. When combustion occurs, the piston is forced downward in the cylinder, moving the connecting rod, which in turn rotates the crankshaft.

piston collapse - when the diameter of the piston skirt becomes less due to heat.

piston head - the part of the piston that is above the rings.

piston pin - see wrist pin.

piston ring - an open-ended ring that fits into a groove on the outer diameter of the piston. Its chief function is to form a seal between the piston and cylinder wall. Most automotive pistons have three rings: two for compression sealing; one for oil sealing.

piston slap - a noise that result from excessive piston to cylinder wall clearance.

pour point - the temperature at which diesel fuel thickens to the point it will not flow or 'pour'.

piston projection - the distance the piston head projects above the cylinder deck surface at TDC; on a diesel engine a measurement that must be made to determine the appropriate head gasket thickness, to prevent the piston from contacting the cylinder head or valves.

positive seal - a type of valve seal that fits tightly around the top of the valve guide.

power circuit - the part of the circuit that is connected electrically to the positive terminal of the battery. Every electric circuit has a power and a ground side. On computer controlled systems, ordinarily power is routed to actuators directly through the ignition switch; the circuit is completed when the computer grounds it. Most manual switches directly connect the power side of the circuit to the load. Fuses are ordinarily positioned as close as possible to the battery on the power side of a circuit.

power stroke - the third stroke of a 4-stroke cycle engine, which begins with the combustion of the air/fuel mixture, driving the piston away from TDC, which in turn exerts turning force on the crankshaft.

powertrain control module (PCM) - on vehicles with computer control systems, the main computer that determines engine operation based on sensor inputs and by using its actuator outputs. The PCM may also control transmission operation.

precombustion chamber - used on indirect injection diesel engines. A small chamber in the cylinder head located over the piston, housing the fuel injector and glow plug and connected to the main combustion chamber by a small passage. As the piston approaches TDC, fuel is injected into the chamber and ignites. The resulting pressure increase in the chamber sends a stream of burning fuel through the passage into the main combustion chamber, completing combustion with the remaining compressed air.

press fit - when a part is slightly larger than a hole it must be forced together with a press.

pressure - the exertion of force upon a body, measured in pounds per square inch on a gauge.

pressure testing - a method for finding leaks in a cooling system. A hand-held pump with a pressure gauge designed for cooling system testing is attached to the radiator or expansion tank, then pumped to the rated system pressure while watching the gauge needle; it should not drop rapidly. If pressure drops, check for leaks at all cooling system components. Also, a crack detection method that is good at revealing hard-to-see internal leaks. After plugging all the external openings of the water jacket, the head or block is lightly pressurized (usually less than 30 psi) with air. A soapy water solution is sprayed on the head or block to check for leaks or the entire head or block is immersed in a tank of water. Bubbles from the soap or in the water indicate leaks.

profilometer - an instrument used to measure surface profiles and surface roughness.

Prussian blue - a paste used to determine the contact area between two parts, such as the height of the valve seat on the valve face.

pump-line-nozzle (PLN) fuel system - a type of diesel fuel system where the injection pump creates the high

Glossary of Terms

pressure necessary for injection and also controls the injection timing. Fuel is delivered under high pressure through individual fuel lines to injection nozzles located on the cylinder head.

pushrod - a rod between the lifter and rocker arm. They are sometimes hollow to allow oil distribution to the valves.

--r--

race - channel in the inner or outer ring of an anti-friction bearing in which the balls or rollers operate.

radial - perpendicular to the shaft or bearing bore.

radial load - load applied at 90 degrees to an axis of rotation.

radiator - the part of the cooling system that acts as a heat exchanger, transferring heat to atmosphere. It consists of a core and holding tanks connected to the cooling system by hoses.

radiator cap - a device that seals the radiator and maintains a set pressure in the cooling system.

ratio - proportion of one number to another.

reaming - technique used to repair worn valve guides by increasing the guide hole size to take an oversized valve stem, or by restoring the guide to its original diameter.

rear main oil seal - a seal that fits around the rear of the crankshaft to prevent oil leaks.

relay - an electromagnetic switch that uses low amperage current to control a circuit with high amperage.

regeneration - the process of using increased exhaust gas temperature to burn off the soot collected in the Diesel Particulate Filter (DPF).

reserve capacity (RC) - the number of minutes the battery can deliver 25 amps at 80°F while maintaining a voltage of 10.5 volts.

resistance - the opposition offered by a substance or body to the passage of electric current through it.

ridge - a raised area at the top of a cylinder bore created by ring wear. The ridge occurs because the piston ring does not travel all the way to the top of the bore, thereby leaving an unused portion of cylinder bore above the

limit of ring travel. This ridge will usually be more pronounced on high mileage engines.

ridge reamer - a tool used to remove the ridge from the top of a cylinder bore.

rigid hone - a hone that removes metal and imparts a precise finish and crosshatch to the bore.

ring end gap - the clearance between the ends of a piston ring when installed in the cylinder bore.

ring file - a tool used to trim the ends of a piston ring to bring the ring end gap within specification.

ring lands - the raised parts between the piston ring grooves.

rocker arm - a pivot lever mounted on a round shaft or a stud. One end of the rocker arm is applied by the pushrod and the other end acts upon the valve stem.

rocker shaft - a round pipe that is mounted parallel on top of the cylinder head. All of the rocker arms on the head are mounted on it.

rocker stud - a stud that is pressed or threaded into a cylinder head on which the rocker arm is mounted.

roller bearing - an anti-friction device made up of hardened inner and outer races between which steel rollers move.

roller lifter - lifters that are equipped with rollers at the bottom that ride on the camshaft lobe, in order to reduce friction.

runner - a cast tube on an intake or exhaust manifold used to carry air in or out of the engine.

runout - degree of wobble outside normal plane of rotation.

--s--

scan tool - microprocessor designed to communicate with a vehicle's on-board computer system to perform diagnostic and troubleshooting functions.

scan tool data - information from the ECM, PCM, or VCM that is displayed on the scan tool. This data includes component and system values on the data stream, DTCs, freeze frame data, system monitors and readiness monitors.

short circuit - a condition that occurs in an electrical circuit when the current bypasses the intended load and takes a path with little or no resistance, such as another circuit or ground.

solenoid - a coil of wire that becomes an electromagnet when current flows through it. It then loses its magnetism when the current flow is turned off. The solenoid contains an iron plunger inside the wire coil that is spring loaded to one position. When the solenoid is energized, the plunger moves to the other position.

specific gravity - the ratio of the weight or mass of the given volume of a substance to that of an equal volume of another substance, e.g., – water for liquids and solids; air or hydrogen for gases, are used as standards.

split-ball gauge - a transfer measuring instrument. Turning the handle on the gauge causes the split ball to expand. It can be used for measuring small holes such as valve guides.

split locks - see valve keepers.

sprocket - toothed wheel that is splined or keyed to a shaft; drives or is driven by a chain or belt.

starter - the electric motor that is used to start an engine.

straightedge - a long, flat steel strip with perfectly straight edges, used for checking surfaces for warpage.

stroke - the distance the piston moves from TDC to BDC.

supplemental coolant additive (SCA) - an additive used in the cooling systems of some diesel engines to combat corrosion due to cavitation.

--t--

technical service bulletin (TSB) - information published by vehicle manufacturers that describe updated service procedures and service procedures that should be used to handle vehicle defects.

thermal cleaning - a parts cleaning method that uses high temperature in a bake oven to turn grease, oil and sludge into a powdery residue. This residue is then removed by washing, airless shot blasting or glass beading.

thermostat - a device installed in the cooling system that allows the engine to come to operating temperature quickly and then maintain a minimum operating temperature.

timing - refers in crankshaft degrees to the position of the piston in the cylinder. When referring to camshaft timing, it is when the valves open. When referring to fuel injection timing, it is when injection occurs.

timing belt - a toothed reinforced belt used to drive the camshaft from a sprocket on the crankshaft.

timing chain - a chain that drives the camshaft from a sprocket on the crankshaft.

timing gears - gears that drive the camshaft from the crankshaft.

top dead center (TDC) - the position of the crankshaft for a specific cylinder when the piston is at the highest point in its vertical travel.

torque - twisting effort on a shaft or bolt.

torque converter - a fluid coupling device used to transfer engine torque from the crankshaft to the transmission.

torque sequence - a specified order in which a component's mounting bolts should be tightened

torque-to-yield head bolts - head bolts that are not reusable. They are torqued into yield, which means that they have purposely stretched beyond the point where they will return to their original length. This provides more uniform clamping force.

torque-turn - the method used to tighten torque-to-yield head bolts. A torque angle gauge is used to tighten a fastener a specified number of degrees after it is torqued to a foot pound specification.

torque wrench - a breaker bar or ratchet wrench with an indicator, which measures the twisting effort applied to a fastener during tightening.

transfer pump - also called the feed or lift pump, supplies fuel to the injection pump or unit injectors. It is usually an electric pump, mounted on the frame rail, and controlled by the PCM/ECM via a relay. However, diaphragm-type mechanical pumps driven off the camshaft are still used in some applications.

Glossary of Terms

trip - a term used to describe a key on, engine run, key off cycle, during which time the vehicle was operated in a way that satisfied the enable criteria for at least one OBD II monitor.

turbocharger - an exhaust driven pump that compresses intake air and forces it into the combustion chambers at higher than atmospheric pressure.

--*u*--

ultra low sulfur diesel (ULSD) fuel - a diesel fuel with a lower sulfur content, designed for use in newer electronically controlled diesel engines with emissions equipment like exhaust gas recirculation (EGR) and diesel particulate filters (DPFs). Using fuel with lower sulfur content substantially reduces particulate emissions (soot) in diesel engine exhaust.

--*v*--

valve - a device that controls the pressure, direction or rate of flow of a liquid or gas.

valve cover - an enclosure fastened to the top of a cylinder head, over the valvetrain.

valve duration - the length of time, in degrees of crankshaft rotation, that a valve is open.

valve face - the area of the valve that contacts the valve seat.

valve float - when valves remain open, usually at high rpm, due to weak or broken valve springs.

valve guide - a bore in the cylinder head that the valve stem fits into.

valve guide knurling - a method of refinishing the inside of a valve guide by restoring its original size.
valve guide liner - a thin bronze bushing installed in a valve guide to restore it to original size.

valve keepers - small locks that hold the valve retainer onto the valve stem. Also called split locks.

valve lash - the amount of clearance in the valvetrain when the lifter is on the base circle of the camshaft lobe.

valve lift - the distance from the valve seat when the valve is fully open.

valve lifter - a small cylinder that fits into a bore above the cam lobe. It acts on a pushrod and rocker arm to open the valve.

valve margin - on a poppet valve, the space or rim between the surface of the head and the surface of the valve face.

valve protrusion/depression - the distance between the valve and the head gasket surface of the cylinder head; a specification that must be maintained when assembling a diesel engine. A valve that extends too far into the combustion chamber could strike the piston; a valve that is too deep hampers combustion.

valve rotator - a part found at the end of some valve springs that rotates the valve each time it opens. This aids in providing even cooling to the valve.

valve seal - a seal located over the valve stem, used to prevent oil from leaking down the valve guide and into the combustion chamber.

valve seat - the machined surface that the valve face seats against.

valve spring - a small coil spring used to keep the valve closed against the valve seat.

valve spring compressor - a tool used to compress the valve spring on a cylinder head. When the valve spring is compressed, the valve keepers can be removed, then the spring is released and the spring, valve spring retainer and valve can be removed from the cylinder head.

valve spring installed height - the specified distance between the machined spring seat on the cylinder head to the underside of the valve spring retainer. Both grinding the valve and grinding the valve seat result in an increase in this dimension. A shim can be installed under the spring to restore the original installed height for proper spring tension.

valve spring retainer - the part that connects the valve spring to the valve and holds the valve against the cylinder head. It is held to the valve by keepers.

valve spring seats - metal shims used, usually on aluminum cylinder heads, to protect the head from the bottom of the valve spring.

valve stem - the part of the valve that is inside the valve guide.

Glossary of Terms

valve stem installed height - the distance from the spring seat to the tip of the valve stem with the valve installed.

valve timing - set rotations of the camshaft and crankshaft to open/close valves at proper intervals during the piston strokes for optimal operation of an engine.

valvetrain - parts that convert camshaft movement to valve movement. These include the camshaft, cam timing parts, lifters or cam followers, pushrods, rocker arms, valve and spring.

valvetrain geometry - the dynamic relationship between the rocker arm and valve stem during the time when the valve is opening and closing.

variable geometry turbine (VGT) turbocharger - a turbocharger with adjustable vanes located around the outside of the turbine that open and close according to engine need. At low speeds, the vanes are closed, creating an obstruction that increases the speed of the exhaust against the turbine wheel, making it spin faster. At high engine speeds, the vanes open to allow the turbine wheel to take full advantage of the increased exhaust flow.

vehicle identification number (VIN) - a number assigned to every vehicle as a unique identifier; includes vehicle specification information and a serial number.

vibration damper - see harmonic balancer.

viscosity - the rating of a liquid's internal resistance to flow.

volt - unit of electromotive force. One volt of electromotive force applied steadily to a conductor of one ohm resistance produces a current of one ampere.

voltage drop - voltage lost by the passage of electrical current through resistance.

voltmeter - a tool used to measure the voltage available at any point in an electrical system.

--*w*--

warpage - a condition that exists when a part is bent or twisted; the degree to which a part deviates from flatness.

wastegate - a bypass valve that limits boost produced by a turbocharger.

water jacket - also called a cooling jacket, it is the hollow area of a casting designed for coolant flow.

water manometer - a tool that measures pressure or vacuum. The water manometer is filled with ordinary water. Antifreeze and other additives change the density of the liquid and affect readings. At rest the water is the same height in both tubes and this point is where the manometer scale is set at zero. When a pressure or vacuum is applied to the manometer, the water will rise in one tube and drop in the other tube. Total movement in both tubes is the measured value.

water pump - device used to circulate coolant through the engine.

wet sleeve - a sleeve, which when installed in a cylinder block, is exposed to coolant.

wrist pin - a hollow metal tube that secures the piston to the connecting rod and allows the piston to swivel on the rod. Also called a *piston pin*